THE
HISTORY OF
PORTUGAL

THE
HISTORY OF
PORTUGAL

James M. Anderson

The Greenwood Histories of the Modern Nations
Frank W. Thackeray and John E. Findling, Series Editors

Greenwood Press
Westport, Connecticut • London

Library of Congress Cataloging-in-Publication Data

Anderson, James Maxwell, 1933–
    The history of Portugal / James M. Anderson.
        p.   cm.—(The Greenwood histories of the modern nations,
    ISSN 1096–2905)
    Includes bibliographical references (p.   ) and index.
    ISBN 0–313–31106–4 (alk. paper)
    1. Portugal—History.   I. Title.   II. Series.
DP538.A56   2000
    946.9—dc21   99–43637

British Library Cataloguing in Publication Data is available.

Library of Congress Catalog Card Number: 99–43637
ISBN: 0–313–31106–4
ISSN: 1096–2905

First published in 2000

Greenwood Press, 88 Post Road West, Westport, CT 06881
An imprint of Greenwood Publishing Group, Inc.
www.greenwood.com

Printed in the United States of America

The paper used in this book complies with the
Permanent Paper Standard issued by the National
Information Standards Organization (Z39.48–1984).

10   9   8   7   6   5   4   3   2   1

For

Gordon and Anne
Bob and Shirley

Contents

Series Foreword

The Greenwood Histories of the Modern Nations series is intended to provide students and interested laypeople with up-to-date, concise and analytical histories of many of the nations of the contemporary world. Not since the 1960s has there been a systematic attempt to publish a series of national histories, and, as series editors, we believe that this series will prove to be a valuable contribution to our understanding of other countries in our increasingly interdependent world.

Over thirty years ago, at the end of the 1960s, the Cold War was an accepted reality of global politics, the process of decolonization was still in progress, the idea of a unified Europe with a single currency was unheard of, the United States was mired in a war in Vietnam, and the economic boom of Asia was still years in the future. Richard Nixon was president of the United States, Mao Tse-tung (not yet Mao Zedong) ruled China, Leonid Brezhnev guided the Soviet Union and Harold Wilson was prime minister of the United Kingdom. Authoritarian dictators still ruled most of Latin America, the Middle East was reeling in the wake of the Six-Day War and Shah Reza Pahlavi was at the height of his power in Iran. Clearly, the past thirty years have been witness to a great deal of historical change, and it is to this change that this series is primarily addressed.

With the help of a distinguished advisory board, we have selected nations whose political, economic and social affairs mark them as among the most important in the waning years of the twentieth century, and for each nation we have found an author who is recognized as specialist in the history of that nation. These authors have worked most cooperatively with us and with Greenwood Press to produce volumes that reflect current research on their nation and that are interesting and informative to their prospective readers.

The importance of a series such as this cannot be underestimated. As a superpower whose influence is felt all over the world, the United States can claim a "special" relationship with almost every other nation. Yet many Americans know very little about the histories of the nations with which the United States relates. How did they get to be the way they are? What kind of political systems have evolved there? What kind of influence do they have in their own region? What are the dominant political, religious and cultural forces that move their leaders? These and many other questions are answered in the volumes of this series.

The authors who have contributed to this series have written comprehensive histories of their nations, dating back to prehistoric time in some cases. Each of them, however, has devoted a significant portion of the book to events of the past thirty years, because the modern era has contributed the most to contemporary issues that have an impact on U.S. policy. Authors have made an effort to be as up-to-date as possible so that readers can benefit from the most recent scholarship and a narrative that includes very recent events.

In addition to the historical narrative, each volume in this series contains an introductory overview of the country's geography, political institutions, economic structure and cultural attributes. This is designed to give readers a picture of the nation as it exists in the contemporary world. Each volume also contains additional chapters that add interesting and useful detail to the historical narrative. One chapter is a thorough chronology of important historical events, making it easy for readers to follow the flow of a particular nation's history. Another chapter features biographical sketches of the nation's most important figures in order to humanize some of the individuals who have contributed to the historical development of their nation. Each volume also contains a comprehensive bibliography, so that those readers whose interest has been sparked may find out more about the nation and its history. Finally, there is a carefully prepared topic and person index.

Readers of these volumes will find them fascinating to read and useful in understanding the contemporary world and the nations that comprise it. As series editors, it is our hope that this series will contribute to a heightened sense of global understanding as we enter a new century.

Frank W. Thackeray and John E. Findling
Indiana University Southeast

Preface

Every country has its unique place in the overall mosaic of human endeavor, and Portugal is no exception. Its history is entwined in the vicissitudes of enterprise, achievements and failings. It is embedded in problems of rigid class structures, warring noble factions, peasant revolts, pestilence, superstition, greed and arbitrary laws often enacted for the benefit of those in power. Further, Portugal was burdened with a church that was heavily endowed with clerics who, more often than not, sided with the wealthy, promoted racial hatred and inhumanity against non-Christians and wielded enormous influence, all too often for its own benefit.

Exclusively, unlike other regions of the Hispanic Peninsula such as Cataluña or the Basque regions—each with its own distinctive heritage—Portugal achieved independence not only once but twice from its giant neighbor, Spain. What determinants and circumstances molded Portugal into a coherent state and propelled it onto the world stage to leave a permanent legacy in Europe, Africa, Asia and South America?

The following pages depict the journey from its beginnings to the present day of this one little nation, which, at its zenith, had a colossal impact on world affairs out of all proportion to its size.

Thanks go to the people of Portugal, proud of their heritage and generous with their help, and more specifically to Dr. Joel Prager, Marilyn Stanton and Dr. Siwan Anderson for materials and suggestions. The assistance of Sheridan Lea in preparing the manuscript was of utmost value.

Timeline of Historical Events

800 B.C.	Phoenicians begin trading along Portuguese coasts
700	Celts begin to settle in Portugal
600	Greeks and Carthaginians initiate trading along coasts of Portugal
218	First Roman legions arrive in the Iberian Peninsula
147	Viriathus begins struggle against Romans
82	Sertorius leads native uprising in Lusitania
60	Caesar establishes camp at Olisipo (Lisbon)
19	Romans pacify Lusitania
A.D. 409	Suevi, Vandals and Alans occupy western Iberia
468	Destruction of Conímbriga by the Suevi
585	Suevic kingdom conquered by the Visigoths
711	Muslim invasion of the peninsula
791	Asturias begins to recover lands between the Minho and Douro Rivers

844	Beginning of Viking attacks
868	Oporto resettled by Christians
1054	Christian Reconquest of Seia, Viseu, Lamego and Tarouca
1064	Definitive capture of Coimbra
1095	County of Portucale established
1109	Henri of Burgundy frees Portucale from feudal dependence on León
1128	Afonso Henriques begins his reign; Battle of São Mamede
1139	Battle of Ourique
1143	Treaty of Zamora and independent kingdom of Portugal
1147	Reconquest of Santarém and Lisbon
1178	Construction of the monastery of Alcobaça begins
1211	First Cortes at Coimbra
1217	Definitive reconquest of Alcácer do Sal
1249	Algarve conquered from Muslims
1254	The three estates represented for first time at the Cortes of Leiria
1288	Foundation of the university
1297	Frontier between Portugal and Castilla established
1340	Battle of Salado
1348	Outbreak of the Black Death
1355	Murder of Inês de Castro and revolt of Prince Pedro
1369	First war with Castilla
1372	Second war with Castilla
1373	Alliance with England
1381	Third war with Castilla
1383	Succession Crisis and Rebellion
1385	Battle of Aljubarrota
1386	Treaty of Windsor
1387	Marriage of João I to Philippa of Lancaster

1388	Construction of the monastery of Batalha begins
1411	Treaty of Perpetual Peace with Castilla
1415	Capture of Ceuta
1419	Discovery (or rediscovery) of Madeira
1427	Discovery (or rediscovery) of the Azores
1434	Cape Bojador rounded
1437	Disaster at Tanger
1441	First slaves from Rio de Ouro; Cabo Blanco reached
1444	Dinis Dias reaches Cape Verde
1449	Battle of Alfarrobeira
1458	Capture of Alcácer-Ceguer in Morocco
1460	Death of Prince Henrique
1471	Tanger captured; islands of São Tomé and Príncipe discovered
1476	Battle of Toro
1479	Treaty of Alcáçovas
1484	Execution of the duke of Bragança
1488	Bartolomeu Dias rounds Cape of Good Hope; Covilhã and Paiva begin overland journey
1492	First voyage of Columbus to America; influx of Jews expelled from Spain
1494	Treaty of Tordesillas
1496	Unconverted Jews expelled from Portugal
1497	Voyage of Vasco da Gama to India
1500	Cabral reaches Brazil
1502	da Gama's second voyage; construction begins on the monastery of Jerónimos in Lisbon
1505	Francisco de Almeida named first viceroy of India
1506	Anti-Jewish riots in Lisbon
1507	Conquest of Ormuz by Albuquerque; fort built at Mozambique

1508	Portuguese fleet defeated by Muslims
1509	Francisco de Almeida defeats Muslim fleet off Diu; Albuquerque appointed governor in India
1510	Conquest of Goa
1511	Conquest of Malacca; trade in the Moluccas
1513	Defeat at Aden; Timor and China reached
1518	Fort constructed in Colombo, Ceylon
1519	Magellan begins voyage of circumnavigation
1524	Vasco da Gama sent back to India as viceroy
1529	Treaty of Zaragoza by which Portuguese acquire the Moluccas
1534	Portuguese occupy Diu
1536	Inquisition established in Portugal
1538	Siege of Diu by Turks and Gujarati
1542	Safi and Azammur abandoned; Francis Xavier arrives in Goa
1543	Private Portuguese traders reach Japan
1547	First index of prohibited books
1549	Alcácer-Ceguer abandoned; Portuguese governor posted to Brazil
1550	Arzila abandoned
1553	Foundation of São Paulo in Brazil
1557	Macão established at the mouth of the Pearl River
1559	Creation of the University of Évora
1570	Asian coalition attacked Goa, Chaul, Damião
1572	Publication of Os Lusíadas by Camões
1578	Battle of Ksar el Kebir and death of Sebastião
1580	Spanish army invades Portugal
1581	Felipe II of Spain confirmed as King Felipe I of Portugal
1588	Armada sails for England

1607	Dutch take the Moluccas
1610	Publication of *Descrição do Reino de Portugal*
1615	Portuguese conquest of Maranhão
1622	Persians and English allies capture Ormuz
1630	Conquest of Pernambuco by the Dutch
1638	Dutch take Ceylon
1640	Portugal achieves independence from Spain
1641	Dutch take Malacca and capture Angola; French and Portuguese attack on Cádiz
1644	Battle of Montijo
1648	Portuguese reconquer Luanda
1654	Portuguese recover northern Brazil from Dutch
1655	Dutch begin conquest of Ceylon and Malabar
1656	Treaty of friendship with England ratified; Battle of Montes Claros
1668	Spain recognizes Portugal's independence
1703	Methuen Treaty with England; Spanish War of Succession begins
1715	Treaty of Utrecht ends Spanish War of Succession
1716	Construction of the Monastery of Mafra begins
1717	Naval battle of Cape Matapan
1720	Foundation of the Royal Academy of History
1729	Diamonds discovered in Minas Gerais, Brazil
1731	Construction of the Lisbon aqueduct begins
1735	Publication of *História Genealógica da Casa Real Portuguesa*
1747	Construction begins on the palace at Queluz
1752	Creation of a captain-general for Mozambique
1755	Great Lisbon earthquake
1758	Attempted regicide of José I
1759	Expulsion of the Jesuits from Portugal and the colonies

1761	Slavery abolished in mainland Portugal
1762	Spanish invasion
1769	Mazagão abandoned, last Portuguese presence in Morocco
1773	Distinction between Old and New Christians prohibited
1777	Pombal's "reign" terminated
1789	French Revolution
1801	War of the Oranges
1807	French occupy Portugal; royal family flees to Brazil
1808	Beginning of Peninsular War
1809	Second French invasion of Portugal
1810	Third French invasion; Wellington repels attack on Lisbon
1811	Liberation of Portugal from French
1820	Liberal revolution begins in Oporto
1821	João VI returns from Brazil to Lisbon; new constitution
1822	Brazil proclaims independence
1823	Constitution suspended
1824	Antiliberal revolt of Prince Miguel
1826	Pedro IV abdicates in favor of his daughter, Maria
1828	Miguel acclaimed king; revolt in the north; revolt in Terceira
1831	Pedro abdicates the throne of Brazil
1832	Civil war begins
1833	Liberal column enters Lisbon; Miguel exiled
1834	Convention of Évoramonte; triumph of liberals
1836	September Revolution; constitution of 1822 restored
1838	Third constitution
1846	Revolts of Maria da Fonte; Bank of Portugal created
1847	End of civil war with the convention of Gramido
1848	Lisbon lit by gaslight

1851	Military coup
1853	Sale of church land; first Portuguese postal stamps
1856	First railroad track laid; telegraph installed
1857	Conflict with France over slave ship
1876	Beginnings of Republican and Progressive Parties
1887	Portuguese Macão recognized by China
1890	Portugal abandons territory linking Angola and Mozambique under British ultimatum
1891	Republican revolt in Oporto
1900	Census reveals 5,016,267 inhabitants
1908	Carlos I and eldest son assassinated in Lisbon
1910	Manuel II abdicates; republic proclaimed
1911	Liberal constitution; Manuel d'Arriaga first president
1915	Resignation of Manuel d'Arriaga; dictatorship of Pimenta de Castro
1916	Portugal enters World War I
1917	Revolution and the New Republic
1918	Assassination of Sidónio Pais
1919	Monarchist revolt; anarcho-syndicalist agitation
1921	Foundation of Portuguese Communist Party; murder of leading political figures
1925	Bank scandal
1926	Military revolt and dictatorship
1927	Revolts against dictatorship in Oporto and Lisbon
1928	Salazar takes over Ministry of Finance
1932	Salazar becomes prime minister and dictator
1933	New constitution, beginning of Estado Novo
1939	Treaty of Friendship and Peace with Franco's Spain; World War II begins
1942	Loss of Timor to the Japanese

1943	Secret accord with allies for air base in Azores
1945	End of World War II
1946	Military revolt fails
1947	Labor leaders and army officers deported to Cape Verde Islands
1948	Portugal joins the OEEC
1949	Entry into NATO
1955	Portugal enters the UN
1956	Gulbenkian Foundation initiated
1958	Humberto Delgado runs for presidency; elections won by Admiral Américo Tomás
1960	Portugal joins EFTA
1961	Goa, Damão and Diu occupied by Indian forces; revolt in Angola; assault on the Santa Maria
1963	Rebellion in Portuguese Guinea
1964	Guerrilla warfare in Mozambique
1968	Salazar suffers a stroke; replaced by Marcello Caetano
1973	Guinea-Bissau declares independence
1974	Military (Carnation) revolution
1975	Provisional government under Vasco Gonçalves; elections for Constituent Assembly
1976	Eanes president; Soares prime minister; new constitution; Timor annexed by Indonesia
1979	Conservative Democratic Alliance led by Sá Carneiro wins majority in Assembly
1980	Eanes reelected as president; Sá Carneiro killed in plane crash
1981	Francisco Pinto Balsemão prime minister
1982	Military Council of the Revolution abolished
1983	Return to office of Mário Soares
1986	Soares succeeds Eanes as president; Portugal enters European Community

1989	Constitution revised and purged of Marxist philosophy
1991	Reelection of President Soares
1992	Portugal signs the Maastricht Accord
1995	President Jorge Sampaio and Prime Minister Antonio Guterres take office
1998	World Trade Fair in Lisbon (Expo '98)
1999	Macão reverts to China

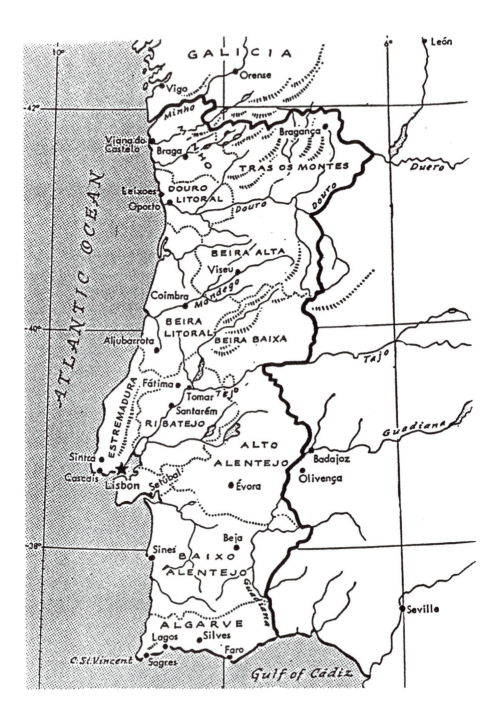

1

Portugal Today

GEOGRAPHY AND CLIMATE

A stretch of the Minho River, which lends its name to the region, separates Portugal from Spanish Galicia in the north, where the land consists of a jumble of granite hills blanketed by forests. To the east, the landlocked region of Tras-os-Montes, "behind the mountains," rises to an exposed, remote and relatively isolated highland lacerated by ragged valleys.

Further south, the Douro River, a continuation of the Spanish Duero, cuts a deep cleavage through vine-carpeted hills to Douro Litoral, Oporto and the sea. In Beira Litoral, where much of the land is low-lying and constitutes marshes and sand dunes along the Atlantic shores, the hills again rise toward the east, culminating in Beira Alta and the lofty peaks of the Serra da Estrêla, the highest mountain range in the country. These mountains give rise to the Mondego River (and some of its tributaries), which passes through Coimbra on its way to the ocean, and to the southwest-flowing Zêzere, a major tributary of the river Tejo and a source of hydroelectric power. Estremadura, once the extremity of the Christian domains in the struggle with the Muslims, is essentially a land of undulating hills and fertile soil interrupted by the jagged outcroppings of the Sintra Mountains. Inland the region of the Ribatejo straddles the lower river valley, much of it a broad alluvial plain. A continuation of the Spanish Tajo, the Tejo flows from the northeast to the southwest and is the principal river of the country. Often cited by its Latin name, Tagus, it enters the sea a little west of Lisbon. In Beira Baixa of the upper Tejo, the northern mountains begin to flatten out onto broad plains.

The southern portion of the country, much of it comprising the Alto and Baixo Alentejo, is primarily a land of rolling, open plains with the exception of a few hills. The climate is hot and dry in the summer and cool and wet in the winter. The olive, cork and holm oaks are the typical trees found here and there in small clusters, but the area is primarily known as *O celeiro de Portugal*, or "the granary of Portugal." The region is drained chiefly by the Guadiana River and tributaries of the river Sado, which exits into the estuary near Setúbal. The Alentejo is separated from the southernmost region of the Algarve by a line of ridges. The Algarve consists of a flat coastal strip across the bottom of the country. With a gentle, frost-free climate and fertile soil, it is conducive to such crops as sugarcane, rice and citrus fruits.

Along the entire Atlantic Coast, breezes moderate temperatures throughout the year. The temperate northern coastal strip with bountiful rainfall and natural forest cover (oak, elm, ash) extends down the western seaboard as far as the Tejo estuary. Inland, mean temperatures fall by four or five degrees in winter and, except on the highlands, rise appreciably in summer. The average yearly precipitation decreases from about forty-five inches in the north to about half that in the south. In summer the Azorean high pressure area dominates, bringing a period of dry, sunny weather that lasts an average of two months at Oporto, three at Lisbon and four on the southern coast.

Mainland Portugal covers an area of 35,516 square miles, occupying about one-fifth of the Iberian Peninsula, and extends between 80 and 140 miles from east to west and 350 miles from north to south.

DEMOGRAPHY

About 80 percent of the total population is concentrated north of the Tejo River, where habitable areas are densely settled. By contrast, except for a compactly settled strip along the Algarvian coast, areas south of the river are sparsely populated, and the landscape, especially in the Alentejo, is one of widely spaced towns and villages and large, relatively isolated farmsteads. Portuguese have traditionally emigrated in large numbers from overpopulated areas of the country, and many still leave for Brazil, the United States and Canada, while others seek temporary employment in the European Economic Community (EEC) countries. Conversely, about 1 million Portuguese of European and black African descent returned to Portugal when Angola, Mozambique and other African colonies became independent in the 1970s.

The population of Portugal, including the Azores and Madeira Islands, established in 1998, is 9,927,556. The overall population density is about 297 persons per square mile. (The United States has about 72 people per square mile.) Lisbon with about 663,315 is the largest city and the leading seaport of Portugal, followed by Oporto with a population of 302,467. Coimbra, an industrial and university center, has 89,639 inhabitants, and Faro in the Algarve, 31,619. Funchal with a population of about 100,000 is the capital of the Madeira Islands.

RESOURCES AND ECONOMIC ACTIVITY

Manufacturing provides less than half the national income but is of increasing importance to the economy, employing about 23 percent of the labor force. Most of it is concentrated in and around Lisbon and Oporto. An oil refinery, petrochemical complex and tanker terminus opened south of Lisbon at Sines in 1979.

Lisbon and Setúbal are the main locations for shipbuilding and repair yards, and much of the country's production of agricultural implements, armaments, hardware and machinery is located in the Lisbon area. Oporto is a center for the manufacture of textiles, Leiria specializes in glass-making, and Barreiro produces fertilizers, insecticides and other chemicals. Products of cottage industries such as lace, pottery and tiles are world-famous.

While Portugal may not boast abundant natural resources, they are not lacking either. There are a few profitable gold, silver and tin mines, and Portugal leads Europe in exports of high-grade copper. Tungsten is mined in ample quantities, as are coal and some pyrites. After Italy, the country is the largest exporter of marble slate and granite. Petroleum and its by-products accounted for about 7 percent of import costs in 1995, but heavy dependence on it for energy was reduced in 1997 with the inauguration of a pipeline carrying natural gas from Algeria via Morocco and Spain.

Commercial fishing, of which more than 25 percent is sardines, is also important to the economy.

Portugal's short-term economic outlook is strong. Figures from 1998 show an inflation rate of 2.8 percent and a rise in the gross domestic product (GDP) of 3.6 percent. Budget revenues were $48 billion, and expenditures $52 billion (1997). The Portuguese monetary unit is the escudo, subdivided into one hundred centavos.

LAND USE

About 47 percent of the land is cultivated: 6 percent in meadows and pasture and 15 percent in heath and swamp, which is potentially reclaimable. Some 11 percent of the employed civilian working population is engaged in agriculture, the chief crops being corn, grapes, olives, potatoes, tomatoes and wheat. Perhaps the best-known product is port wine from the Douro region; but many other wines of various types are made and exported, along with natural mineral water, with which the country is well endowed. Approximately 32 percent of the land is forested, and pine trees are cut for lumber and pulp and also supply large quantities of resin and turpentine for export. Cork oak occupies an additional one-third of the timberland, and Portugal supplies about half the world's cork requirements.

TOURISM

Tourism, a strong and growing sector of the economy, accounted for foreign exchange receipts of more than $3.2 billion annually in the early 1990s, which helped compensate for the chronic trade deficit. In January 1999, Pina Moura, minister of the economy, announced government expenditures to expand the industry, professionalize it and coordinate tourist promotion with the lucrative industry of Spain. The primary area for tourists is the Algarve, visited by hundreds of thousands of vacationers every year. Many people worry about the degradation of the environment and see the past haphazard construction of villas and apartment buildings as an ominous sign of irresponsibility among contractors. But, a vital source of income, this fast-growing industry provides about 14 percent of the jobs.

GOVERNMENT AND POLITICS

Portugal is a parliamentary democracy governed under a constitution promulgated 25 April 1976 and revised in 1982, 1989, 1992 and 1997. The president is popularly elected to a five-year term as head of state. The president, in turn, appoints the prime minister, who is leader of the majority party or majority coalition as head of government. The prime minister presides over a cabinet of about fifteen ministers. A Council of State acts as a consultive body to the president. Legislative power is vested in a unicameral parliament, the Assembly of the Republic, with a total of 230 seats. Members of the Assembly are elected by popular vote under a system of proportional representation and serve four-year terms.

Political parties are the Socialist Party (PS), the Social Democratic Party (PSD) (which strives to promote greater private enterprise), the Communist Party (PCP), the center-right Popular Party (PP) (which espouses a market economy and less public sector intervention), the National Solidarity Party (PSN) and a number of small leftist groups.

The judicial system is headed by the supreme court, made up of a president and forty judges appointed for life. Below this are courts of appeal and ordinary and special district courts. Local authority is vested in the district governors and legislatures. Each of the districts, subdivided into parishes, has an elected assembly and council. The autonomous regions of the Azores and Madeira elect their own governments.

THE PRESS

Under the dictatorship from 1926 to 1974 the state and the church were allied in the struggle to combat materialism, communism and the dilution of Portuguese customs and traditions through foreign influences. Censorship of the press, radio and television was established to meet these ends. Events such as suicides, assassinations, strikes, child abuse and abortions, matters concerning the ubiquitous poverty, homosexuality, working-class unrest, emigration, civil burials and especially political prisoners were all taboo subjects. Newspapers could be shut down for reporting an increase in pollution along the beaches. Nothing could be said with regard to Soviet Russia, as communism was an outlawed subject. When sputnik captured the attention of the world, Portuguese papers were permitted to quote only a patriotic astronomy professor who declared it was all a fabrication. In a country with endemic illiteracy the censors were sometimes as unlettered as the audience and lumped together evil influences, equating writers such as Lenin and Racine.

Under the constitution of 1976 freedom of the press is guaranteed, and legislation to return seven state-owned newspapers to private ownership was approved in early 1988, with privatization of the press being completed in 1991. By 1998 some twenty-six daily newspapers were published.

MILITARY AND DEFENSE

Military service is compulsory. Male citizens serve four to eight months in the army and four to eighteen months in the air force and navy. Conscientious objectors are permitted to select alternative community service. Portugal has modern, well-equipped armed forces, the total strength of which in mid-1997 was 59,300, including 12,700 conscripts. The paramilitary National Republican Guard (GNR) totaled 20,900, and the Public Security Police, 20,000. Some 1,050 U.S. troops were stationed in Portugal, mainly at the air force base of Lajes in the Azores. In 1996 military expenditures were 1.9 percent of the GDP.

CULTURE

In Lisbon there are a number of important libraries, including the Academy of Sciences, the Ajuda, the National and the Military Library. The National Archive of Torre do Tombo, also in Lisbon, is noteworthy for its collection of historical documents dating from the ninth century. Libraries in Oporto, Évora, Braga and Mafra contain many rare books and large collections of manuscripts. In addition, various specialized libraries are attached to the universities. Museums of archaeology, art and ethnography are found in the principal cities and towns. The art museum in Coimbra is famous for its sixteenth-century sculpture, and that of Évora for Roman sculpture and sixteenth-century paintings. Lisbon is replete with world-class museums, which include the National Museum of Ancient Art, the museums of Contemporary Art, Natural History, Ethnography, Azulejos (tiles), the Coach Museum and the National Museum of Archaeology. The superb Calouste Gulbenkian Museum has a collection of fine art.

Music

Portuguese folk music ranges from very lively songs and dances to sad laments. Until the seventeenth century formal training in music was in the hands of the church, and clergy dominated musical composition. It is little wonder that it reflects Roman Catholic influences. Among classical composers, the best known is probably João Domingos Bomtempo, head of the National Academy of Music in the early nineteenth century, while in Romantic music, Alfredo Keil, a student of Franz Liszt, is of note.

At the end of the twentieth century, as in other countries, Portugal suffers from a lack of money to support the arts. The Gulbenkian Foundation, however, has been instrumental in sponsoring opera, ballet, choirs and an orchestra, along with festivals (often held in historical settings such as cathedrals and monasteries).

Associated with Portugal probably above all is the fado, haunting songs of yearning and longing expressing profound passion and sorrow. Accompanied by guitar, the melancholy music is generally sung by women, often of middle age. In contrast there are today many jazz clubs, especially in Lisbon.

Art

Of singular interest is Paleolithic art and rock sculpture found in caves or grottos scattered throughout the country. Employed in the drawings were vegetable dyes and sometimes blood for bonding. Oil painting began to develop in the fifteenth century in which court painters were employed to depict the monarchs. Portuguese artists in general adhered to the various European schools—Italian, Dutch and French. Some of the most successful Portuguese artists lived in Paris, such as Amadeus da Sousa Cardoso, who studied under Paul Cézanne. Today there are many established artists such as Júlio Pomar and Paula Rego, whose outstanding works are on display.

The Monument of the Discoveries at Belém, constructed in 1960 to commemorate the 500th anniversary of the death of Henrique the Navigator, and the giant statue of Christ across the Tejo estuary are the most visible of modern sculptural works, but the art is alive and healthy in various studios throughout the country.

The founder of the Portuguese theater, Gil Vicentes, who staged plays for the nobility beginning in 1502, still enjoys some popularity today. Perhaps not the country's strongest medium, the theater has some good playwrights whose works appear on the Lisbon stage along with those by other world-famous authors.

Film festivals are organized by enthusiasts, but often small towns do not have cinemas, so the audiences are limited. Many who work in this medium have their films appear on television, where there is no lack of viewers for the multiplicity of channels now available.

Architecture

Portugal exhibits many different styles of architecture: prehistoric dolmens, ancient megalithic stone burial chambers found in various parts of the country—the largest at Valverde near Évora—are the earliest architectural monuments. Other structures and designs manifest the ages in which they were built. Celtic round stone houses of the castros, Roman forums, villas or country manor houses and the temple of Diana at Évora are only part of a bygone heritage still visible today. Subsequent occupations by the Visigoths in the fifth century and by the Muslims in the eighth can be discerned in the styles of many buildings and churches, while medieval castles dot the landscape. There are Romanesque cathedrals in Lisbon, Oporto, Évora and Coimbra; the monasteries of Alcobaça and Batalha are Gothic, while the Renaissance style is seen in the great monastery and palace of Mafra, the baroque in Lisbon's church of Santa Engrácia, neo-classical in the national theater of Dona María, again in Lisbon, and modern architecture in the new buildings of the major cities.

Unique to the country is the sixteenth-century Manueline architectural design named after the Fortunate King. It symbolizes Portugal's grand Age of Discovery, elaborately reflecting its maritime eminence. Manueline motifs are derived from the sea, including shells, coral, waves, fish, anchors, ropes and nautical instruments, combined with such Gothic forms as pointed arches and finials. It is especially visible today in the monastery of São Geronimos in Lisbon and the Convento de Cristo at Tomar.

Folk architecture developed in accordance with earlier influences and varying climate. In the Algarve are numerous whitewashed houses with Roman red-tiled roofs and Moorish-style filigree chimneys. In the Alentejo, squat, often nearly windowless farmhouses are generally painted white to keep out the heat, with a blue trim to ward off evil, and in the Sado River estuary square houses with thatched roofs are frequent. To the north, near Aveiro are the distinctly striped wooden houses called *palheiros*, and in the Minho region the granite dwellings are constructed to keep out the cold, often with two stories, the farm animals being installed on the ground floor. Most have an adjacent *espigueiro*, or covered storage bin, resting off the ground on stone pillars—probably of Celtic origin. The azulejos, or Portuguese tiles, are a distinctive feature of architectural decoration, continuing the Moorish tradition. Initially polychromatic, they generally now follow the Dutch blue delft style.

On the outskirts of the major cities growing populations and the influx of peasants from the country have spawned cardboard and corrugated tin slums, especially around Lisbon. Ubiquitous drab apartment buildings also disfigure the skyline. In the Algarve, excessive construction has been the source of many complaints.

Literature

Portuguese literary output dates back to the thirteenth-century inventive talents of the troubadours, who composed songs of chivalry and love, and to the prose works of the lives of saints and of miracles. The early fifteenth century saw a second flowering of literature brought on by the Renaissance and Age of Discovery in both poetry and prose, and historians recorded the rise and fall of the empire and chronicled the reigns of kings.

The philosophy of humanism, which emphasizes the dignity and value of the individual and contains the basic premise that people are rational beings, inspired some famous sixteenth-century writers. The man regarded as the foremost Portuguese humanist, Damião de Góis, historian and diplomat, is best remembered for his *Chrónica do felicíssimo rei Dom Manuel* (*Chronicle of the Very Fortunate King, Dom Manuel*). The most outstanding of Portugal's literary figures was Luís Vaz de Camões, the greatest of Portuguese poets, whose principal work, *Os Lusíadas*, is considered the national epic.

Another surge in world-class literature came in the nineteenth century with the poet-playwright Visconde de Almeida Garret and the historian-novelist Alexandre Herculano. Antero de Quental, poet and aristocrat of the French positivist persuasion, influenced the "generation of 1870," which included Teófila Braga, Joaquim Martins, the original novelist Eça de Queiros and José Ortigão, among others.

Although comparatively small in volume, Portuguese literature equals other major European works in quality and innovation. Well into the twentieth century, poetry was shaped by French literary trends, although the avant-gardist Fernando Pessoa also brought English influences to bear. Since the revolution of 1974, contemporary Portuguese writers have turned to questioning the myths of Portuguese history in a search for new ways of defining the nation. Once suppressed works are now published.

New freedom of expression has encouraged the publication of writings by Portuguese Africans and of many fine women writers, of whom novelist Olga Gonçalves is the most prominent. José de Almeida Faria's trilogy about the past two decades, especially its final volume, *Lusitania* (1981), is ranked as one of the most important recent works of fiction. In the 1990s young writers draw on their experiences of the revolution, decolonization and social and class injustice. In 1998, José Saramago was awarded the Nobel Prize for Literature.

RELIGION

Roman Catholicism is the faith of about 97 percent of the Portuguese people, while Protestantism is the faith of about 1 percent, and the remainder are of diverse faiths. There are three ecclesiastical provinces under archbishops at Lisbon, Braga and Évora. The constitution guarantees freedom of religion, and some Protestant churches and Jewish synagogues have been established. Strong anticlerical sentiments appeared in the late eighteenth century with the tardy arrival of the ideas of the Reformation on the Iberian Peninsula. During the era of the First Republic relations with the Vatican were broken, church property was confiscated, religious holidays were abolished, sacred oaths ceased to have legal force and religious instruction in schools and theology in the universities were prohibited. During Salazar's dictatorship the church was given special recognition and privileges. A concordat with the Vatican in 1940, while maintaining the separation of church and state, reversed the anticlerical stance of the republican period, and the church was restored to a position of exclusive control of public school education, moral instruction in the army, the right to own property and reclaim that taken by the republic, made exempt from taxes and given state subsidies, among other privileges. Naturally, the church supported the dictator.

In the north people are generally more devout than in other parts of the country, often making agonizing pilgrimages, sometimes for miles on their knees, to hilltop shrines and chapels. The basilica at Fátima, on the spot where three peasant children reputedly witnessed apparitions of the Virgin Mary in 1917, is a focal point for this kind of religious activity. At the same time many peasants in rural areas believe in witchcraft and magic and good and bad spirits, along with saints. Belief in the evil eye is still widespread, and "witch" burning occurred as late as the 1930s.

LANGUAGE

Although Portugal occupies the same peninsula as Spain, the country is very different from its large neighbor in architectural styles, art, cuisine, temperament and, of course, language. A descendant of Vulgar Latin, Portuguese, the official language of the country, is a Romance language. It contains vocabulary borrowed from Arabic and other foreign tongues and is closely related to Galician in the northwest corner of Spain. Both began to separate from Hispano-Latin in late Roman times, before the Muslim conquest of the peninsula in 711. It was first committed to writing in the twelfth century, although Latin as the written medium was still used officially for centuries afterward. Portuguese is spoken by about 200 million people around the world.

SOCIETY

The original Portuguese stock derives from Celtic immigrants, Romans and Germanic settlers, Moors and Jews who were absorbed into the population and Africans, once imported as slaves. Despite such complex origins, the population today is one of Europe's most homogeneous, and the only important minority is fewer than 100,000 black colonial refugees recently arrived from Africa.

By the end of World War II the country was still composed of its traditionally small upper class, a middle class of no great numbers, a modest urban working class and a large mass of rural peasants. Roughly divided into occupations, the upper class consisted of owners and managers of major industry, high-ranking government officials and military officers, large landowners in the Alentejo and many lawyers, physicians and university professors. The middle class was composed of rural proprietors, company and midgrade officials and officers, owners of small businesses, shopkeepers, schoolteachers and low-level civil servants. The lower class was made up of small-plot peasant farmers, especially in the north, or landless peasants, especially in the south, and an urban proletariat concentrated mostly around the industrial centers of Lisbon and Oporto.

This system remained largely unchanged until the 1970s, when through more widespread education, new career opportunities emerged, creating a group composed of skilled technicians, computer specialists, entrepreneurs and commercial farmers (often involved in cooperative efforts), giving more mobility within the class hierarchy and blurring many social distinctions.

Among the peasant class disparities still exist between the north and south of the country due to differences in long-standing property tenure dating back to the time of the Reconquest. In the hilly north, a small parcel of owned or rented land worked by an independent farmer is the dominant form of agricultural holdings. Entire families work the land, reinforcing the family as a self-contained unit. The people are more conservative and church-oriented. A more class-conscious peasantry has been created in the south due to the large landed estates (a legacy of the old military orders that conquered it from the Muslims), leaving the peasants landless. Many migrated to Lisbon seeking work, fueling the growth of the proletariat in the city and contributing toward the breakdown of the traditional structure of family and church. This, in turn, led to a more progressive or radical disposition for change since there was no strong ancestral attachment to the land.

The differences in outlook between the north and south are clearly seen in the voting behavior of each region. The north has strongly endorsed conservative or right-wing political parties, while the Left draws much of its strength from the south and the industrial employees.

TRANSITIONAL PERIOD

The 1960s were good years for Western Europe, which was optimistic about a better future. Only the Cold War cast a long shadow over the continent. In general, economies were prosperous, social change was taking place throughout, freedom of expression and civil rights were proclaimed, inventions were making domestic life easier, people had achieved space travel, the churches, both Catholic and Protestant, appeared open to change and autocrats had fallen almost everywhere. But Portugal still had over a decade more to endure a severe dictatorship. The Salazar regime looked upon the changing morals and viewpoints of the post–World War II years as a degenerate breakdown of traditional customs through lack of discipline brought on by liberal ideas. To combat liberalism, a resurgence of the Catholic faith and censorship was considered indispensable to protect society against radical misconceptions.

As late as 1974 newspapers, magazines and films were mutilated by the censors to conceal progressive ideas, public demonstrations were prohibited and even modern dancing was officially frowned upon. When girls' skirts went up above the knees, the youth of Portugal (even on the beaches) were obliged to wear long, unrevealing apparel. Mothers continued to keep a fixed eye on their daughters and stand between them and any potential untoward relationship with young men. Pop music was seldom heard, and concerts were forbidden. The church kept a strict eye on such sinful activity.

Over the years and in the head-on confrontation with students, workers and intellectuals, Salazar's popularity and influence waned as the twin pillars of his power, the church and the military, began to vacillate in the support they had always shown for the regime, the former realizing it was losing the youth of the country and the latter tired of its unappreciated role, especially in colonial Africa.

The church, not unlike the lay sector, split into liberal and conservative factions, and a delegation of clergy now dared to criticize the government. In 1963 a new magazine, *O Tempo e o Modo* (*Time and Style*), reflected the spirit of the times and came into conflict with the conservative elements. The most pronounced issues concerned the relationships between the sexes and the conflict between generations involving the changing role of the family. Throughout Europe and slowly encroaching on Portugal the extended familial structure with grandparents, parents and children all under the same roof was decreasing. Instead, the nuclear family was replacing the traditional one that Salazar had championed for decades.

CRIME AND POVERTY

Appalling poverty exists in the two major cities, Lisbon and Oporto. Many thousands of people live in squalor in dwellings that are illegally constructed and lack any form of sanitation, running water or electricity. Like most large cities in other countries they have their share of the poor, the hungry and the addicted. Car break-ins, pickpockets, especially at tourist resorts, and burglaries for quick cash are probably as common as elsewhere in similar circumstances.

With its miles of coastline and open borders, the country is vulnerable to drug traffickers, who wasted little time exploiting the situation after the advent of democracy. Homicide and other violent crimes occur from time to time, especially in the drug-infested depths of the underworld, but they are less of a problem in Portugal than in many other countries. In the countryside and villages any kind of crime is practically unknown.

Perhaps, the most dangerous thing to do in Portugal is drive. Portugal has the highest death rate from automobile accidents of all the European Union (EU) countries.

EDUCATION, HEALTH AND WELFARE

The Inquisition stifled intellectual life in the sixteenth and seventeenth centuries, and the Jesuits exercised nearly complete control over education until they were expelled from Portugal in the middle of the eighteenth century. In 1964 compulsory schooling was increased from four to six years, and both public and private institutions now provide formal studies at all levels. While preschool attendance for three- to six-year-olds is not compulsory, it is available free of charge. Between the ages of six and fifteen basic education is mandatory and is also provided free of charge at public schools. Special programs are available for handicapped children, and, besides the university, higher education is offered at technical schools. The adult illiteracy rate declined from 29 percent in 1970 to 10.4 percent in 1995. Government expenditure on education in 1994 was 12.9 percent of total spending. New universities were founded in Lisbon and Oporto in 1911, and three more followed in 1973 at Braga, Évora and Aveiro.

In the realm of health (based on 1998 figures), life expectancy at birth for Portuguese males is seventy-two years and seventy-nine for females (United States: seventy-three and eighty, respectively). There was one hospital bed for every 235 persons (United States: one for 218) and one physician for every 344 people (United States: one for 391). Infant mortality per 1,000 live births was 9.2 (United States: 8). In 1993 the state budget allocated 10.5 percent of total spending to health services. The state-run social welfare system includes family allowances, health insurance, maternity benefits, old-age pensions, workers' compensation, unemployment and disability payments and veterans' pensions.

THE ROLE OF WOMEN

The status of women has traditionally been subordinated to that of men; hence, they have had few economic, political and personal rights. For centuries this subservient role has been inflicted on them so that it has become ingrained in the mentality of both sexes, and even today in the villages and hamlets escape from it is extremely difficult since the women's self-image is often that of an inferior.

Under Salazar a woman could not vote unless she were literate and head of a household and could not sell family property or enter into any economic arrangement, obtain a passport or open a separate bank account without the consent of her husband. Women were considered the moral backbone of the all-important family—docile, obedient and faithful as wives and mothers. The regime went to great efforts to keep women in this role, affirming that the decadence of modern society was, in part, due to excesses in capitalism, with the corollary of the recruitment of women into the workforce. Feminine participation in the labor market was discouraged, and the political and social climate for women remained reactionary until the end of the dictatorship.

In 1972 Maria Isabel Barreno, Maria Teresa Horta and Maria Velho da Costa collaborated to produce *Novas Cartas Portuguesas*, subsequently published in the United States as *The Three Marias*. Its recurrent theme is the oppression of women in a male-dominated society. The women were charged by the state for writing about the forbidden topic of women's sexuality and not acquitted until after the 1974 revolution.

Since then, a women's liberation movement has developed, and by 1975 everyone, male or female, over eighteen was given the vote, with women forming more than half the national electorate. In 1979 the prime minister was a woman (albeit for only six months). By 1987 four women were included in the government, nineteen were members of parliament and three were civil governors. In 1989 Assunção Esteves became a judge in the constitutional court, two women were elected to the European Parliament and by 1991 Judite Correia, the first woman accredited to the stock exchange, began her own stockbroking company. Divorce and abortion under certain circumstances are now legal, and many women are prominent, excelling in universities, medicine, the law, banking and the arts.

Although discrimination against women has officially been abolished, in fact, especially in rural areas, many are still trapped in brutal marriages, have less access to education, are frequently paid less than men and are nearly always the first to be laid off from work.

ANIMALS AND THE ENVIRONMENT

Since the standard of living and level of education have improved for much of the populace, some attention is now being paid to protection of nature and the environment. The powerful EU has rules and standards, backed by plenty of money to enforce them, and has proved to be an important catalyst for passing laws in Portugal dealing with environmental protection. Current issues include soil erosion, air pollution (caused by vehicle emissions and industry) and water pollution, particularly in coastal areas.

In general, the average Portuguese has not been concerned with the welfare of animals, wild or domestic, but there are today some active organizations such as the Nature Conservation Institute, the Portuguese Animal Association and the Grupo Lobo—the latter formed in 1985 to protect the remaining wolves in the country along with their habitat. The Liga Portuguesa dos Direitos do Animal represents the country in the Eurogroup for animal welfare.

2

Early History

The earliest immigrants to the Iberian Peninsula appear to have come from Northwest Africa over half a million years ago. Remains of campsites, bones of the animals they hunted and primitive, stone hand axes attest to these primordial peoples. When ancient people learned to exercise their artistic talents, they began to depict animals on the walls of caves and rock faces, probably as magical symbols to bring good luck to the hunt.

PREHISTORIC MAN

From about 40,000 to 10,000 years ago, a legacy of paintings and stone engravings of animals such as the mammoth, ibex and bison has come down to us in Portugal and other places. As the climate changed, and temperatures rose globally, many of the animals migrated northward or died out, and as a result, the growing population turned to the sea and rivers in order to exploit the food sources there. Fish, crustaceans and various other remains accumulated over the ages have been found in large mounds (shell middens). About 5000 B.C., in search of a more stable food supply, prehistoric communities learned to cultivate the land, domesticate animals such as sheep and goats, plant crops and manufacture pottery. This, in turn, resulted in a more settled population in villages instead of caves and allowed for leisure time away from hunting and fishing. More free time gave rise to intellectual and spiritual interests as people also cultivated their innate curiosity. Threatening natural phenomena, for example, lightning storms, as well as the idea of death and the unknown led humans to seek an authority superior to their own. The gods and goddesses they envisioned induced religious beliefs and rituals, of which the most salient today relate to the care and preparation of the dead for an afterlife. Dolmens, or tombs made of large, upright stones, roofed over with stone slabs and covered with earth, were constructed for the repository of bodies, often accompanied by personal articles of the deceased. Many of these dolmens, mostly built between about 4500 and 2000 B.C., still dot the Portuguese landscape.

Other palpable evidence of early spiritual beliefs may be seen in the erection of menhirs, large, single, standing stones, often phallic symbols, that appear to have represented some kind of appeal to gods or goddesses of fertility. Such monuments would not be surprising in cultures concerned with high mortality, especially among the young.

Leisure time also enabled early settled peoples to experiment with new ideas and methods of adornment and the manufacture of better weapons. While the discovery of shaping metal such as copper into decorative objects or tools and axes may have been an accident when it was noted that copper ore melted in a hot fire, early societies learned to mix copper and tin ore, which resulted in bronze, producing a much stronger tool or weapon. These activities, in which societies were no longer completely dependent on stone, ushered in the new, more advanced period of the metal ages.

Those who cared for the dead, studied the heavens for signs of disasters or propitious events and advised the populace about such matters as the best time to plant or make war on neighbors passed on their knowledge to their kin. Those who became skilled in metallurgy taught the methods to their offspring, and the field-workers and hunters likewise passed on their experiences. Thus, social classes began to form based on knowledge and skills in which priests, artisans, hunters and farmers made up society. Prowess in battle often singled a man out for leadership of the village, and he might then become the chief, surrounding himself with a coterie of warriors. The most revered members of the society were, no doubt, the priests or priestesses (who believed they had direct communication with the supernatural), followed by the warriors, then the artisans and finally the farmers.

CELTS

The land that is now Portugal constantly received new immigrants from the east seeking fresh pastures and living conditions more secure from marauding tribes. Celtic peoples began arriving on the peninsula as early as the tenth century B.C., bringing with them knowledge of the use of iron, which they had learned from more advanced eastern peoples. They took over the fortified hilltop Bronze Age villages of the local people or constructed new ones. The remnants of these stone villages, known as *cîtanias* or castros, are numerous throughout northern Portugal. In time, the Celts replaced the native inhabitants in this region of the country.

They cultivated the land, gathered honey, brewed beer, used the wool, milk and meat from their domesticated animals and produced weapons, jewelry and utensils from bronze, iron, lead, gold and silver. They lived in clusters of round stone houses with thatched roofs.

PHOENICIANS AND GREEKS

The rich metal deposits in the south of Portugal lured ancient Phoenician and, later, Greek mariners from the eastern Mediterranean in search of commerce about the same time as the Celts were settling in the north of the country. They established trading posts along the southern coasts and exchanged eastern finished products such as pottery, wine and arms for raw gold, silver and tin. With them came writing, and the local, Bronze Age populace of the southern part of the country adopted a modified Graeco-Phoenician script to their own language requirements, which, to this day, has not been deciphered. Most of the inscriptions that remain are on tombstones and can be seen in museums.

ROMANS

The Romans invaded eastern Iberia in 218 B.C. to deprive their enemies the Carthaginians under Hannibal (at the time attacking Italy) of their resources in manpower, horses and mineral wealth. About 202 B.C., they penetrated and conquered southern Portugal, where the tribes were relatively peaceful, and from there moved farther north. The closer they came to the villages of the warrior-like, independent Celts, whom they called Lusitanians, the more resistance they encountered. Matters were made worse when the Romans tricked the Lusitanians into a peace treaty, promising them better land. They gathered thousands of them in one place and then turned the legions loose on them, slaughtering a large number. Those who were not killed were taken prisoner and sold into slavery. The incensed Lusitanians now found a leader, a courageous and aggressive shepherd named Viriathus, who rallied his people against the enemy.

Employing guerrilla tactics of hit, run and ambush, he caused the Romans a good deal of trouble, even annihilating a Roman army in 147 B.C. The Romans finally defeated Viriathus by once again pretending friendship but secretly bribing assassins to murder him while he slept. After his death, the Romans killed thousands of Lusitanians and enslaved many others. The legendary name of Viriathus lives on in folklore to this day, however, immortalized by the poet Camões in *Os Lusíadas.*

Some Lusitanian Celts in their mountain bastions of central and northern Portugal continued their resistance to Roman rule even after Julius Caesar established his headquarters in 60 B.C. at Olisipo, present-day Lisbon. Not until the reign of Emperor Augustus, whose legions finally subdued the last of the freedom-loving mountain warriors in 19 B.C., did the Lusitanian wars come to an end, after which people no longer needed to live in protected, mountaintop villages where access to cultivated fields and fresh water often proved difficult. Attracted by the amenities and prospects of an easier life, they moved down onto the fertile plains.

Some of the *cîtanias* developed into Roman towns themselves, although others, removed from the main Roman centers, were abandoned. Many of these remain today, the best preserved being those at Briteiros (near Braga) and Sanfins (northeast of Oporto).

As Roman settlers from Italy moved into Lusitania, and ex-soldiers settled on land they had once fought over, the Roman or Romanized towns developed the luxuries they were used to (e.g., baths, circuses, theaters, temples and forum with a variety of shops and administrative offices). Lusitanians flocked to these centers, abandoning many of their old self-sufficient and simple customs whereby clothes were produced on primitive, home-made looms, wheat was ground on hand-powered stone mills and flocks of sheep were moved from the lowlands in winter to the higher pastures in summer. The Roman towns offered employment and a more animated lifestyle for many of the young people.

The choice of location of Roman towns was based on economic considerations. On the broad plains of the Alentejo, for example, the agricultural towns of Évora and Beja developed. The important industry of mining copper and silver led to the Roman settlement at Aljustral. For fishing and the manufacture of garum, a fish sauce exported all over the Roman empire, Faro and Tavira were ideal, and salt production at Alcácer do Sal became a fast-growing business.

The economy was enlarged to include the manufacture of building materials, ceramics, textiles and marble quarrying. Roads, dams and bridges (some of which are still used today) were constructed, and opulent villas were laid out with such refinements as under-floor heating, pools, rich, decorative mosaics and beautiful gardens. Roman law generally replaced the unwritten, local tribal traditions.

In the second century A.D., when Christianity was introduced and began to spread, pagan worship was still active in Lusitania. The old Celtic deities, gods and goddesses of fertility, of the sacred forests, rivers and mountains, of thunder and lightning, slowly lost their significance. At first, the Christians were severely persecuted by the Romans, who insisted that their gods, along with their emperor, be venerated. Not until Constantine I (emperor 306–337) became a Christian did this persecution mostly cease, but the pagan beliefs continued to be tolerated at the same time.

GERMANIC TRIBES

At the beginning of the fifth century, barbarian tribes, mostly of Germanic origin, crossed the Rhine and Danube Rivers, invaded the Roman empire, proceeded westward and crossed the Pyrenees Mountains into Hispania. By late summer 409, they had settled on the peninsula, and central Portugal was occupied by the Alans, a non-Germanic tribe that had accompanied the invasions. Vandals and Suevi settled in Galicia, the northwest corner of the Iberian Peninsula, while still other Vandals took up residence in the south. Meanwhile, the once-mighty Roman empire disintegrated under the advance of these hordes, and chaos, plundering and burning of towns characterized the new era.

Some Roman towns were abandoned during the barbarian invasions and were not rebuilt. Similarly, many villas were left to be covered over by the encroaching sands of time, only to be later unearthed by archaeologists. Outstanding remains can be seen today at Conímbriga (near Coimbra), Miróbriga (south of Setúbal), the Roman temple of Évora and the villa of Pisões near Beja.

Another Germanic people, the Visigoths, were enlisted by Roman emperors to help regain control of the Iberian Peninsula, and after successfully eliminating the southern Vandals and scattering the Alans in

Lusitania, they retired to Gaul until 456, when they returned. After a series of battles they defeated the Suevi and took over most of the Hispanic Peninsula. Few in numbers, the Visigoths almost entirely adopted the more advanced Roman culture over which they ruled as well as the Latin language. In addition, they embraced Christianity, earning the support of the church.

Emerging from the turmoil brought on by the barbarian invasions was a new political and social system in which the Visigothic warrior class, headed by a king, developed into a landed military aristocracy whose barons maintained control over a much larger Hispano-Latin population consisting of a poor peasantry often tied to the land as serfs and a class of slaves, many of whom were enrolled in the army. A politically powerful clergy often dictated policy, while its bishops lived in sumptuous palaces. Trade was generally controlled by a prosperous, but despised and persecuted, Jewish minority. These basic elements of society would, to a large degree, characterize the Christian kingdoms of the Middle Ages to follow.

In the year 700, starvation and death spread throughout the Iberian Peninsula due to crop failure and disease. At the same time, Arab and Berber pirates from across the Mediterranean plundered the southern coasts.

MUSLIM CONQUEST AND CHRISTIAN RECONQUEST

The first major invasion of the peninsula by the Moors of Mauritania in North Africa took place in the year 711. (Moors were descendants of Berber-speaking tribesmen who, conquered by the Arabs in the seventh century, converted to Islam. The term in eighth-century Portugal and Spain denoted any one of the mixed Arab and Berber conquerors.) Under the command of Tariq Ibn Ziyad, they crossed the straits and landed near Gibraltar (*gebel* meaning "mount," *tar* meaning "Tariq") and, shortly after, defeated the Visigothic forces under King Roderick. Tariq and his army then seized the Visigothic capital of Toledo, and within a few years most of the peninsula was under Moorish control. In what is now Portugal, Moorish domination lasted for about 500 years.

The conquerors took over the towns, which again became centers of commerce and trade, with the inhabitants living in relative harmony. Landowners who had not resisted were permitted to keep their property, but those who had stood against the Muslims lost it and were reduced to serfs or slaves. At first, Muslims, Jews and Christians lived side by side in their own communities and with their own houses of worship. A person was defined not by race or language but by religious creed. Those who did not profess the Muslim faith simply paid a head tax.

As new immigrants arrived from Africa, the Muslim population was far from socially homogeneous. Syrians, Arabs, Egyptians and Berbers, among others, made up the population, often quarreling and fighting for power. The vanquished Christians who absorbed the culture and language of the conquerors but not the Muslim faith were later to be called Mozarabs or "almost Arab." Those who converted were known as Muladí.

Where Arabs took over the Visigothic estates, production of the land was increased by new methods and development of irrigation canals, water wheels and cisterns. New crops were introduced such as oranges, peaches, saffron, dates, sugarcane and cotton.

In time the caliphs became patrons of learning, encouraging the collection and translation of Greek classics in philosophy, mathematics, medicine and botany. The Muslims cultivated science and technology, mapmaking and shipbuilding, among other disciplines. By the tenth century the feared caliphate of Córdoba was the envy of Christian Europe for its splendor and learning.

Christian Visigothic nobles who had fled from the invading Moors found sanctuary in the small, northern territory of Asturias in the northern Cantabrian Mountains. The snowy peaks and deep and foggy valleys did not attract the desert peoples from Africa, and they left the Christians pretty much to themselves. Under their leader Pelayo and subsequent kings, these refugees began to expand and challenge the Muslims in the northern plains along the southern edge of the mountains. Capitalizing on Muslim internal dissension, they began what was to become known as the Reconquest.

In the western part of the peninsula, the area between the Minho and Douro Rivers was hotly contested in a series of brutal battles as Christians and Muslims fought over the land. Much of it became ravaged and depopulated. As each side won, houses and farms were rebuilt, and areas were repopulated by the victors, but the situation remained unstable for many decades. Often Christian forces would occupy a region but, lacking manpower and resources to maintain control, would lose it again to the Muslims.

Dynastic politics involving struggles for power and prestige threatened to tear the Christian realms apart just as they did the Muslim lands. Both Christian and Muslim princes or others of noble birth would challenge the authority of the king, generating local civil wars within the context of the larger struggle. When it was convenient, each side made alliances with the other, but few lasted very long.

Arab raids extended far north into Portugal and Galicia, leaving the towns of Braga and Oporto in ruins and deserted, the inhabitants dispersed, seeking shelter in the forests. Counts and their men-at-arms in the service of the neighboring, expanded Christian kingdom of León raided south and established urban centers to which the populations could return. These towns were placed under the jurisdiction of a nobleman or bishop. In spite of battle lines moving back and forth as each side rebounded, by the year 868 the old Roman fort of Cale, which had once dominated the crossing over the Douro River, was definitively conquered by Christian forces. The area was given the name Portucale (Port of Cale), a name that would later become Portugal.

With the Muslim capital at Córdoba in the south of Spain where the caliph resided, a desirable, lush region of palm trees and fertile land nestled in the lee of the Sierra Morena, the Islamic court was far from the troubled frontier where the wars were taking place. Muslim settlers were not enamored with the idea of living in a far-off combat zone where unpredictable enemy raids could destroy the farm and family in minutes. The northern Christians, on the other hand, were fighting on their own doorstep. As their population expanded, so did their land to the south at the expense of the Muslims. The counts of Portucale were vassals of the kings of León but far enough from court to conduct their affairs with minimum interference.

In 1064 Coimbra was reconquered from the Muslims and governed in the name of King Fernando of León. Many Christian settlers came, and the city became mostly Christian in religion and administration while it retained its Muslim customs and architecture. The wars fought between the opposing religions were not total wars. Christians continued to live under Muslim suzerainty in the south, and followers of Islam were often tolerated in reconquered Christian towns. In both cases they generally lived in their own urban enclaves and avoided problems with the authorities.

Such was not always the case, however, and the Christian lands in the north grew through the influx of immigrants from the south escaping Muslim tyranny and persecution, which occurred from time to time. These acts of suppression in Córdoba and in other southern cities were often self-induced by Christian martyrs' openly and publicly defying the laws of Islam or blaspheming the Koran.

In the early eleventh century Alfonso VI of León gave the county of Portucale as a dowry to his daughter, Teresa, who married Henri (Portuguese Henrique), a French Burgundian knight who had come to Spain to participate in the Reconquest. In 1095 Henri was given control of the area south of the Minho, and soon his name appeared in documents as count of Portugal. On his invitation, the monks of Cluny built over 100 monasteries in the area, the most famous being the cathedral at Braga. On his death in 1112, Teresa, who took to calling herself queen, was left as governor, but since she was much disliked by the barons (in large part due to the fact that she now married a Galician nobleman, and they were afraid of becoming subject to the Galicians), attention began to be focused on her son, Afonso Henriques, who was sympathetic to the barons' concerns.

Portugal was still a province ruled by, and dependent on, the neighboring kings of what had now become through further Christian expansion Castilla-León, while south of Coimbra it was still a Muslim province of the caliphs of Córdoba. Culturally, differences between Castilla-León and Portugal had been well defined for some time. The Portuguese language, for example, was already rather distinct from that of their neighbors, partly due to the geographic isolation from the Hispano-Roman speech of the rest of the peninsula. Among other things this language had already developed the nasalized vowels that make it so different from Spanish, and the earliest documents written in Old Portuguese in the late twelfth century confirm these distinctions. Living in a region that was cut off culturally, politically and geographically from the center of power must have contributed to the desire for independence from Castilla-León, where decisions were made without much concern for the inhabitants of Portugal.

3

House of Burgundy, 1097–1385

AFONSO HENRIQUES

The independence of Portugal took place over a period of time in the twelfth century beginning with the revolt in 1128 of Prince Afonso Henriques against his mother, Teresa, and her lover, the Galician Fernão Peres. At the decisive Battle of São Mamede, near Guimarães, both of them were taken prisoner and exiled across the Minho River, while the victory gave Afonso Henriques, supported by many local barons, dominion over Christian territory from the Minho to Coimbra. During the years 1130–1135, the lands of the king of Castilla-León were raided several times by Afonso Henriques, who rejected the idea of subservience. Further, to secure his southern border from attack by the Muslims, he built a castle at Leiria south of Coimbra.

In 1139 a Christian victory at Campo de Ourique over a Muslim force turned out to be significant for the Portuguese Reconquest, giving it a separate sense of identity from similar struggles in Castilla-León. After this, Afonso Henriques began calling himself king. In 1143 he sent a letter to Pope Innocent II to request protection from the Holy See, establishing Portugal as a vassal state of the Vatican, a long way away, and thus avoiding vassalage to Alfonso VII, his more powerful Castillian neighbor. The title of king for Afonso was not formally confirmed by the pope until 1179, when the substantial sum of 1,000 gold coins was paid for the privilege.

A continuing, alternating state of war and peace prevailed along the Christian-Muslim frontier, and as one town after the other fell into the hands of Afonso Henriques, he was able to extend his territory to the far side of the Tejo. In 1162, in a southeasterly move toward the Alentejo, the strategic town of Évora was attacked and taken by one of his lieutenants, Geraldo Sem-Pavor ("Geraldo without fear"), who, using guerrilla-style tactics reminiscent of Viriathus over a thousand years before, generally took his opponents by surprise.

As the struggle for dominance of southern Portugal continued, the Muslim society underwent profound changes. These fierce men of the North African deserts succumbed to the easy living in the bountiful south of the peninsula, and their communities became riddled with factions seeking power and wealth. Moors fought with Arabs, Arabs with Syrians, and nobles fought each other for control of territory.

The Muslim lands became divided into small kingdoms called taifas, often mutually hostile, and as they found themselves easy prey to Christian expansion, they called on the fanatical Almoravids of Morocco, a Muslim sect that had taken over that country, for assistance. Answering the call, an Almoravid army crossed the Strait of Gibraltar. Besides attacking the encroaching Christians and driving them back, the Almoravids also reduced the taifas of their coreligionists one by one. By the beginning of the twelfth century, they controlled a unified Muslim territory on both sides of the strait, but as their society, too, degenerated, taifas reappeared, and in 1146 the even more zealous Almohads, who had forcibly replaced the Almoravids in Morocco, began to make an appearance on the Hispanic Peninsula. The Almohad court developed into a center of art and learning, but their religious conservatism did not appeal to the Hispanic Muslims, creating anew social divisions and unrest.

In the meantime, with a growing reputation for daring and skill in warfare, Afonso Henriques set out in 1147 to capture Santarém, north of Lisbon, the most important town of the middle Tejo River valley, strategically situated at the focal point of several Roman highways. Enlisting the help of the religious military order of the Knights Templar, his army surprised, captured and sacked the town, slaughtering many of its Muslim inhabitants. In the same year, with the assistance of an army of crusaders about 13,000 strong who had put in at Oporto for provisions on route to the Holy Land, the city of Lisbon was taken after some weeks of siege. As a result, the surviving Muslims were ordered to leave without their possessions, and the crusaders and the Portuguese soldiers shared the booty. With the capture of Lisbon, Sintra was cut off from Muslim aid and surrendered, while the fortress of Palmela on the south side of the Tejo was abandoned, giving the Christians a strong outpost for further attacks southward.

In 1169 the Portuguese attacked Badajoz, but assistance to the Muslims came from Fernando II of León, who considered the insolent attack an affront to his sovereignty since it was directed at a city he deemed to be in his sphere of interest and eventually his own prize. Fernando II took Afonso Henriques and his commander, Sem-Pavor, prisoner and released them only in exchange for a large amount of gold and the surrender of castles held by the Portuguese north of the Minho and east of the Alentejo. Badajoz meantime remained in the hands of the Muslims, who agreed to be vassals of the Leonese king.

Afonso Henriques' son, Sancho, was knighted in 1170, whereupon he became coruler of the country with his father, who, injured in the battle at Badajoz, was unable to continue taking an active role in governing the country. The newly acquired territory south of the Tejo was now granted to the Templars for protection and development.

The Portuguese capital under Afonso Henriques was at Guimarães, but as the Muslim society was pushed back, the capital was reestablished first at Coimbra, then at Lisbon. When Afonso Henriques, now Afonso I, died in 1185, his son Sancho became the second king of the Burgundian dynasty.

SANCHO I AND AFONSO II

The first few years of Sancho's reign were peaceful. He set about strengthening the eastern frontier with Castilla, restoring Covilhã and founding Guarda. He is mainly remembered as a colonizer, resettling areas that had been depopulated, constructing or improving towns, roads and castles and offering privileges to encourage people to live in the territory. Municipal charters were granted guaranteeing such privileges as alleviation of taxes and freedom to serfs and runaway captives after a period of residence. Even though most of Sancho's reign was devoted to strengthening and consolidating his domain, he attacked by sea and captured Silves on the southern coast, which was later lost to the Almohads, and enhanced commerce by decrees that made travel easier for merchants. Portugal, meanwhile, was becoming a force in its own right. In 1211 Sancho died, a wealthy man, and was succeeded by his son, Afonso II "the Fat."

Unable personally to indulge in drawn-out military campaigns against the Moors because of his health, Afonso II devoted his time to matters of law, administration and further unification of the country. Disputes within his own family over property rights occupied much of his reign, along with investigations into the property rights and privileges of the church and the nobility. Beginning in 1218, a series of inquiries into the legalities of landholdings was initiated as a means of protecting the crown against fraudulent land claims on which no taxes were paid. The first law of mortmain was also initiated whereby land was not permitted to be donated to the church. He was excommunicated by the pope for his interference in ecclesiastical affairs, and his kingdom was placed under an anathema.

Early in Afonso II's reign, extraordinary meetings or assemblies called Cortes, comprising members of the nobility and clergy, to which grievances were addressed, came into being. The Cortes was not a legislative body at this time, but one of its concerns was the question of public money.

Meanwhile, the Templars were granted large properties on the eastern frontier with the obligation to develop and protect the town of Castelo Branco, and the Knights of Calatrava, soon to be known as the Knights of Avis, were granted the town of that name to build a castle and settle the district. Military orders were soon given large tracts of reconquered land in the south, which were later leased to farmers who worked them and maintained the knights. This legacy of subservience to the owners of the large estates continued up to the nineteenth century. In 1223 Afonso II died from leprosy.

ECONOMIC DEVELOPMENT AND SOCIAL ORDER

As Portugal emerged as an independent nation, agriculture was the primary economic activity, but some mining took place, allowing local manufacture of iron implements such as horseshoes, nails and farm tools, and salt was mined or panned to preserve produce. Trade developed with Northern Europe and the Moors, with the Jewish population acting as intermediaries between Christians and Muslims. While trade gave rise to a small, urban middle class, only three divisions were recognized in society: clergy, nobility and the rest of the population, which consisted of peasants, serfs and slaves.

The clergy controlled the parishes within the dioceses and administered the monasteries and convents, and the pope claimed supreme control over all, including kings. With enormous wealth and political power at its disposal, the church dispensed its own justice, was immune from taxes and frequently received large legacies of property, all of which led to much conflict between the clergy and the state. The clergy's spiritual mandate gave them added power, which they did not hesitate to use to gain their ends. Many a king, fearing what awaited him in the next world, gave in on his deathbed and bequeathed to them land and wealth, even though these endowments had been forbidden.

The nobility consisted of the wealthy, estate-owning *ricos homens*, who were of the highest rank; the *infançoes*, or lesser nobles, whose only influence came from their birthright, and the *fidalgos*, who had a warrior status and were part of the king's or other nobles' households. All castles belonged to the king, and no one else was permitted to own or construct them, and when armies were raised, again only the king had the legal power to do so. As time progressed, the land north of the Tejo became the domain of the king, church and nobility, while south of the river it belonged to the military orders and municipalities that had been granted to the early settlers after the Reconquest and retained feudal privileges.

Peasants formed by far the largest part of the population. In the rural areas of the south, many owned nothing and were forced into conditions approaching slave labor. Although technically free, they had to support the clergy by paying tithes and were subject to the arbitrary decisions of their noble or clerical lords, to whom they had to pay rent. They, like the serfs bound to the land, had no voice in affairs of state. At the bottom of the heap were the slaves, who were mostly captured Moors, often kept chained to prevent them from escaping.

When commerce started to take on more importance, especially in Lisbon and Oporto, and a bourgeoisie began to emerge, the class structure showed signs of change. The towns, rather than the landed estates, became more powerful, but in the south farming remained vital to feed an ever-growing population.

SANCHO II AND AFONSO III

Afonso's son Sancho II was about ten years old when he inherited the title of king. His reign was chaotic, characterized by ongoing conflict with the Muslims as well as by revolts of both the nobility and the church, both of which resisted the growing power of the royal family. The rich landowners who, with their illegal private armies, ruled the country, committed acts of murder, extortion, lawlessness and conflict, producing anarchy and violence and creating a crisis of gigantic proportions. In 1245 the pope, who had been assailed on all sides by complaints, called together a church council, which conspired to remove Sancho from the throne, giving the crown to his brother Afonso, then in exile in France.

Before leaving Paris, Afonso confidently proclaimed that he would restore order in Portugal and that all the people would have what was rightfully theirs. Hence, he was welcomed by the populace, much of the aristocracy, and the church. Sancho's death in 1248 at Toledo gave Afonso III's claim to the throne legitimacy, and during the early part of his reign the country flourished under a period of relative stability.

Meanwhile, conquest southward made steady progress until in 1249 the southern coastal towns of Tavira and Faro fell into Christian hands. The Muslim Algarvian capital of Silves on the river Arade, with its sandstone castle and stout walls, definitively fell to the Portuguese about the same time. The remainder of the western Algarve succumbed to Christian forces in 1250, allowing Portugal to consolidate its natural boundaries.

In 1254 a Cortes was held in Leiria, where, for the first time, common people, representatives of the towns, on the initiative of the king, were in attendance, forming the first parliament of the three estates: nobility, church and commoners. New laws were instituted that curbed privileges of both the nobility and the church and that, at the same time, gave more justice to the people from whom the king gained much of his support.

In 1258 inquiries into land illegally held by nobles and church were revived, which led to threats from Rome. In 1277, through lack of success in reaching any agreement, an act of impeachment freeing the king's subjects from his rule was issued by the Vatican. Two years later, Afonso, ill and bedridden and fearing his impending death, decided to make peace with the church and receive absolution by swearing an unconditional oath of obedience to the pope. His son, Dinis, made a like declaration.

The reign of Afonso III had seen development in the growth of Lisbon as the seat of government, the augmentation of international trade, representation given to the common man in the Cortes and, in the realm of culture, the encouragement of the poetry of the troubadours, wandering minstrels of Provence.

DINIS

Dinis came to the throne in 1279 at age eighteen to rule over nearly 1 million subjects. He had been raised partially by his grandfather, Alfonso the Wise of Castilla, who profoundly influenced the young man's education. Peace and relative harmony characterized Dinis' reign, and his court was a center of culture, the economy prospered and Lisbon was fast becoming a city of international importance. Castles were restored and refurbished, and some fifty fortresses were built along the Spanish frontier, while forests were planted and land reclaimed and made arable.

Dinis considered agriculture a major source of his country's wealth, and his reforms led to unused land being put in the hands of peasants who could make it productive. He guaranteed the transmission of cultivation rights and encouraged the draining of marshes, planting of crops, reforestation, and greater mineral exploitation. Through his efforts such exports as grains, dried fruits, olive oil, salt, cork, almonds and raisins were produced, making it possible for Portugal to import needed goods such as lead and linen cloth. Foreign trade was encouraged, and an agreement drawn up in 1293 provided a sum as security against losses at sea—the first kind of basic marine insurance in Europe. Under Dinis, laws and documents were written in the vernacular instead of Latin, education was promoted, and a university was opened—originally to provide training for clergy. It began in Lisbon, was transferred to Coimbra for a hundred years and then came back to Lisbon before it finally settled in Coimbra.

Dinis inherited a domain that had been excommunicated, but he seemed in no hurry to do anything about this. In 1285 the Cortes met to deal with the religious problem, but reconciliation with the pope was not achieved until 1289, when most of the outstanding questions were resolved to Dinis' advantage, the frontiers with Castilla being definitively confirmed. King Dinis further took control of the military orders and settled the Knights of Santiago at Palmela. After a dispute over the Knights Templar, Pope Clement V abolished that order in 1312, giving their property to the Hospitallers, but he made exceptions of the Hispanic states, and the Portuguese crown fell heir to the many Templar castles in that country. Dinis suggested to the pope that a new order be created, and in 1319 the Portuguese Order of Christ came into being from the ashes of the Templars, which immediately took over any Templar estates that the crown had not confiscated. The Order of Christ was settled at Castro Marim in the south so that they could defend the country from possible Muslim invasions and contest any potential incursions from Spain into Portugal along the Guadiana River frontier.

Political turmoil brought on by family feuds clouded Dinis' later reign, culminating in a civil war in 1320 that was to last three years. Dinis' son, Afonso, rebelled against his father, accusing him of failing to maintain proper social order. Time and again, Afonso's mother, Isabel, acted as intermediary between them, but in 1325, after a military defeat by his rebellious son, Dinis fell ill and died at Santarém, and the crown went to Afonso.

AFONSO IV

In 1340 the Battle of the Salado River in southern Spain took place, in which the kings of Portugal and of Castilla joined forces at Sevilla and marched against Muslim contingents from Granada and North Africa, winning a resounding victory, but as soon as this was over, the differences between them resumed. Afonso IV was more of a warrior than his father, but he did continue to encourage trade and commerce. Under his rule, the Cortes met regularly, the land inquiries were reinstituted and a law was passed prohibiting interest to be charged on loans.

In 1348 the populace of Portugal, like that of the rest of Europe, was decimated by the worst outbreak of the plague in known history. All segments of society were affected, and nowhere was safe. Those who sought shelter away from the cities simply took their deadly fleas with them, unaware that they were the cause of the problem. Hundreds of thousands of people perished, a situation that led to an acute labor shortage and left much of the land idle. Increased work demands by landowners caused many remaining peasants to flee to the cities to seek better conditions. In 1349 a new law obliged the peasants to remain in the countryside, but it proved rather ineffective.

War broke out once again between Portugal and Castilla when the Castillian king refused to permit the daughter of a member of his opposition in Aragón to cross his territory in order to marry Pedro, son of Afonso IV. As a result, Pedro had to wait four years to meet his betrothed, Constanza. When she finally arrived in Lisbon, they were married, but her lady-in-waiting, a Galician woman named Inês de Castro, stole the prince's heart. She became his mistress, and on the death of his wife in childbirth in 1345, they took up residence together. It had been Afonso IV's policy to stay out of the wars of succession taking place in Castilla at the time, and it was brought to his attention that Inês de

Castro was involved along with her brothers in a plan to persuade Pedro, grandson of Sancho IV of Castilla, to claim the Castillian throne.

His councillors led Afonso IV to believe that Inês and her two ambitious brothers were dangerous, and, as a result, she was murdered on the king's orders. Pedro openly rebelled against his father, and a short, but bloody, civil war ensued, devastating much of the north before they were reconciled. Pedro now insisted for the benefit of the three children he had sired with Inês that, contrary to opinion, he had secretly married her and that his children were thus legitimate. He then gave her an elaborate funeral and a magnificent sarcophagus in the monastery of Alcobaça.

PEDRO I

Afonso died in 1357, and Pedro ascended the throne, determined to avenge Inês' death. Her assassins were extradited from Castilla, where they had fled, and were brutally put to death, after which he spent the rest of his reign following his interests as a self-styled judge dispensing rough justice throughout the country. He had, for example, a nobleman beheaded for maliciously destroying the wine vat of a peasant and a bishop whipped for adultery.

Prosperity increased a little under Pedro, who managed to maintain peace. He fathered another son out of wedlock who would become the Master of Avis. In 1367 Pedro died at age forty-seven. He is buried at Alcobaça, facing the tomb of his beloved Inês and with the inscription *Até ao fim do mundo* (Until the end of the world). He was succeeded by his eldest son, the twenty-one-year-old Fernando, destined to be the last of the Burgundian dynasty on the throne of Portugal.

FERNANDO I

In Castilla civil war raged between Pedro the Cruel and his half brother, Enrique de Trastámara, over succession to the throne. In 1369 Enrique personally assassinated Pedro, but several Galician towns on the Castillian/Portuguese frontier refused to recognize him as king and turned instead to Fernando of Portugal. The throne of Castilla was also claimed by John of Gaunt, duke of Lancaster, who had married a daughter of the late Pedro the Cruel. Fernando agreed to support Lancaster, but in the meantime Enrique gained the backing of the French. The inevitable war that was to take place between Portugal and Castilla on the peninsula was but a reflection of the Hundred Years' War going on between England and France. This, in turn, led to the Portuguese nobility's splitting into two factions, one group supporting Lancaster and England, and the other, Enrique II of Castilla and France. Enrique invaded northern Portugal, but his attention was suddenly diverted to hostile Moorish activity in the south of Spain, and he returned to Granada to deal with them.

The pope undertook to bring about a peace settlement, and in 1371 the Treaty of Alcoutim was signed, whereby Fernando agreed to marry a daughter of Enrique in exchange for extension of the Portuguese frontier to the east. In the meantime, he fell in love with Leonor Teles de Meneses, a Galician noblewoman who was not only already married but also thoroughly disliked by the Portuguese populace. In spite of delegations from Lisbon and ensuing riots demanding Fernando forsake Leonor, the couple fled to the north and were married. Thereafter, she wasted little time in taking reprisals against those who had objected to her.

Enrique, indignant over the slight to his daughter, marched on Lisbon in 1373. The country was in such shambles and the populace so demoralized that he met only token resistance, and although royal troops withstood the siege, much of the city was burned. In March of that year, the pope arranged the Peace of Santarém, forcing Fernando to accept humiliating terms such as abandoning support for Lancaster, providing galleys to the king of Spain when he might need them and handing over castles and hostages.

Suffering from the shame of this treaty, Fernando longed for revenge. He embarked on a third war with Castilla in 1381. This time his people were even more alienated from their king, enraged by the useless wars they were forced to fight and the mortifying terms Fernando had been obliged to accept, so once again when the Castillians marched on Lisbon, they met very little resistance. A pact was signed, however, with Juan of Castilla (who had succeeded Enrique) providing, among other things, for the betrothal of Fernando and Leonor's daughter Beatriz to a son of Juan I.

When Juan I was widowed, the ambitious Leonor arranged for Beatriz to marry the father instead, offering him the throne of Portugal when Fernando should die. A despondent Fernando, completely dominated by Leonor, who had taken on a new lover, Andeiro, count of Ourém, passed on in 1383. The country broke out into riots against the possibility of losing their independence to Spain, engineered by the hated Leonor Teles, named by Fernando as regent for Beatriz.

A group of nobles and merchants plotted the assassination of the influential count of Ourém, who was leading the faction in favor of Beatriz and Juan I, and João, Master of the Order of Avis, illegitimate son of Pedro and half brother of Fernando, was selected to do the deed. Once accomplished, João was hailed as defender and governor of the realm.

Taking advantage of the disorder in Portugal, Juan I invaded in January 1384 to defend the rights of his wife, Beatriz, and take the crown he considered justifiably his. At Santarém he met Leonor, his mother-in-law, but no longer needing her meddlesome presence he had her confined to a Spanish convent. Meanwhile, João and Nuno Alvares Pereira, his friend and later constable of the realm, fortified Lisbon for the expected attack. It soon came. In February Juan's forces reached Lisbon, while his fleet sailed into the Tejo, completing the blockade of the city by land and sea. The fortunes of war favored the Portuguese, however. Pestilence broke out among the attackers, reaching epidemic proportions, and the king of Castilla with the loss of numerous men abandoned the siege.

4

House of Avis: João I–Manuel I, 1385–1521

In 1385 a Cortes was assembled at Coimbra in which João das Regras, the chancellor and friend of the Master of Avis, persuaded the members to accept João as king. He was elected and began a new dynasty—the House of Avis. At this time Juan, along with many of the Portuguese nobility who supported Beatriz, recruited a fresh army and invaded Portugal again.

BATTLE OF ALJUBARROTA AND THE TREATY OF WINDSOR

The Castillian forces marched across the country to Coimbra, then turned south toward Lisbon. To block the route, the Portuguese army took up position just north of the village of Aljubarrota on a spur between valleys. The Castillians arrived late in the morning on 14 August 1385, but the commanders decided not to attack. Instead, by a long, hot, cross-country march, they bypassed the Portuguese position and regained the road to the south in order to attack on better ground and in the rear of the enemy. During the afternoon, João and Nuno Alvares reversed their order of battle, which exposed them to open ground in front but with flanks still protected by the valleys. Portuguese morale, an essential ingredient in winning battles, was high, whereas the Castillians, approaching in the late afternoon from the south, were exhausted from their protracted flanking maneuver.

A ferocious cavalry charge pushed the Portuguese back but failed to break their ranks. A contingent of expert English archers then unleashed their lethal shafts into the advancing Castillians, taking a heavy toll and allowing the Portuguese to advance. As evening approached, the enemy standard went down, and the Castillians panicked and fled the field. Juan I made haste back to Sevilla, while the victor, according to custom after formidable battles, passed three days encamped on the field of carnage.

An estimated 7,000–8,000 Portuguese had overcome an enemy of several times their number. The Castillians lost some 2,500 men slain, and many others were captured, while their defeat immensely strengthened João's position, as many of the Portuguese nobles who fought for Juan I were among the dead at Aljubarrota. The Portuguese frontiers were still vulnerable, however, as Juan, with more manpower at his disposal, could in time gather together another army. No doubt, with this in mind, once back in Lisbon, João set about encouraging John of Gaunt of England to act on his neglected claim to the Castillian throne.

João's representatives to England were well received. Richard II would have been more than pleased to send his powerful uncle, John of Gaunt, the duke of Lancaster, off to rule a foreign land. He would then be busy elsewhere, and, as a bonus, Spanish galleys, often in alliance with those of France in the Hundred Years' War, would no longer pose a threat to southern English coastal towns.

According to his promise if victory ensued from the Battle of Aljubarrota, João I began the construction of the great abbey-church of Santa Maria de Vitória at Batalha near the scene of the battle. Today the tombs of João and his wife, Philippa, can be seen there, their stone effigies eternally linked hand in hand.

On 9 May 1386, João I signed the Treaty of Windsor, which assured perpetual peace and friendship with England and affirmed that between the reigning kings, their heirs and successors and the subjects of both kingdoms there would be an enduring and true league of friendship, and each would have the obligation in perpetuity to assist and give aid to the other against all people who might threaten the peace of one or the other state. The treaty endures to this day, giving England and Portugal the longest lasting alliance between sovereign states.

Reasserting his family claim to the throne of Castilla through his wife,

Constanza, daughter of Pedro I, the duke of Lancaster landed in Coruña in July 1386 with some 5,000 men. He achieved initial military successes, but as the season for campaigning drew to a close, he set up headquarters in Orense for the winter. Negotiations with João I led to the agreement that the Portuguese would maintain an army against the Castillians in exchange for the hand in marriage of Lancaster's daughter, Philippa, whose dowry would bring a considerable piece of Castillian territory, once conquered, to João. The marriage was celebrated in Oporto in February 1387. In the spring the English and Portuguese armies marched around western Castilla without doing any serious damage. Lancaster and Juan I of Castilla then came to the agreement in September 1387 that Lancaster would renounce his claims to the Castillian throne and marry another of his daughters, Catherine, to the heir of the Castillian king, the future Enrique III. He then took ship for home, and the Portuguese and João I were forgotten. In 1390 Juan I died, and Enrique III, still a boy, assumed the throne.

CONQUEST OF CEUTA

In 1411 the war with Castilla came officially to an end, and attention was turned toward the traditional foe. Having been born too late for the glorious adventures in the struggle for independence against Castilla, the elder sons of João I and Philippa, anxious to prove their knightly abilities, countenanced a plan to attack Muslim-held Ceuta across the strait from Gibraltar. The Enterprise of Ceuta, as the plan was called, also attracted bored and restless aristocrats. The machinery of government, in the hands of professionals appointed by the king, offered few opportunities for many of the often poorly educated and idle nobles. War in the service of God and king was still the hallmark of a brave knight, and battle with the heathen Moors could not fail to bring credit in the eyes of God, pope and country. Besides glory there was booty to be gathered, all of which was preferable to the daily rounds of the estate. To conceal the purpose behind amassing of troops and armaments, rumors were circulated that an attack would take place against the Moorish stronghold of Granada.

The prospect of a crusade did not much appeal to the merchant class, but one of new markets was a different matter. Portuguese products of fish, salt, cork, wine and olive oil were staple trade items to England and Flanders, but the Mediterranean, commercially controlled by Venice and Genoa in the supply of lucrative luxuries to Europe, whose sources were in Muslim hands, could partly end up in the Portuguese net if the city of Ceuta were to come under Portuguese jurisdiction.

Ceuta was a terminus of the trans-Saharan trade, a staging center for merchandise and some of the gold from Guinea on route to Europe brought across the desert by camel caravans. Similarly, the weavers of the kingdom of Fez made cloth that was shipped from Ceuta to Europe. The town, in a strategic position overlooking the strait, already attracted the attention of Castilla and even Genoa. It should not be allowed to fall into rival hands. As a base for Portuguese vessels attacking Muslim merchant men along the Barbary Coast it was ideal. Not least among the attributes of Ceuta was the fact that, at the time, the hinterland produced agricultural products, including wheat, that also found their way to Europe and to Portugal.

On 25 July, six days after the death of Queen Philippa, the fleet sallied forth. Surprised and unprepared for the onslaught, Ceuta fell in a single day of fighting. For their part, the princes Pedro and Henrique were made dukes of Coimbra and Viseu, respectively, the first duchies to be created in Portugal. Along with the elder brother Duarte, who was heir apparent, they were knighted by their father in the captured mosque hastily converted to a Christian church. In addition, Henrique was made Master of the Order of Christ, and João received the direction of the wealthy religious military order of Santiago. Fernando, the youngest of the brothers, was not old enough to participate in the battle.

A garrison was installed, and the city became the first Portuguese possession in Africa. The prize proved a disappointment. Palaces and warehouses of wealthy Arab merchants had been looted and burned by the soldiers in a reckless search for gold and silver. Expensive silks, furniture, tapestries and carpets, along with valuable stores of pepper and cinnamon, had been mostly destroyed. Little was left to pay for the cost of the expedition, let alone for the upkeep of the garrison left behind. Muslim trade that had previously flowed through the town quickly dried up and went to other ports along the Mediterranean coast as the Moors kept up a steady stream of counterattacks. Instead of the wealth that was to accrue to the crown, the king found his financial resources strained in maintaining the Portuguese presence in Ceuta. At age seventy-seven, João I succumbed to a long illness on 14 August 1433. For some time prior, Prince Duarte, his eldest son and heir, had borne much of the responsibility of government.

DUARTE

Scholarly and pious Duarte, eldest of the five legitimate brothers, came to the throne at age forty-two. He was a man of integrity with a conviction of noblesse oblige toward his subjects. He was also vacillating, impractical and fatalistic, finding solace from the country's problems in his books. At the beginning of Duarte's reign, a Cortes was summoned at Santarém, where the king set about revising and codifying the body of law. His *lei mental* (mental law), so-called because it was supposed to have been in João I's mind at the time of his death, declared all crown grants inalienable and indivisible and to revert to the crown in default of a male heir. Only the eldest son in the family could inherit the property on the death of the owner. By this decree the king expected to make up much of the revenue that his father's generosity had greatly diminished. This legislation remained in effect until 1863. In addition, by offering two-thirds of the family property to any Jew who converted to Christianity, he hoped to solve what was perceived as a Jewish problem. This was ignored by the Jewish communities, however.

The king was often caught up in familial problems when responding to the wishes of his wife, Leonor of Aragón, and his brothers, all of whom he held in high esteem. Traveled and experienced, brother Pedro was the king's closest adviser. Prince Henrique, thirty-nine years old when Duarte ascended the throne, had the reputation of being devout and inquisitive. He was also keenly interested in profiting from trade. Committed to the prosecution of an offensive against the Muslims, he attributed the costly defense of Ceuta (which could be supplied only by sea) to the failure of further conquest in North Africa, as opposed to others who considered that the excessive costs to hold the town would lead to further disasters if more wars were fought against the Moors in Morocco. His brothers, Pedro and João, opposed future conquest in this sphere.

The youngest brother, Fernando, aged thirty-four, longing to demonstrate his prowess in an engagement, sided with Henrique. They appealed to the king to launch a campaign against the Muslim city of Tanger. Duarte acquiesced and successfully solicited the Cortes, meeting that year in Évora, to grant finances for the undertaking. Henrique exhorted the pope to issue a bull of absolution for those who should die in the crusade.

EXPEDITION AGAINST TANGER

The attack on Tanger, August 1437, began adversely with too few ships available for transport. More significantly, the preparations were no secret to the Moorish general, Sala-Bin-Sala, who had ample time to make his defensive preparations.

The success at Ceuta may have caused Henrique to underestimate the fighting qualities of the Moor, or he had too much faith in the righteousness of his cause. After moving ponderously along the road from Ceuta to Tanger, he made costly attacks with inadequate siege machinery on the walls of the city. Then, waiting for longer ladders and bigger cannons, he wasted his men in useless skirmishes, finally permitting his army to be surrounded by a larger enemy force. He was obliged to agree to a truce whereby Sala-bin-Sala demanded the return of Ceuta in exchange for safe conduct back to Portugal, while Fernando remained behind as a hostage until the surrender of Ceuta to the Moors was arranged. Back home, the Cortes, with Prince Henrique's approbation, was prepared to make any sacrifice to save the young prince, except surrender Ceuta. Fernando was destined to die in prison at Fez. Not long after the inglorious battle of Tanger, Duarte died in the old Templar town of Tomar, probably a victim of the plague, and Henrique retired to Sagres on the southwestern tip of Portugal, distancing himself, perhaps, from humiliation in Lisbon.

REGENTS QUEEN LEONOR, PEDRO AND AFONSO V

Afonso was six when his father, Duarte, died, and his mother, Queen Leonor, was appointed regent. She was supported in the main by the clergy and by most of those advocating further conquest in Morocco headed by Henrique and his half brother, Afonso, count of Barcelos. Duarte's other brothers, Pedro and João, rallied against Leonor, who was also out of favor with the bourgeoisie and the lower classes of Lisbon, who distrusted her as an Aragonese and an adversary of the popular Pedro. The townspeople were anxious to see the appointment of the educated and prudent Pedro, duke of Coimbra, as regent, especially since the prince was opposed to the landed aristocracy, which was championed by his half brother Afonso. Pedro advocated exploration and commerce and opposed destructive war in Morocco.

The Barcelos faction feared and opposed Pedro's regency, and both

Pedro and Afonso, bitter rivals, endeavored to gain influence over the young king, Afonso V. The turmoil in Lisbon and resentment toward the queen mother alarmed her, and she ordered the populace assembled before the monastery of São Domingo and given a sermon on the duty of obedience. Decidedly unimpressed, the crowd chased the preacher-monk from the platform into the church. Only the intervention of Pedro prevented it from being burned.

At the next Cortes the burghers of Lisbon, through their representatives, successfully demanded the election of Pedro to the regency. The queen insisted that she maintain the education of the children and the treasury—or nothing. So, with nothing, she retired to the palace at Sintra, where conspiracy became her only weapon. The Portuguese nobles were not strong enough to thwart the will of the House of Avis, so the queen made contact with political allies in Castilla. In October 1440 a Castillian embassy arrived and demanded her reinstatement. It proposed to visit the principal Portuguese cities and towns and read to the populace a proclamation of the queen's rights. These provocative requests were refused, and two days later, further instructions in favor of the queen arrived. The extraordinary speed with which the letters arrived from Castilla prompted suspicion among Pedro's adherents, and it was soon verified that the letters has been fabricated by Queen Leonor, who then prudently departed in haste for Castillian territory.

Pedro, meanwhile, arranged the marriage between his daughter Isabel and her cousin the young king, Afonso V. An oral dispensation was obtained from Pope Eugene IV. A further demand from the Castillian embassy in 1442 for the rehabilitation of Leonor with an implied threat of war was rejected by the Cortes meeting in Évora, which only served to increase Pedro's popularity. At long last Afonso, count of Barcelos, came to terms with his half brother Pedro and was forgiven and honored with the title duke of Bragança.

Animosities were renewed when the regent elevated his son (also called Pedro) to the post of constable, a hereditary position claimed by the count of Ourém, a son of the duke of Bragança (also called Afonso). In January 1446, Afonso V reached his fourteenth birthday, his legal majority, and assented to the marriage with his cousin Isabel. The young monarch asked his uncle Pedro to continue administrative authority until he himself felt ready for the duties of king. The Bragança faction, however, persuaded the vacillating and susceptible young Afonso V, whose manifest desire was to please, to dispense with the services of Pedro.

The king dutifully dismissed his uncle, and Pedro retired to his estates. Nevertheless, the marriage between his daughter and the king took place in 1447.

The once popular Pedro now became the object of defamation throughout the realm, as he was accused of poisoning Queen Leonor, who had died in Toledo in 1445 as well as his brothers Duarte and João (the latter had died in 1442). He was further charged with having planned to remove the present king and claim the throne for himself. The Barcelos-Bragança clan, including the exiled archbishop of Lisbon, ardently engaged in lies.

Now accused of treason by Afonso V, Pedro raised a force and marched on Lisbon. He and most of his faction were massacred by royal troops at the Battle of Alfarrobeira in Estremadura in 1449, which closed the chapter on the struggle for control of the boy king and the resultant civil conflict. The high nobility won the day, ensuring their position and privileges. Peasant and middle-class support for Pedro had already eroded, and nowhere did his death result in popular uprisings. Further, his family suffered persecution. The eldest son, deprived of his post as constable, became an exile in Castilla and was eventually offered the contested kingdom of Cataluña, where he died in 1466 among civil strife. One of his brothers, Jaime, fled to an aunt in Burgundy and later became a cardinal; the other, João, became king of Cyprus through marriage. Isabel, wife of Afonso V, could do little to assuage the disgrace of her father and family.

THE BRAGANÇAS: SPOILS OF VICTORY

The Bragança family took full advantage of the victory at Alfarrobeira, extracting all they could from the monarchy. Afonso V introduced the new title—marques—into Portugal, given to the eldest son of the duke of Bragança. One member of the family, Jorge da Costa, cardinal of Alpedrinha, was not shy in his quest for power. He amalgamated under his authority three archbishoprics: Braga, Lisbon and Évora, as well as several bishoprics, priories and abbeys. Further, he ousted the abbot of Alcobaça from his post and personally assumed full rights over the greatest monastery in the kingdom. Complaints against the king's munificence, expressed at the Cortes of 1461, were to no avail.

During Afonso V's thirty-year rule, the amount of royal land and royal jurisdictions given away rose to proportions previously unheard of. Lands were distributed to fifteen families, the most powerful of which were the Braganças, the Meneses, the Coutinhos and the Melos. They lived in splendor on their grand estates, acquired most of the titles, furnished many of the bishops and important abbots to the church, occupied high offices and enjoyed exalted privilege. The king's brother Fernando received two duchies, the mastership of two religious orders and many other lordships.

Besides this upper echelon of some 500 people, many royal vassals or lesser nobility received income from the crown independently of their patrimony, along with wedding allowances and subsidies given for no particular reason except being a favorite of the king. Handed out year after year they tended to become hereditary. The vassal had to be prepared to aid the king with a fixed number of riders and footmen in full armor. By the end of the reign of Afonso V, about 2,000 vassals were obliged to own a horse and weapons and collected revenues from the crown.

NOBLES, MERCHANTS AND PEASANTS

Many members of the less powerful aristocratic families were often short of money. To possess an expensive wardrobe—perfumes, saddles and horses adorned with gold and silver, luxuries sold by the merchants of the towns—was a requirement of their class. No longer could the nobility pay in bushels of wheat. Silver and gold coins were now demanded. With the decline of the labor force on the estates and inflation eating up profits, many of the lesser aristocracy were hard-pressed to maintain their grand style of living. As a result, they became poorer as merchants became wealthier.

To maintain their lifestyle, the upper class resorted to various strategies. The practice of giving land to the peasants for a proportion of the produce was an inducement to keep them on the estates. Intimidation through violence was often employed when peasants refused to support them. When all else failed, work might be the last resort for a few, but labor outside one's own estates entailed a renunciation of the noble life and its privileges. Blatant robbery was not beneath the dignity of the aristocracy. Bands of nobles and their retainers often ranged the countryside seizing what they wished. They installed themselves in the best houses of the villages during their forays and stayed as long as they liked, taking what clothes they fancied and eating what they could find to their taste, often forcing the peasant to slaughter his best cattle for their consumption. Frequent complaints to the king and government officials had little impact. Younger sons of the nobility looked to fighting in Morocco to establish their endowments from the crown and to the profits brought home from pirate expeditions.

WARS WITH MOROCCO AND CASTILLA

In 1454 Enrique IV succeeded to the crown of Castilla and in the following year married Joana, sister of Afonso V. Afonso and Enrique met on the frontier, swore allegiance to each other and pledged to make war on Islam. Commanded by the king and accompanied by many nobles, a Portuguese army of about 25,000 descended on Morocco in 1458, conquered and garrisoned the small town of Alcácer Ceguer (Ksar es Seghir) on the coast about halfway between Tanger and Ceuta. The town then withstood two long sieges by the emir of Fez under its governor Duarte de Meneses. Fresh attempts to take Tanger in 1463 failed, but in 1471 the situation changed. The confusion brought on by the demise of the Merinid Dynasty in Fez created an opportunity for a further attempt on the city. Afonso assembled the largest army yet engaged in Africa—some 30,000 men, according to accounts—and captured the town of Arzila (Asilah) on the Atlantic Coast southwest of the main objective. The citizens of Tanger panicked, and the city was evacuated, leaving Portugal in possession of the western tip of the continent. The government in Fez agreed to recognize Portuguese suzerainty as far south as the river Loukos (Lukkus), which flows into the Atlantic at Larache some fifty miles south of Tanger. Afonso V would now be known to the chroniclers as Afonso the African. War with Castilla, then, brought a halt to further adventures overseas.

The arrogant and cowardly behavior of the king of Castilla had lost him much support. His wife, Joana, gave birth to a daughter in 1462, commonly held to be the illegitimate offspring of the queen and one of the courtiers named Beltrán de la Cueva. Because of this, the infant was nicknamed the Beltraneja. The king, known as Enrique the Impotent, proclaimed the child heir to the throne, but numerous nobles and churchmen objected, declaring for Enrique's sister Isabella. Several times she had turned down royal suitors who Enrique had tried to have marry her, including the now widowed Afonso V of Portugal. Instead, she had married in 1469 a man of her own choice—Fernando, prince of Aragón and heir to the second largest kingdom in Christian Spain. Afonso V and his court must have been concerned. If, upon assuming their respective thrones, Fernando and Isabella united the two most powerful kingdoms of Castilla and Aragón, thus drastically altering the peninsular balance of power, Portugal could be swallowed up in the process. In one way or another these two kingdoms and the neighboring states, Navarra and Moorish Granada, would amalgamate into one colossus of Spain and threaten the existence of Portugal. At the end of the fifteenth century these future events were already casting a shadow over the Portuguese land.

When Enrique died in 1474, Isabella was proclaimed queen. Afonso V announced that he would marry and support the claim of his niece, the half-Portuguese princess, the Beltraneja, to the Castillian throne. His ambitions were bolstered by an anti-Aragonese faction in Castilla. This policy would mean war between Portugal and Castilla, but to win would result in unification of much of the peninsula under the Portuguese crown. The Beltraneja's faction was small, but some Spanish nobles were undecided whether to support Afonso V or Isabella and Fernando.

Afonso invaded Castilla in 1475. After occupying much of León, the army came up against a Castillian force at Castro Quemado near Toro, a little north of Salamanca. The Catholic monarchs, Isabella and Fernando, emerged victorious, and the Portuguese withdrew across the frontier. From then on, having lost the respect of the Castillian nobility who had earlier sided with him, Afonso's fortunes plummeted. He attempted to enlist the aid of Louis XI of France in his cause, hoping for a French attack on Castilla from the north. Receiving no positive results and against the advice of his councillors, he traveled by ship to France to personally request military aid from the king. He found himself in the middle of a dispute between Louis XI and Charles the Bold, duke of Burgundy. Both dismissed him as a nuisance, and he returned a discredited and dispirited man.

For two more years negotiations with Castilla absorbed much of the king's time, but the matter was finally resolved by the Treaty of Alcáçovas in 1479. Afonso V renounced his claims to Castilla and to the Canary Islands in exchange for Castillian recognition of a Portuguese monopoly over African coastal trade and exploration south of the Canary Islands. Until his death in 1481, Afonso V and his son João were nearly corulers. The son was entrusted with control of overseas policies.

THE LEGENDARY NAVIGATOR

Born at Oporto in 1394, the third son of João I and Philippa, known to the English-speaking world as Henry the Navigator, is celebrated as a great patron of exploration. After the disaster at Tanger in 1437, he made his residence near Sagres and there established an observatory and, it has been alleged, a school for navigators. Henrique's chronicler, Eanes de Zurara, a man in his service, mentions the prince's burning curiosity to know what lay beyond Cape Bojador on the coast of Morocco opposite the Canary Islands, the southern extremity of the world then known to Europeans. He wished to ascertain how far south the Muslim lands extended and if Christians, with whom it might be beneficial to trade and enlist as allies in war against the Muslims, lived somewhere beyond. There had long been rumors of a Christian kingdom somewhere in Africa or Asia.

The legend of the Navigator has come down through history, depicting him as an inspired, studious, scientific man of broad learning who gathered around himself other erudite men at Vila do Infante at Sagres, where he worked on maritime charts, trained pilots, designed or improved a new ship—the caravel—and advanced navigational devices. With determination and foresight he sent his mariners to seek a sea passage around Africa to Asia.

None of these attributes of Henrique were mentioned while he was alive or verified since, and there is no contemporary reference to a school, the first mention of it having been made in the seventeenth century by an Englishman. However, it does seem that Henrique took more interest in African exploration and conquest than perhaps any other person in Portugal at the time. He gave focus to the country's restless energies in an age when medieval society was awakening to the new promises of the Renaissance.

Of all the known voyages between 1415 (the conquest of Ceuta) and his death in 1460, about one-third were due to Henrique's initiatives. Others were directed by the king or the regent Pedro, feudal lords, private merchants and wealthy landowners.

CANARY AND MADEIRA ISLANDS AND THE AZORES

An expedition was sent to Gran Canaria about 1424, but the island was abandoned after fierce resistance from the natives. The islands provided a source of slaves, and Castillians, French and Italians all engaged in the trade. Similarly, the Portuguese raided them and transported slaves to Madeira, but competition was intense, preventing Portugal from using the islands as a permanent slave center. There were other reasons also: opposition came from Castilla, which had already colonized some of the Canaries and claimed them all, and from the islanders themselves, who were difficult to capture, making better fighters than slaves.

The first step toward exploration and colonization of the Madeira archipelago began about 1419, not long after the capture of Ceuta. Two captains in Henrique's service, blown off course by storms, ran into Porto Santo, one of the Madeira Islands. The uninhabited islands were not entirely unknown since they appear on fourteenth-century maps. Around 1429 fear of Castillian hegemony on Madeira led to permanent Portuguese settlements there. Dyestuffs, fish and timber exported to the mainland were lucrative propositions. From about 1450 to 1470 the production of wheat there helped sustain the demand on the mainland, and sugar and wine began to make an appearance. Trade and population grew, and slaves were imported to work the plantations.

To reach the Azores required a more remarkable voyage in open seas, yet the islands appear to have been reached by Diogo de Silves in 1427. A royal charter was issued in 1439 authorizing Henrique the Navigator to begin a settlement on the Azores, and, as was the case with Madeira, the archipelago was granted to him. As on Madeira, the exemption of customs duties on goods shipped to the mainland helped promote settlement. Cattle and wheat became major export commodities, but sugar production did not develop in that climate, and few slaves were imported. Commodities other than slaves, however, interested Portuguese merchants.

TRADE ROUTES AND THE AFRICAN COAST

For many centuries there had been three main trade routes from the east to the Mediterranean and Europe: the long, overland caravan journey from China across the steppes of Central Asia to the Black Sea, by ship from India to the head of the Persian Gulf and then overland via Baghdad or Damascus to Mediterranean ports, and through the Red Sea to Cairo and Alexandria. These lucrative arteries had long been controlled by Semitic Muslim peoples and increasingly since the fourteenth century by Turkish Muslims anchored in Anatolia and the Balkans. When goods reached the Black Sea or the Mediterranean ports, they were then monopolized by the northern Italian city-states, especially by Venice or Genoa, which distributed the products, transshipped by galleys, throughout Europe. The merchandise included precious metal and stones, porcelain, perfumes, silks, exotic woods and many spices. Prices in Europe for such luxuries were high, and profits were good. A lesser

The Conquests of
Afonso de Albuquerque

Map of The World
showing
the Principal Travels and Voyages
of the Portuguese

Coasts discovered by the Portuguese are shaded.
The eight modern Portuguese Colonies
are underlined.

Reprinted from Harold Livermore, *A History of Portugal* (Cambridge University Press, 1947), by kind permission of the author and publisher.

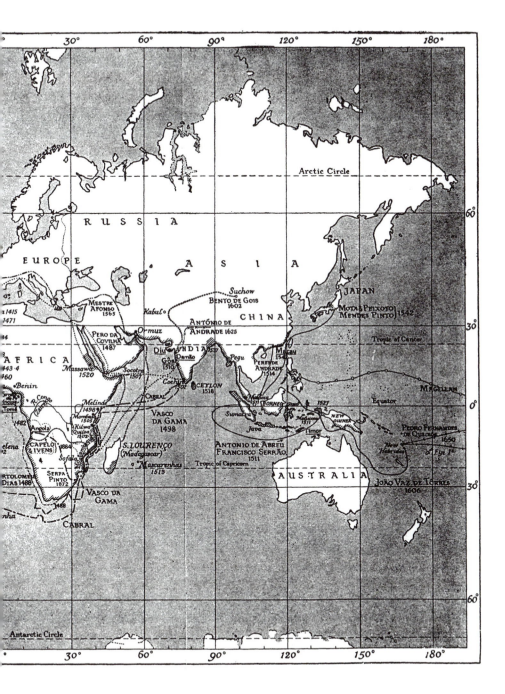

trade route but of particular interest to the Portuguese crossed the Sahara from Central Africa over the vast western desert to Tripoli, Tunis, Fez and Ceuta, where many of the goods were purchased by Italian merchants. The Portuguese had hoped to capitalize on this trade by the earlier conquests of Ceuta and Tanger.

By the middle of the fourteenth century the notion that it was possible to take advantage of this trade by sailing down the coast of Africa and indeed even reach the East by sailing around Africa was widely accepted by cartographers and learned men. Nevertheless, the objective of the first voyages, as stated by contemporary Portuguese chronicles, was Guinea, where the gold was mined in the region between the Senegal and the Niger Rivers. It has been estimated that until about 1350, two-thirds of the world's supply of gold came from West Africa.

Many uneducated people believed in sea monsters, huge whirlpools and other diabolical dangers in the outer regions of the Atlantic Ocean. To sail too far from home might mean never to return, and there were precedents to sustain this anxiety. It was widely believed that life near the equator was unsustainable, that a searing sun burned the body black and that boiling seas liquidated all life. Farther on lay the Antipodes, where, according to many clergy, monsters lived, since no man derived from Adam could cross the tropics. Fabulous treasures were said to be guarded by dragons, and giants could wade into the sea and grasp a ship in one hand. Women with eyes like gems could slay a man with a single glance. These ominous hazards were not taken lightly by many ordinary seamen, but, motivated by profit and curiosity, they overcame their fears of unknown seas.

After repeated efforts, Henrique's navigators achieved their first important success in 1434, when Gil Eanes, a squire of Henrique's household, rounded the famous and dangerous Cape Bojador (Boujdour). Antão Gonçalves was sent out in 1441 to bring back a cargo of skins, but he exceeded his mandate and returned with two natives from the region of the Rio d'Ouro—the first captured beyond Cape Bojador. Nuno Tristão, a gentleman in Prince Henrique's household, sailed on as far as Cape Blanco (Mauritania), the farthest point south yet reached. In 1443, the year that Henrique was granted the monopoly on trade and conquest beyond Cape Bojador by his brother Pedro, acting as regent, Tristão sailed beyond Cape Blanco and took more captives among the islands of Arguim Bay. With exclusive rights to the new regions, Prince Henrique had charts prepared for the recently discovered coasts. As Africans were brought back to Lagos near Henrique's headquarters as slaves, merchants of the town, seeing an opportunity, began to solicit him for a license to sail south and participate in the trade. In 1444 six caravels sailed to the area around Cape Blanco and, after killing a number of resisting natives, filled their ships' holds with human cargo, a fifth of which was turned over to Henrique, some forty-six people in all.

Nuno Tristão was now forced farther afield as the Africans became wary of ships. He sailed on and reached the Senegal River in 1445. Shortly after, Dinis Dias rounded Cape Verde before bad weather drove him home. On another voyage in 1446, Tristão reached about 200 miles south of Cape Verde, where he met his death in a slave raid, and in the same year Alvaro Fernandes reached an area the farthest south of Cape Verde.

In 1449 Henrique gave orders for a fort and trading post to be constructed at Arguim just south of Cape Blanco and leased it for ten years to a private entrepreneur. Many caravels are said to have visited the fort every year to take away gold, slaves, silk and cotton in exchange for cereals, cloth and horses. From the accounts of Alvise da Cadamosto, a Venetian nobleman in the service of Henrique, historians have learned much of the sailing conditions as well as about flora and fauna along the African coast. In 1456 Diogo Gomes went beyond the Gambia River still farther down the coast discovering the river Geba, and in 1460 he explored more of the Cape Verde Islands, as did Diogo Afonso the following year. About the time of Prince Henrique's death in 1460, one of his captains, Pedro de Sintra, reached what is today Sierra Leone.

Lacking sufficient agricultural workers, Portugal was the first modern European nation to meet its labor needs by importing slaves—some 700–800 slaves annually—and for more than a century Portugal virtually monopolized the African seaborne slave traffic. The population of Lisbon about this time has been estimated at about 100,000 of which some 10,000 were black Africans. Between sixty and seventy slave markets are thought to have existed in the city.

In 1468 the crown contracted the merchant Fernão Gomes of Lisbon to carry on trade along the African coast for a period of five years, provided that he explored 100 leagues (320 miles) of coastline each year. The starting point was Sierra Leone, where Pedro de Sintra had turned back. For a time as the coast turned eastward it was thought that the long sought passage around Africa had been discovered. No one could imagine just how far there still was to go. Gomes' captains João de Santarém and Pero Escobar reached what is now Ghana in 1471. Fernão do Pó pushed on farther east as far as present-day Nigeria-Cameroon and discovered the large island, Bioko (that formerly bore his name), in the angle of the continent as it turns again from east to south. Gabon was reached by Lopo Gonçalves and Rui de Sequeira in 1474, passing over the once-dreaded zero degrees of latitude. By this time, other islands around the equator had been found: São Tomé, Príncipe and Ano Bom.

JOÃO II

Unlike his father, Afonso V, who died in 1481 and who allowed the feudal lords to gain power at his expense, João II opposed them to centralize authority in his own hands. Upon his accession he convoked the Cortes at Évora, where he ordered the nobility's loyalty in an oath of allegiance and demanded proofs of grants and privileges that each of them claimed and of the titles by which each held lands, towns or castles. He forced them to swear to deliver to the king, on demand, property held from the crown. The powerful families that had benefited handsomely under Afonso V now had their wealth, privileges and prestige threatened.

The commoners at the Cortes had their say and asked for the abolition of private justice in the hands of the nobles, the termination of aristocratic interference in the affairs of the districts, the correction of abuses in the collection of tribute such as levying of taxes without authority and compelling the peasants to work on the estates of the great landowners without pay. The king was asked to reduce the throngs of parasites who revolved around the court and to extend the system of magistrates (corregidores) throughout the land. Instead of ignoring such complaints as his father had done, João II promised redress and established the supremacy of royal judges, abolished offices held by nobles as deputies of the crown, replacing them with magistrates, and asserted the right of royal corregidores to inspect private administration throughout the kingdom. At the same time he cut back on the royal grants and stipends. Such measures greatly enhanced the popularity of the king among the public.

The current duke of Bragança held over fifty cities, towns and castles and could easily command 3,000 cavalry and 10,000 foot soldiers. To his surprise, his holdings were not confirmed by the new king, but instead he was compelled to produce the titles of his domains. Meanwhile, the king quarreled with the duke's brother, the marques of Montemór, and exiled him to the remote Castelo Branco. The humbling of the House of Bragança had begun. The noble landowners struck back with a widespread conspiracy against João II, headed by the duke of Bragança. Compromising letters between the duke and Isabella and Fernando of Spain, which conveniently fell into the king's hands, however, were said to have been discovered on his estates, revealing that he was in touch with the queen of Castilla, encouraging her to lay claim to the throne of Portugal. The duke was arrested and tried for treason, while two of his brothers, the marques of Montemór and the count of Faro, fled to Castilla. On 29 June 1484 in the main square of Évora the duke was beheaded for treason.

The second great feudal lord of the realm, the duke of Viseu, Diogo, nephew of Afonso V and cousin of João II, was summoned the following year to an interview with the king. It was reported that the duke was involved in a conspiracy to assassinate the king and eliminate the heir, Prince Afonso, so that he himself could usurp the throne. Diogo was of royal blood and could not be tried by the courts as was the duke of Bragança, so the king invited his cousin into the royal apartments at Setúbal and in the presence of three loyal councillors stabbed him to death. His followers either died at the stake or fled the country. Within three years after ascending the throne, João II had managed to rid himself of most of the upper feudal lords whose titles he abolished and whose huge estates he confiscated. He gained popular loyalty by promoting legists (specialists in law) and civil servants to top positions often reserved for the upper strata of the aristocracy.

With domestic issues in check, João II turned his attention to Africa and beyond. But it was equally important to protect what was already in Portuguese hands. Encroachments by foreign traders in Portuguese African waters had prompted him to construct a fort at El Mina, and he chose for this enterprise Diogo de Azambuja, dispatching him to the Gold Coast with instructions to build a trading post and a fort with or without the agreement of the local people. Diogo selected a sheltered bay about sixty miles west of the modern town of Accra for the fortress of São Jorge da Mina. The fort was built in 1482, and Diogo kept sixty men with him to garrison it, sending the rest back to Portugal. He remained at São Jorge for two years, overseeing the gold that now began to move over the forest trails to the fort's storehouse. The earlier trade routes that had been oriented northward across the Sahara to the Muslim world were redirected to the coast. João II and his advisors now conceived and undertook the task of reaching Asia by sea, subordinating all else to the project.

How far beyond the farthest point reached some ten years before by the captains of Fernão Gomes before one could again turn east toward India was anyone's guess. Diogo Cão, an experienced captain, was selected as the man to find out. He had already proven his value when, in 1479, he had captured Eustace de la Fosse, a French pirate whom he had brought back to Lisbon in chains. Cão had found and explored the lower Congo River, where he erected a stone pillar in 1483. On a second voyage the next year with the celebrated pilot Pero Escobar, they surpassed his earlier distance and began to encounter land that was again dry, desolate and treeless. Food and water ran short. He carried on almost to the Tropic of Capricorn, but at 21° 50' south, where they placed their last pillar at Cape Cross, they turned back. The seemingly endless landmass still ran southward.

COLUMBUS AT THE PORTUGUESE COURT

Sometime in 1484 Columbus came calling at the Portuguese court and lay before the king his idea of reaching Asia by sailing west. He asked for three caravels and crews to carry out his plans. He also demanded to be made Admiral of the Ocean Sea and be given the hereditary title of viceroy of all lands he discovered as well as one-tenth of the profits he brought back. João did not reject the offer out of hand and established a committee consisting of geographers, mathematicians and cartographers to look into it. There were reasons to believe that undiscovered land existed to the west apart from the fact, probably unknown at European courts, that Norsemen had reached it in the eleventh century. From time to time various objects of unknown provenance drifted onto the shores of the Azores, other islands and even mainland Europe. A few captains driven off course on the way home from Guinea had reported lands far to the west. It was well known by educated men that the earth was round; hence, land to the west was a certainty, but the question was how far away it was and, as Columbus claimed, if it was the islands of Cipangu (Japan) or land of the Indies.

Opinions differed among fifteenth-century cartographers, resulting in estimates of the earth's circumference that could vary by as much as 4,000 miles. The width of Asia, which Columbus proposed to reach, was also unknown. How far would he have to sail? There was a strong possibility that he would sail off into the setting sun, never to be seen again.

João II had good reasons to reject Columbus. Apart from the uncertainties of distance and time, winds and weather, the court had invested a good deal of money in the African route to the Indies. Dissipation of royal resources would be dangerous, and little investment could be expected from merchants for such a doubtful undertaking. The demands and, perhaps, arrogance of the foreigner, Columbus, may have also deterred the king, who had many competent navigators in his own realm. At any rate, his answer to Columbus' request was no, and the yet-to-be Admiral of the Ocean Sea went off to seek his fortunes in Spain.

BARTOLOMEU DIAS

João II may have been in a hurry to reach the Indies after Columbus proposed sailing west for the same purpose. He selected Bartolomeu Dias to lead the next voyage south to seek a route around Africa. Dias sailed in 1487 with two caravels and a store ship. He called in at São Jorge da Mina, sailed on past the mouth of the Congo River, past Cape Cross, and about Christmas dropped anchor in a sheltered bay at 29° south. (Cape Agulhas, the farthermost point on the African continent, lies at nearly latitude 35° south.) Brisk, steady, adverse winds made going difficult, and the supply ship was left in the bay. Resuming the voyage, the two caravels were forced farther out to sea by storms that relentlessly carried them onward toward the southwest and into the unknown, then southward through a belt of variable winds until they picked up the westerlies that propelled them back toward Africa. They could calculate latitude only by dead reckoning but decided after days of heavy sailing that they might be approaching 40° south. Turning north, Dias sighted the mountains of the African continent.

The coastline now tended to run northeastward. Having rounded the southern cape, although at the time they could not be sure, they made landfall in what is now Mossel Bay. The local Hottentots were decidedly unfriendly, and so the ships sailed on. Promontories projecting southward suggested that perhaps they had not reached the end of the continent after all, but by the time they arrived at what is today Port Elizabeth, all doubt was cast aside as the land turned northeast, and a warmer current caressed the hulls. With tattered, weather-beaten ships and exhausted companions, Dias sailed on for three more days as far as the Great Fish River near present-day Port Alfred. The crew by now had had enough and clamored to return home, but Dias knew that he had achieved what before had been only a dream. He turned back and passed a great promontory that he called the Cape of Storms, as he had missed it earlier while driven out of sight of land by gales. His ships reentered the Tejo after a voyage of over a year. They had a good deal to report to the king, but the most important news was that they had rounded the Cabo Tormentoso, as Dias called it, into the Indian Ocean. João saw a more fitting name for the cape and called it Cabo de Boa Esperança (Cape of Good Hope), as it now offered high hopes of reaching India. The voyage, like others from Portugal, was secret, and still today few of the details are known. Also, about the time Dias set sail, João II directed two emissaries on dangerous overland journeys—one to investigate eastern trade routes, the other to establish the veracity and whereabouts of the legendary Prester John and the rumored Christian realm.

THE SEARCH FOR THE KINGDOM OF PRESTER JOHN

Prester John appears in the chronicle of the German bishop and historian Otto of Freising in the twelfth century. It was believed that the Nestorian Christians had built up a rich monarchy ruled by a priest-king named John. Letters from this mysterious personage addressed to the Byzantine emperor or the pope were circulated, describing the size and wealth of the territory. In the fourteenth and fifteenth centuries the home of Prester John was generally believed to be located in Africa, where it was frequently identified with the kingdom of Abyssinia.

Henrique the Navigator had been much interested in the legend of Prester John and hoped that his captains would find such a man or his descendants in Islam's rear. From time to time a Coptic monk appeared in Jerusalem or even in Rome confirming what was now known by the late fifteenth century, that the kingdom was in Ethiopia. The name Ethiopia was not precise and might include the larger part of Africa south of the Sahara. Some believed that Prester John ruled over a vast territory, that he was served by seven kings and sixty dukes and that thirty archbishops sat to the right of his throne and twenty bishops on the left. How much of this João II believed is unknown, but he was anxious to make contact with the great Christian potentate of the East. It was, he knew, a long haul to the Indies, Portuguese ships would need ports of call to restock food and water and Prester John could be of great help. João had instructed his captains to ask, whenever possible, about the mysterious king, but nothing had come of such inquiries.

In 1487 he took a more direct approach, selecting Pêro de Covilhã and Afonso de Paiva, sturdy men from villages on the slopes of the Serra da Estrêla, to undertake a difficult mission. Both were versed in Arabic. Covilhã was instructed to travel overland to India and discover what he could about the routes of the Muslim traders who sailed the Indian

Ocean. Afonso de Paiva was given the formidable task of penetrating Africa and searching out the mysterious kingdom. In Alexandria they disguised themselves as Moors and traveled with Arab merchants as far as Aden, where they separated. Covilhã traveled by dhow to India, where he spent a year observing the spice trade, where junks from China and the East Indies unloaded their cargoes, which, along with pepper and ginger from the Malabar Coast, were then stowed aboard Arab dhows for shipment to East Africa and the Persian Gulf on their way to Europe. The intrepid traveler eventually made his way back to Cairo for a rendezvous with Paiva, who, he learned, had died in Africa. Messengers from the king were waiting for him and his report, however, with new instructions to proceed in Paiva's place on the mission to find Prester John. He reached the court of the priest-king in the mountainous region of Lake Tana on the Blue Nile, where he met the emperor Iskander, or Alexander, and was welcomed. But the emperor died suddenly, and his brother Naod was not interested in an alliance with his Christian colleague in Portugal. The customs of the country prohibited foreigners from leaving, and Covilhã was given land and a wife and told to remain.

Meanwhile, João II sought to guarantee the stability of his growing empire by maintaining good relations with Spain through matrimonial alliances and treaties. Afonso, his son, married Isabella, the eldest daughter of Fernando and Isabella in 1490, but the following year Afonso was killed in a riding accident, and João's nearest legitimate male relative was now his cousin Manuel, duke of Beja, Master of the Order of Christ and brother of Queen Leonor. A year later, the king had to contend with a fresh problem from his Spanish neighbor.

The Catholic kings of Castilla and Aragón, upon completion of the conquest of Granada in 1492, expelled the nonconverted Jews from Spain. Many of these people considered Portugal a friendly and peaceful country and offered João II a large sum of money for admittance to the kingdom. Thousands of skilled and resourceful newcomers came to Portugal at the price of eight cruzados each, but the king allowed them to remain only eight months. More than 50,000 are reported to have arrived, but most had to leave within the allotted time. Some remained illegally, while only 600 families succeeded in buying permanent residence, settling into the established Portuguese Jewish communities. Also in that year, Columbus reached the New World, claiming to have discovered Asia, and with Spain now in the field of discovery, jurisdictional disputes arose with Portugal.

TREATY OF TORDESILLAS

In 1494, on the high plateau of Castilla in the village of Tordesillas, João II's advisors negotiated a treaty that ratified first the Treaty of Alcáçovas, confirming that Granada and the Canary Islands belonged to Spain and that João II was king of the Algarve (meaning southern Portugal) and beyond the sea, that is, his possessions in Africa. It further established a line of demarcation between Spanish and Portuguese spheres of influence drawn 370 leagues west of the Cape Verde Islands. All islands and continents discovered or to be discovered on the east side of the line went to Portugal, the west side to Spain and to the respective monarchs and their heirs forever. It was also agreed that one or two caravels from each side were to meet in the Canary Islands with pilots, astrologers, mariners and other knowledgeable persons and set sail for the Cape Verde Islands. From there they were to voyage westward to the agreed-upon line of demarcation, and then, sailing north and south along the line as far as possible, they were to set up towers or other marks of identification on any land they encountered. This, then, would constitute the boundary. The arrangements for determining the exact position of the line of demarcation were never carried out, and at the time it was probably not possible to do it.

MANUEL I

João II died in 1495, and Manuel I "the Fortunate" assumed the throne at age twenty-six. He pardoned nobles who had been exiled ten years before and returned fifty properties to the new duke of Bragança. Manuel was to marry the widowed Isabella, daughter of Queen Isabella and Fernando, but her pious mother demanded the union be made conditional on the expulsion of unconverted Jews from Portugal. Issued in 1496, the eviction order of Jews and Moors who were unwilling to undergo baptism offered only the alternative of confiscation of property and death. For fear of retaliatory laws against Christians living in Muslim lands, the edict including Moors was not enforced, but in October 1497, about the time of the royal marriage, all the Jews in the country who had not converted to Christianity were ordered to Lisbon for embarkation. The 20,000 or so who thus gathered were then told that they should have previously departed and were now the king's slaves and subject to forced conversion. The Jews who staunchly resisted this treatment were at last allowed to depart, while those who converted were promised that no inquiry would be made into their beliefs for at least twenty years. The exercise was to convert Jews by any means, fair or foul, but not to deport such a large and productive segment of society. Many Jews who had accepted conversion no longer wished to remain in Portugal, however, and the government then had to enact laws to keep them in the country! They were not allowed to leave without a special permit, which was issued only for commercial purposes provided the man's family remained behind. The general populace resented the royal twenty-year edict, which theoretically allowed Jews to relapse into the practice of their Hebraic rites and forgot that their contributions to society in medicine, science, law and printing and as skilled artisans went far beyond tax collecting and moneylending—the only things the common people remembered.

VASCO DA GAMA

After the return of Bartolomeu Dias to Portugal, João II had ordered a new voyage under the command of his admiral Estêvão da Gama. Both the king and the admiral died before the ships were prepared to sail, but Manuel carried on with the venture. The admiral's heir, Vasco da Gama, was put in command of four vessels that left Lisbon on 7 July 1497. One of the ships carried supplies for three years, another was da Gama's command ship the *São Gabriel* and the other two were captained by his brother Paulo da Gama and by Nicolau Coelho. The crews consisted of 168 men, including convicts assigned to especially dangerous work. Da Gama bore letters from Manuel to the king of Calicut and to Prester John in case the latter might be contacted. For three months the ships battled heavy seas as they penetrated deeper into the South Atlantic. On 8 November they came ashore at Angra de Santa Helena about thirty leagues short of the Cape of Good Hope, where they encountered a small, dark people with whom they engaged in a sharp clash, wounding da Gama. After days of delay in rounding the cape against contrary winds, they arrived at the Great Fish River, the farthest point reached by Dias, where they remained for a fortnight reprovisioning until a quarrel with the natives compelled them to set sail. Sighting a new coastline on Christmas Day, they gave it the name Natal.

On 2 March the little flotilla (the supply ship had been lost) continued northeast as the sea gradually became warmer, and they knew they were well round the tip of Africa. They put in at Mozambique. Unfamiliar-looking merchantmen were anchored in the harbor, and Arab and local traders crowded the quays. Da Gama was greeted by a luxuriously dressed sultan who, unlike the previous African chiefs who became excited over a few trinkets and bells, treated the Portuguese trade goods with disdain.

After securing a local pilot, they were recognized as Christians, and an attack by a Muslim throng precipitated a hasty departure. Mistaking some islands for the mainland, one of the ships went aground but was refloated on the high tide. The pilot was flogged for the mistake. Finally, reaching Mombasa, another thriving port (in present-day Kenya), local Arabs made an attempt to capture the *São Gabriel*. Taking two of their number prisoner, da Gama extracted information from them by pouring boiling oil on their bare skin. At least one of the crew, having been a prisoner of the Muslims, spoke passable Arabic and served as a translator. It is not clear what, if anything, da Gama learned from his method of interrogation, but before long the crews hoisted sail, and the ships slipped away over the northern horizon.

At Melindi, the next stopover, the sultan proved amicable and provided a new pilot, an intelligent and able Gujarati, to take them across the Indian Ocean. The Hindus living in the city were thought by da Gama to belong to a Christian sect, so he concluded (wrongly) that Prester John could not be far away. After nearly another month's voyage, the fleet arrived off the Indian port of Calicut, presumably already known from the report sent home by Covilhã in 1490 as one of the important trading centers on the Malabar coast.

Vasco da Gama immediately sought an audience with the samorin (ruler) of Calicut. The Arab and Persian merchants who dominated the trade between India and Africa and the Mediterranean found the few Europeans who had visited the area previously to be no commercial threat. A fleet of ships was a different matter. Friendly at first, the samorin sided with the hostile merchants, and the proposal to exchange goods made in Portugal for spices was ill received. Only a small quantity of spices was taken on board. A threat uncovered against da Gama's life dismayed the Portuguese, believing as they did that the Hindu samorin was a Christian of some kind. With little point in remaining at Calicut, and as disease and accidents had taken a toll of his men, da Gama set sail for Portugal on 29 August 1498. Against strong head winds and shifting currents, the three-month voyage across the Indian Ocean took so many lives through scurvy that one of the ships had to be abandoned and destroyed near Mombasa for want of a crew to sail it. The cape was again rounded homeward-bound 20 March 1499. At Terceira in the

Azores an ill and weak Paulo da Gama died. The admiral finally reached Lisbon in September 1499, concluding a voyage of two years and two months and 24,000 nautical miles. Of the 168 men who had begun the voyage, 44 returned. The hold of the *São Gabriel* contained specimens of pepper, cloves, nutmeg, cinnamon and gems—all coveted in Europe. To contemporaries this was a much more useful accomplishment than Columbus' voyage to the New World. King Manuel wrote to the pope for confirmation of his authority over the discoveries and to Isabella and Fernando of Spain reveling in his accomplishment. After this historic voyage, which so drastically changed the course of European history, da Gama was welcomed with praise, rewarded financially and permitted to use the prefix Dom with his name. With such a prize, coupled with the knowledge that Columbus brought back of a New World in the West, what other treasures might lie out there beyond the immense ocean? The Portuguese were going to find out.

THE NORTH ATLANTIC

To João Fernandes Lavrador of Terceira in the Azores, King Manuel granted a license in 1499 to seek out and discover islands on the Portuguese side of the demarcation line. He appears to have rediscovered Greenland, but the dates of the sailing are uncertain. The name Lavrador was later associated with the mainland, although there is no evidence of his having been there, and what happened to Lavrador after 1501 is unknown. On 12 May 1500 the king issued a license to the brothers Gaspar and Miguel Corte-Real. They reached Newfoundland, which they explored in some detail. It is not clear if they had known about the previous voyages to that part of North America by John Cabot on behalf of Henry VII of England several years before, or about the license granted to Lavrador in 1499. On a second voyage with three ships a year later, Gaspar reached Labrador (Lavrador), Newfoundland and Nova Scotia. Then he set off to the south alone and was never heard from again. His brother Miguel set off with two vessels in 1502 for the same area, and he, too, disappeared.

PEDRO ALVARES CABRAL: BRAZIL

Six months after Vasco da Gama's return to Portugal, the largest fleet yet assembled sailed out of Lisbon harbor on 9 March 1500 to demonstrate Portuguese power in the East and open diplomatic and commercial relations by whatever means. The thirteen ships were placed under the command of Pedro Alvares Cabral, a nobleman of good education. Among the total of some 1,200 men there were also provisions for eighteen months. The departure was an occasion of grand and solemn ceremony. Sailing southwest from the Cape Verde Islands for about a month to avoid adverse winds and in order to make a position east of the Cape of Good Hope where he could pick up westerlies to take him around the cape, Pedro Alvares sighted land on 22 April 1500. It was the coast of Brazil.

Cabral, who called the new land Vera Cruz, sent a ship home to inform the king of the discovery and continued his journey toward India on 2 May. Many of his ships were lost during the course of the voyage, including the one captained by Bartolomeu Dias, who drowned at sea. Only six reached Sofala (Mozambique) in July and Calicut on 13 September.

This time, pleased with the gifts from King Manuel, the samorin was friendly to the visitors, but before Cabral could firmly establish a relationship at his court, the Muslim merchants of the city, viewing the Portuguese as trespassers threatening their commerce, instigated a fight in which some of the Portuguese were killed. Cabral bombarded the city with ships' cannon and set ablaze some of the local commercial boats.

Having learned that the Raja Trimumpará of Cochin was hostile to the samorin of Calicut, Cabral sailed south to Cochin, until then an unknown location to the Portuguese, quickly established friendly relations and loaded a cargo of pepper. The city was situated closer to the pepper fields than Calicut and had a better harbor. Before returning to Lisbon, Cabral visited Cannanor, a pepper principality north of Calicut. At odds with the samorin, the raja there was also friendly.

When Cabral sailed for home, he carried with him ambassadors of the rulers of Cochin and Cannanor and left a party of Portuguese to set up a trading post at Cochin. From this time on Portuguese liaison with India was established. The discovery or rediscovery of Brazil passed almost unnoticed as attention focused on the East. A fleet sent out in 1501 under João de Nova contained only four vessels and set up a post at Cannanor, where it was well received and returned with spices. This was the first of six voyages between 1501 and 1505. The generally tranquil exploration and opening up of the African coasts would not be duplicated in India, however, due to the presence of numerous hostile Muslims. But with Cabral's report, the king and his councillors now had a clearer idea of what awaited the Portuguese in the East, and, when necessary, the Indian policy would become more bellicose and threatening.

SECOND VOYAGE OF VASCO DA GAMA

Vasco da Gama, now Admiral of India, was chosen again to lead twenty ships, fifteen under his direct command and five sent out later under the captaincy of his cousin. They sailed in February and March 1502 with intentions less than peaceful. In the Indian Ocean, da Gama's fleet captured and set fire to a large vessel out of Calicut ladened with wealthy pilgrims, their families and goods on the way home from Mecca. The passengers were burned alive or drowned in the sea.

Next, the fleet sailed into Calicut harbor for a showdown with the samorin, who showed a congenial demeanor in the face of a strong force. He was also envious of the agreement with Cochin and now desirous of trade with the Portuguese. Coming to terms, he offered to turn over the men who had been responsible for the trouble two years earlier when some of the sailors under Cabral had been killed. He was adamant, however, in refusing da Gama's orders that Muslims be expelled from the city, insisting that Calicut was open to all traders.

The Portuguese response was unexpected. Da Gama brought his ships close to shore and opened fire. Cannonballs rained down on the city the entire day, starting fires and killing indiscriminately. Then, as he prepared to sail, he committed a further barbarous act: several hundred local fisherman on their boats just out beyond the fleet were slaughtered. It can only be surmised that da Gama's actions were designed to instill fear along the Malabar coast and force the expulsion of Muslim colonies from the Hindu kingdoms. Da Gama filled his ships with spices at Cochin and Cannanor and sailed for home. With his departure, the samorin of Calicut invaded Cochin and drove the ruler and the Portuguese garrison left there to seek refuge on the island, from which they were rescued by one of the fleets sent out in 1503 bringing Duarte Pacheco.

In anticipation of further attacks on Cochin, Pacheco was left in charge of 160 men-at-arms and three ships. The expected assault on the fortress began early in 1504. Pacheco's brilliant defense against great odds made him a Portuguese national hero. He received from King Manuel congratulations for his exploits in India but little else. Finally, in 1520 he was appointed governor of the fort at Mina. There he was accused of embezzlement and sent home in irons. Acquitted after an inquiry, he lived in poverty until his death in 1530. In September 1504 a fleet of thirteen ships under Lopo Soares de Albergaria arrived in India and again bombarded Calicut and burned a Muslim fleet in Cannanor. Five ships and 300 men were left behind to safeguard the Portuguese posts.

FRANCISCO DE ALMEIDA

Francisco de Almeida, appointed viceroy, arrived in India in 1505 with twenty-two ships and 2,500 men, of whom 1,500 were soldiers. He carried instructions for the organization of forts on the coasts of Africa, which were constructed at Kilwa (Tanzania), where da Gama had already made an alliance with the ruler, and at Mozambique. He entered into an alliance with the sultan of Melindi and burned hostile Mombasa, all of which assured Portuguese naval supremacy in East Africa. De Almeida also had a mandate for the conclusion of alliances with Indian rulers, and the construction of forts was begun on the west coast of India at Cannanor and Cochin, where a stone fort replaced the earlier wooden one.

Almeida's next step was the most provocative. Through a system of licenses, he sought to control all eastern trading ships, making them subject to arrest if they failed to have his authorization. This move threatened immediate ruin to Portuguese commercial rivals, and the struggle was soon under way. The samorin gathered a fleet but was badly mauled by the firepower of the Portuguese vessels. The Arab merchants then began to collect their spices in Malacca and the Sunda Islands and to sail via Ceylon or the Maldives directly to the Persian Gulf or the Red Sea. An attempt to cut off this trade brought the Portuguese to Ceylon.

Under Lourenço de Almeida, son of the viceroy, they arrived in 1505, landing at Colombo, where they immediately began the construction of a fort. They were made welcome by the king of the lowland Sinhalese, Parakrama Bahu, at his capital of Kotte. Impressed by their guns and armor, he solicited their protection in return for an annual tribute to be paid in cinnamon. The king hoped to gain support of the Europeans in his struggle against the Tamil peoples in the northern part of the island as well as the highland King Kandy and the Muslim traders. Building forts along the western coasts of the island, the Portuguese soon dominated the spice trade from Ceylon.

Meanwhile, back home, trouble was escalating between Christians and Jews.

PERSECUTION OF JEWS

Food shortages and price increases in 1503 were blamed on the Jews, along with any other ills that assailed society, and some demonstrations involving stoning took place in Lisbon. The following year an outbreak of anti-Semitism occurred in Évora resulting in the destruction of a synagogue. Like a gathering storm, other towns were caught up in similar incidents. Anti-Jewish sentiment struck with full force in Lisbon in April 1506, when the city was again afflicted by the plague, which was blamed on the Jews. One Sunday after mass a New Christian (a Jew converted to Christianity) was murdered in the street by a gang, and his body was set on fire. This kindled an uncontrolled frenzy of hatred. Two Dominicans ran through the streets of the city waving crucifixes, shrieking heresy and inciting the crowds. Mobs at fever pitch of excitement and hostility battered down doorways, dragged Jews from their shops and houses and murdered them on the cobblestones. Some 500 died, and the bloody performance was repeated the following day and again on the next. The carnage numbered in the thousands.

The king had been out of the city, as was usual when the plague visited. When the news of the massacre reached him at Avis, he set in motion an inquiry that resulted in a death sentence for some fifty of the instigators, including the two Dominicans, the closure of the monastery of São Domingos and the confiscation of the property of all those implicated in the pogrom. The Casa dos Vinte e Quatro, the Lisbon guild hall, considered to be a source of anti-Semitism, was closed. The city was deprived of its titles of noble and loyal. To mollify the New Christians, the king repealed the orders of 1499 against their leaving the kingdom but hoped to persuade them from doing so by confirming the promise that no inquiry would be initiated concerning their religious beliefs for twenty years. At the queen's request the punishment of the city of Lisbon was terminated in 1508.

CASA DA INDIA

The Casa da India was the center of all overseas commerce and administration. It supervised exports, the disembarkation of merchandise and the distribution of products among interested parties. All sales were controlled in the name of the king. The crown office and warehouse were situated on the ground floor of the royal palace on the waterfront of

Lisbon, where the king could observe the loading and unloading of the ships. In 1506 the king declared an official state monopoly on all imports and sale of such items as spices and silk and on the exports of gold, silver, copper and coral. In the sixteenth century spices, gold and slaves were the commodities most traded.

The most profitable item of trade, slaves, had its source all up and down the coast of Africa wherever Portuguese forts and trading posts were found. Slaves from West Africa supplied the labor markets of Europe, the Madeira Islands, Cape Verde and São Tomé. Later, Brazil became the chief importer.

AFONSO DE ALBUQUERQUE

Two more fleets left Lisbon in 1506, one under Tristão da Cunha and the other under Afonso de Albuquerque. With fifteen ships da Cunha explored the coasts of Madagascar and then sailed north and seized the island of Socotra at the entrance to the Gulf of Aden with a view to controlling the Red Sea. He built a fort on the island before sailing on to India, but the site proved to be too impoverished and too easily bypassed to make a useful naval base. It was abandoned in 1510. The fleet under Afonso de Albuquerque, the man who carried secret orders to succeed Almeida as viceroy when his term finished, had other ideas.

Navigator, statesman and consolidator of the Portuguese empire in the Orient, Albuquerque spent his youth at the court of King Afonso V. In 1503 he made his first trip to India, traveling with a Portuguese fleet. Three years later King Manuel appointed him viceroy of all Portuguese possessions in Asia.

On his own initiative Albuquerque attacked the cities of the Oman coast. Some surrendered and supplied him with provisions; others resisted and were plundered. His six ships next appeared off Ormuz on 25 September 1507. The busy market town was crowded with merchants and sailors, Persians, Arabs and Turks, and numerous ships stood at anchor in the barren inlet. Greatly outnumbered and with only about 400 men at his disposal, Albuquerque boldly demanded tribute. When it was not forthcoming, he bombarded the town and attacked the ships in harbor until the regent made a gift of considerable money, promised to pay more annually and submitted to the construction of a Portuguese fort, which was begun on 24 October.

To work as stonemasons under a blazing sun in a desiccated land was not the reason the Portuguese captains and crews had braved the Cape of Good Hope. Their thoughts were apparently on plunder, prizes and wealth. One night, three of Albuquerque's ships slipped anchor and stole away, leaving the commander little choice but to retire. Albuquerque proceeded to India, where he arrived in December, took up residence in Cannanor and claimed the office of viceroy from Almeida, whose three-year term had expired. In the process of preparing an expedition against Egypt, Almeida refused to turn over command and declared that he had not been ordered to leave India.

The Egyptians and Turks had resolved to protect their interests and with the aid of the Venetians constructed a fleet. In a surprise attack at Chaul in 1508 it intercepted some Portuguese ships under the command of Almeida's son, Lourenço. The young captain was mortally wounded in the battle, and his ship was captured. Some escorting vessels escaped and reported the matter to Almeida, who collected nineteen ships and 1,600 men to meet the threat. The Egyptian fleet sailed into Indian waters and made its base at Diu, where it was supplemented with ships and arms of the samorin of Calicut. On 2 February 1509, the forces met in a large naval engagement fought off the coast of Diu. The total destruction of the Muslim fleet and its Indian allies guaranteed Portuguese sea power in the Indian Ocean for the immediate future.

On renewal of his demand to be recognized as viceroy, when Almeida returned from Diu, Albuquerque was arrested and locked up in Cannanor. He was freed when Fernando Coutinho arrived in India with fifteen ships in October 1509, armed with confirmation of Albuquerque's appointment and orders to attack Calicut.

The attack was a failure and resulted in the death of Coutinho and many of his men, while Albuquerque himself was wounded. The new viceroy now chose Goa as the seat of his authority, as it seemed best to fulfill the strategic requirements. He captured the town with little difficulty since, as luck would have it, the local army was away on a venture when he arrived. When the army returned, however, he was driven out, and he sailed to Cochin. At the end of 1510, a second attempt to take Goa was successful. The city was sacked, fortifications built, administrative offices set up, intermarriage with Indians encouraged and merchants from Ormuz welcomed. His predecessor, Francisco de Almeida, with the laurels of victory at Diu, never returned home. He was killed in a skirmish with natives near the cape.

CONQUEST OF THE CITY OF MALACCA

Albuquerque went on to complete the conquests of the Malabar coast, and with a firm grip on the trade of the Arabian Sea and much of the Indian Ocean, he set off to appropriate the richest source of the spice trade, the Moluccas or Spice Islands, today islands of eastern Indonesia. By a stroke of good fortune a large chart of the Indian Ocean, the South China Sea, and the islands of Indonesia compiled by a Javanese pilot was acquired by the Portuguese. The viceroy departed in May 1511 with seventeen ships to subdue Malacca, the center of the trade, on the southern tip of the Malay Peninsula. The site was not unknown to the Portuguese since some eighteen months before, Diogo Lopes de Sequeira had made a voyage there from India but, encountering a hostile reception, had returned. A second fleet of four ships had fared no better.

Albuquerque arrived at Malacca, sailing into the harbor with flags flying and cannons roaring in salute with a view to intimidating Sultan Mohammed. The viceroy demanded the surrender of the city and the release of the Portuguese prisoners whom the sultan had held from the time when Sequeira attempted to construct a fort on the site. Stalling for time, the sultan hastily began erecting defenses, and Albuquerque burned some of the Gujarati ships in the harbor and some waterfront buildings. The sultan then released the prisoners but continued to procrastinate while the defenses were improved.

The crowded city was divided in half by a river spanned by the Malacca Bridge. On 25 July 1511 at first light, the Portuguese rowed boats up the river, landed men at both ends of the bridge and, after fierce fighting under showers of poisoned arrows, captured it. They held it for a time, waiting for the sultan to sue for peace, but nothing happened, and they withdrew to their ships. Sultan Mohammed with a large garrison of about 20,000 soldiers and plenty of artillery was not in a mood to negotiate a surrender.

Albuquerque had at his disposal some 900 Portuguese and 200 Indian mercenaries. Another attack on the bridge with a fortified junk was made as a diversion, while the majority of the soldiers came ashore elsewhere. With a furious charge they stormed the barricades in the narrow streets of the city, sweeping them first with cannon fire. The sultan then suddenly appeared with his full strength of war elephants. The astonished Portuguese held their ground. The lead animals, confined in the narrow lanes and jabbed with long pikes, reared up, bellowing, furiously unsettling their mounts, including the sultan. The panicked elephants then wheeled and charged through the Malaccan troops advancing behind them.

Twenty-eight Portuguese had been killed in the battle, and many had been wounded when they retired to the ships. A week-long lull then occurred, but on 24 August, when they again attacked, the sultan had fled. The city yielded an enormous fortune in gold, silver, jewels, silks and spices. A Portuguese administration was established in Malacca, and a fort was built using the stone from nearby mosques and tombs of former sultans. Albuquerque then sent three ships eastward to find the Moluccas, the source of nutmeg and cloves, and left a squadron to patrol the straits and protect Malacca. Returning to Goa, the viceroy's ship, *Flor de la Mar*, a large, worm-riddled and leaky carrack (beamy sailing ship), sank off Sumatra in a storm with most of the looted treasure on board. Albuquerque escaped on a raft and was rescued the following day.

Reaching Cochin in 1512 and after having made peace with the samorin of Calicut, Albuquerque established a fort there and set about in earnest to destroy the remainder of Arab trade. Just as Ormuz closed off the Persian Gulf, so the city of Aden in Portuguese control would close off access to the Red Sea from the Indian Ocean. An attack on Aden in March 1513, however, failed for lack of scaling ladders and fresh water. On his way back to India, suffering from dysentery, the viceroy learned that his enemy, Lopo Soares de Albergaria, had been appointed his successor.

Afonso de Albuquerque died shortly after his ship crossed the bar into Goa. Only the peripheral Red Sea remained in enemy hands, but Albuquerque's larger dreams of complete control of the sources of spice, the ruination of the Muslim lands and the seizure of the body of the prophet Mohammed from Mecca in order to ransom it for Jerusalem were never realized.

Lopo Soares de Albergaria, leader of the court intrigue against Albuquerque, which was fed by complaints from India concerning the discipline instilled by the viceroy, immediately relaxed the rule of his predecessor that prohibited private trading by Portuguese subjects. It was an invitation for all and sundry to fill their own purses, and piracy and disorder quickly resulted. In other major miscalculations he failed to catch an Egyptian-Turkish fleet in the Red Sea and failed to establish a fort at Aden when invited to do so by the sultan, whose city walls were in shambles from an assault by the Egyptian fleet and who wanted Portuguese protection pending another attack. On the same expedition, in spite of the contrary counsel of his captains, he avoided a battle at

Jeddah in which the city could well have been his. Now short of supplies, his fleet became trapped in the summer doldrums of the Red Sea and put ashore at Kamaran Island (off the Yemen Red Sea coast). Before the winds permitted his departure a month or so later, some 800 Portuguese and nearly all the accompanying slaves were dead. He stopped again at Aden, where the city walls had now been rebuilt, but the sultan refused to renew his offer of a Portuguese garrison in the city. The one opportunity to gain a foothold at Aden and close the Red Sea had slipped away. Too weak to fight, Albergaria was reduced to begging for water at the city gates.

He was replaced by Diogo Lopes de Sequeira, whose timid performance as governor fared little better. Ordered to capture Diu, he twice lost his nerve when it appeared a ferocious battle was in the offing. He fortified Chaul but failed to hold it. Complaints reached Lisbon from the merchants of Cannanor, among other places, that vessels issued Portuguese licenses to trade along the Malabar coast were seized and pillaged sometimes only hours later by the very officials who issued the licenses. De Sequeira seems to have done little or nothing to prevent his captains from robbing the natives under their command. In fact, the governor was the first among chief officers to return to Portugal weighed down with the illegal riches of office. To maintain their silence, large amounts went to members of the royal family, who were aware of how he acquired his wealth. Duarte de Meneses, the fifth in the series of governors appointed by King Manuel, once a successful governor of Tanger, followed the example of his predecessor to build his personal fortune. He was incapable of staving off disaster in India.

PORTUGUESE DOMINION IN MOROCCO

By the end of the fifteenth century the Portuguese grip on North Africa consisted of four towns on the northern tip of Morocco of no great commercial value. During the reign of Manuel I, interest in Morocco again increased, and from 1505 to 1514, a chain of fortresses was built along the length of the Atlantic Coast. Eight in all were constructed or occupied. Bishoprics were established in the port cities, while the Portuguese language written with Arabic letters was introduced for native use. For the most part, the areas controlled by Portuguese coastal fortresses extended only a few miles inland and had little effect on Moorish commercial and military activities, but they impeded piracy along the Atlantic Coast. Maintenance of the forts cost more than they brought in, and as there was little money to be diverted to Morocco, and many ordinary Portuguese were not interested in serving there, the forts remained poorly garrisoned, with Spanish mercenaries and local Moroccan auxilliaries serving under the Portuguese crown. The military aristocracy, nevertheless, found a partial outlet for their crusading ideals, for the greater of glory of church and purse. Raiding the countryside rather than enaging in commerce was generally the practice.

In 1515 an armada left the Tejo estuary with the mission to construct fortifications in Mamora and Anafé near the present city of Casablanca. The Moors attacked the undertaking with disastrous results for the Portuguese. About 4,000 men, 100 ships and all the artillery were lost. Those chosen to become the colonizers of the new sites were taken and sold into slavery. Up to this time no expedition had been so costly. With revenge on his mind, the king immediately announced the creation of a new fleet, but neither men nor money for ships and arms was available. The king appealed to the Cortes for money and to the people and the church for their valuables to finance the continuation of the war, but the appeal failed, and the new expedition never sailed.

Meanwhile, the Portuguese governor of Safi, Nono de Ataide, ranged the Moroccan countryside for booty and slaves. He failed in an attempt to take Marrakech, but in spite of this, his compatriots attempted an assault on Fez and were soundly defeated. The next year Ataide met his death near Marrakech in another great raid on Muslim towns in a further effort to carve out a Moroccan empire at the expense of the Moors. These unprofitable crusades, in the manner of a holy war, were a waste of manpower and money and often opposed at home.

ETHIOPIA REVISITED

Another mission under Rodrigo de Lima reached Ethiopia in 1520, and after a grueling five-month journey from Massawa (in present-day Eritrea on the Red Sea), the embassy found the tent city of the emperor, or negus, as he was called. It was greeted in Portuguese by an old man— Covilhã, who had settled and raised a family. After many delays and endless questions about Portugal, Lima was granted an audience with the elusive negus, who hid himself behind a curtain even from his own people. Portuguese aspirations remained basically the same. The subject of the interview was to build a fort in the strait of Bab al Mandab at the mouth of the Red Sea and deprive the Muslims of access and trade in the Indian Ocean. The negus promised to supply provisions to the fort when it was completed. The party was not hindered leaving the kingdom for the return journey, but no ships awaited Lima and his men at Massawa, nor were there any the following year, 1522. Returning to the tent capital, they tried again the next year but arrived too late. The fleet had come and gone. This process was repeated again in 1524. Not until 1526 were they rescued, and they reached Portugal in 1527.

DECLINE OF THE CORTES

By the end of the fifteenth century the growth of royal power and income through overseas sources and regularization of tax collection under João II and Manuel I allowed the crown to dispense with frequent meetings of the Cortes. Manuel called it to meet only four times in twenty-six years. Less dependent on that body, the kings became more autocratic. The commoners, or the third estate, on whom the kings had often relied to keep the nobility in check, now found their means to power not so much through the Cortes but through overseas enterprises and wealth derived from them. The rise of professional administrators to advise the monarch on problems of state and bureaucratization of the central government also made the crown more politically self-reliant.

Overseas, Manuel's fortunes seemed boundless. His ships sailed home from the Far East laden with wealth, in Morocco his captains were completing a chain of forts from Tanger to Mogador depriving the Muslims of access to the Atlantic Ocean and sugarcane was beginning to appear from the Brazilian settlements that would soon rival the brazilwood imports.

FERNÃO DE MAGALHÃES (MAGELLAN)

Fernão de Magalhães, or Ferdinand Magellan, was the first European to cross the Pacific Ocean, and some of his crew were the first to circumnavigate the globe. Born in Sabrosa of noble parentage, Magalhães spent his early years as a court page, participated in several exploratory expeditions in the Spice Islands and by 1510 had been promoted to the rank of captain. Wounds acquired in Morocco left him lame for life. Request for an increase in his royal allowance was rejected by King Manuel, who was indifferent also to Magalhães' scheme to seek a westward route to the Moluccas. Renouncing his Portuguese nationality, he offered his services to the king of Spain, Carlos I, and secured approval for an expedition that would attempt to reach the Moluccas by sailing west.

The success of the voyage, it was hoped, would circumvent the African route to the islands controlled by Portugal.

On 20 September 1519 Magalhães sailed from Sanlucar in Spain with five ships. In November he reached South America, sailed through the passage that bears his name, the Strait of Magellan, and entered an ocean that he named "Pacific" because of its calmness. He reached the Marianas, or Ladrone Islands, on 6 March 1521. Landing on the island of Cebu in the Philippines on 7 April, he was mortally wounded in a skirmish with local natives.

With only two vessels remaining, his captains reached the Moluccas on 6 November 1521, where the Portuguese commandeered one of the ships. Only the ship *Victoria*, commanded by the Spanish navigator Juan Sebastián del Cano, completed the circumnavigation of the globe, arriving in Sevilla on 6 September 1522. The cargo of spices carried back to Spain by the remaining ship paid for the expenses of the expedition, but passage through the Strait of Magellan was too long and difficult to be a practical route from Europe to the Moluccas. Spain sold its interests in the East to Portugal.

DEATH OF KING MANUEL

King Manuel benefited greatly in wealth and prestige from trade with the Indies. The first voyage is said to have paid for itself many times over even by the small amount of pepper Vasco da Gama brought back. In Cochin the price of pepper was two cruzados the quintal (or two Portuguese gold coins for about 220 lbs. of pepper) but that brought back by da Gama sold at eighty cruzados the quintal. In spite of the loss of ships, the voyage of Cabral returned two to four times its cost in profits. With the opulence of the Indian trade Manuel maintained grants and pensions for some 5,000 people.

By the time Manuel died in 1521, the nobility, having been greatly reduced in number during the reign of João II, were once again well entrenched at court. The efforts of the crown to centralize administration and fiscal policy, eliminate local privileges and improve tax collection reached their apex in his reign. A revised compilation of Portuguese law involving town charters, the *Ordenações Manuelinas*, was completed the year of his death. He kept the country free of European entanglements and the second half of his reign has been considered the most prosperous period in Portuguese history.

CULTURAL PERCEPTIONS

It was no easy matter for the Portuguese to deal with people halfway around the globe. It was believed by the king and others that in India if one was not a Muslim, then one was some sort of unorthodox Christian. The Hindu religion was new and strange. It was not known what kind of gifts to bring to the rajas or what their views of the world were. Offering the king of Calicut little red cloth hats, bells and mirrors to place among his gold and silver, jewels, ivory and rich plumage in exchange for pepper was an insult. Such gifts served to enthrall only primitive African tribes. Da Gama and his men were so badly informed that they mistook Hindu temples for churches and statues of the Goddess Dewaki nursing the infant Vishnu for the Virgin Mary. Paintings on the wall of gowned figures with long, protruding teeth and four or more arms were thought to be saints. Disagreements arose from cultural differences and did not abate until the Portuguese became more integrated in local society, generally through intermarriage. Portuguese women were usually not allowed to go and live in the overseas possessions.

5

House of Avis: João III–Cardinal Henrique, 1521–1580

João III's reign gave way to a conservative lack of compromise under the influence of Jesuits and rigid counter-reformationists. Born in 1502 to King Manuel and his Spanish wife, Maria, the pious João succeeded to the throne in 1521. Portugal was at the height of its international power, and during his reign overseas expansion in commerce and settlement continued. At home, however, the country was deeply in debt, old problems intensified and new ones appeared.

The relationship between João and his father appears to have been strained. In agreement with a faction of the king's council, the son opposed some of the policies of his father, including further territorial extension in Morocco and construction of forts in East Africa. The relationship between son and father was no doubt not improved when, on the death of his second wife, Manuel married Princess Leonor, sister of Carlos I of Spain (Carlos V, emperor of the Holy Roman Empire), twenty years his junior, in spite of the fact she was contracted to marry his son. In 1523 the widowed queen Leonor departed for Castilla along with her considerable fortune.

In the first year of his reign João III began negotiating for a double marriage alliance with Spain, which was concluded in 1526 by his marriage to Catarina, the sister of Emperor Carlos V, and that of the emperor with his sister Isabel. João's marriage to Catarina cost the country an enormous sum in gold for the emperor's coffers, as Carlos refused the dowry payment of 50,000 quintals of pepper. João III lacked both imagination and astute advisors to develop major policies that would benefit the country. The nobles assumed more power at his expense, and the wealth from commerce was spent in conspicuous consumption at court and on aristocratic luxuries rather than on beneficial capital investments. His religious views, in accordance with those of the times, may have been intensified by personal tragedies. The fact that his ten children all died before him might help account for his somber outlook.

DOMESTIC AND INTERNATIONAL ISSUES

Agriculture continued to decline in João III's reign. The Alentejo wheat farms, worked by slaves or not worked at all, produced little, and in the green, fertile north of small landholdings the peasants had been leaving in droves to look for work in the large towns or had shipped out to the East, seeking a better life, few of whom ever returned. Many died on the six- or seven-month voyage from Lisbon to Goa or on the fever-stricken tropical coasts of India, Asia or Africa. Living conditions in the tropics brought on many more deaths from disease than occurred in the numerous conflicts on land and sea. The cost in material and manpower of the passage to India was prodigious. It has been calculated that during the first half of the sixteenth century about 472 ships left for the East carrying about 180,000 men. The eight- or nine-month voyage under the most primitive sanitary conditions often cost the lives of half the crews and passengers before the destination was reached. The homeland was drained of healthy young men as several thousand left the country each year. At home, plague and other manifestations of the Fourth Horseman carried off thousands annually. Men-at-arms and experienced sailors were in short supply to man the fleets that brought home the spices that, in turn, were needed to finance the royal tastes and buy grain from abroad to feed the populace.

The supply of manpower required to control such a large area of the world by a relatively small nation meant that the number of Portuguese throughout the empire was never large. The military was often inadequate for the jobs at hand, and the tendency for soldiers to drift off into freebooting or better-paid mercenary occupations in which they were prized by local Eastern sultans made the situation worse. Portuguese society in the East and later in Brazil was largely founded on miscegenation and native Christian converts. While greatly outnumbered by local inhabitants in most areas, the Portuguese relied on their naval power, the prowess and determination of their soldiers in battle and the disunity of native states to maintain control.

The city of Lisbon grew rapidly during this time, becoming a haven for both rich and poor. The royal monopoly on trade concentrated here prompted a decline in other coastal cities. But instead of developing into a town of new enterprises, Lisbon was becoming a center for consumption of profits, creating a burden on the empire. It was poorly situated to disperse the commodities from Eastern trade throughout Europe, so merchants had to send their products to other capitals, particularly Antwerp, for distribution. Overseas, the continuing struggle against the Muslims in Morocco and the maintenance of outposts along the trade route required vast sums of money and manpower.

Clansmen of the Sadid Dynasty streamed into Marrakech out of the Sahara Desert in 1524, giving rise to a revitalized Moroccan resurgence. Portuguese strong points along the southern and central coasts came under hit-and-run attacks, and what little trade they did was curtailed. The king was in favor of withdrawing many of the economically unremunerative garrisons, but not until Agadir fell in 1542 and Safi, under great pressure, was abandoned the following year did the crown act. During the next five years all the Portuguese fortresses on the Moroccan coast, with few exceptions, were abandoned. After 1550 only Ceuta, Tanger and Mazagão to the south remained in Portuguese hands.

Like his father, João III tried to keep clear of European entanglements, preferring to buy his way out of difficulties. To protect Portuguese shipping from predatory European enterprises, he tried to buy off the leading French ship owners and the French admiral Chabot, who was aiding, abetting and outfitting pirates. Little changed, however, as problems between Spain and France left Portugal, in the eyes of the French, as simply an appendage of Spain and subject to the same acts of plunder. João tried other methods to protect his interests. A convoy system of fast caravels was commissioned to protect the heavily laden vessels. Battered by the long voyage, the cargo-carrying ships from the Indies often put in at the Azores for refitting before crossing the open sea to Lisbon. As this last lap consisted of favorite cruising waters of French pirates, a fort was built at Terceira, and heavily armed caravels were employed to ply the waters off the islands during the season when the India ships were expected.

During the first ten years of João III's reign some 300 Portuguese vessels of all kinds were lost to French pirates. That François I shared in the spoils is clear from some of the letters found on French ships. But French corsairs were not the only parasites feeding on Portuguese shipping. In 1535, at great cost, João III raised an armada to join the Genoese admiral Andrea Doria in an expedition to destroy the Muslim pirate fleet in Tunis. The successful outcome freed thousands of Christian slaves. In the background the ominous Ottoman Turkish threat was ever present. Turkish corsairs were making Mediterranean ports dangerous places for commerce, and farther afield, with the Turks building a fleet at Suez at the head of the Red Sea, the Portuguese lifeline to its Indian possessions was in jeopardy.

INQUISITION

With the implacable animosity of João III and his anti-Semitic Cortes, the Jewish communities were in for a bad time. Secret societies were formed to hunt down Jews who relapsed into the faith of their ancestors, and the Inquisition was introduced into Portugal. The New Christians made up the bulk of the Portuguese middle class, and as entrepreneurs, financiers and skilled craftsmen, they were the only economic and social competition to the aristocracy. Their wealth and influence could thus be controlled by the power of an inquisitorial body. The corrupt and profligate members of the clergy, of whom sixteenth-century Portugal had its share, could also be brought into line by the crown through a regulatory watchdog. By projection, the renascent holy war against Muslims, in Morocco and elsewhere, might be aided by a more unified Christianity at home.

The bull announcing the Inquisition was read before the king and local dignitaries at Évora in 1536. It allowed thirty days for anyone guilty of a sacrilegious act to confess and repent. This included any act of heresy or apostasy or any rite associated with Judaism, Lutheranism, Islam or any magic ritual. More specific pronouncements that required atonement soon followed, including celebrating the Sabbath on Saturday, fasting for Ramadan, bathing the whole body, praying shoeless, refusing bacon or wine and denial of paradise, hell, the articles of faith or mass, the Virgin Birth, the power of priests to absolve and witchcraft.

João's brother Henrique was appointed inquisitor-general, who, vindictive, bigoted and vain, took up his duties with enthusiasm. The Inquisition vigorously performed its duties in six cities: Lisbon, Oporto, Évora, Coimbra, Lamego and Tomar. This was the very time when the country was having major difficulties meeting the military and economic commitments of the empire, a problem compounded by the persecution of the New Christians, which retarded the development of a prosperous (taxable) middle class. Of the approximately 24,522 people investigated over the following two centuries 1,454 were condemned to death, the last victim being burned at the stake in 1739.

The Inquisition shielded Portugal from the currents of the Reformation taking place in Europe. Strict control was exercised over the book trade, and all books, imported or locally published, had to have the stamp of the Holy Office. Previously published books were censored or banned and possession of a book not on the Index was a crime. The Dominican Order in charge of the Holy Office could thus control exposure to new ideas and keep Portugal intellectually isolated and backward. Also contributing to national decline, rural areas became more and more neglected and impoverished as a general contempt for manual labor and farmwork developed. A man could work hard for a lifetime and have nothing at the end of it except more taxes, while a short sojourn of plundering in the Indies could harvest a fortune. Lack of fertile holdings and the ownership of the best land by the church contributed to the feeling of futility. Many of those in the country were driven into the towns. The more adventurous set out for distant lands, such as the 4,000 men and boys who went with Diogo do Couto to India, but through piracy, shipwreck and disease only half reached Goa.

CORTES

Under João III the Cortes met on average once every twelve years. The Cortes of 1525 had considered some of the difficulties of the country, both moral and financial, including vagabonds, gambling, extravagance, court parasites, appointment of nobles to well-paying sinecures, redundant servants and offices and dishonest and fraudulent officials, along with ecclesiastics who demanded payment but failed to perform their duties. The crown did precious little to address these abuses.

Many complaints were again expressed in the Cortes of 1535. In an attempt to alleviate some of the problems, ordinances were issued in 1538. Begging by all who were of a healthy nature was banned, masters were directed to pay their servants, judges and officers were forbidden to demand food and lodging or establish their slaves as constables. To inhibit personal expenditures edicts proscribed wearing silks, silver or gold, and gambling was forbidden. Such laws did little to remedy the underlying causes of economic stagnation, even less so the earlier ban on Gypsies who had arrived in Europe from India by the second half of the fifteenth century. Their nomadic practices and proclivity to traits not found acceptable such as witchcraft and fortune-telling, led to an official prohibition against their entry into the country. Renewed periodically, the ban never achieved the desired result.

When the Cortes was called in 1544 at Almeirim to swear the oath to the heir, Prince João, sickly son of João III, the financial state of the country was presented to the representatives. Dynastic marriages had cost 1,400,000 cruzados, and about as much again had been spent to hold India and buy off Spain over the Molucca problem. Money to finance expeditions and defend Africa was raised in Flanders on three-month bills, which were usually not redeemed but left to ride at rates as high as 16 percent. The few hundred thousand cruzados that the cortes could raise was a drop in the bucket. There had been no attempt to pay off the debts, and the betrothal of João's daughter Maria to Prince Felipe in 1543 (the heir of Emperor Carlos V) cost the country another fortune.

Of the nine children of João III only one, the ailing Prince João, survived. In December 1552 at age fifteen he married a Spanish girl, Doña Juana, but lived only two more years and died 2 January 1554. The princess was pregnant, however, and gave birth on 19 January to a boy, Sebastião. The widowed mother soon departed for Spain with all her money, leaving the boy to be brought up at the Portuguese court in the care of his grandparents João III and Queen Catarina. João III was struck down by a stroke on 11 June 1557, and a royal council appointed Doña Catarina, his widow, a Spaniard and sister of Emperor Carlos V, as regent.

VASCO DA GAMA: VICEROY

Duarte de Meneses proved a disappointment as governor in India. Muslims occupied the hinterland of Goa, threatening a rich source of revenue, and Ormuz was in turmoil and revolt, cutting into the lucrative trade. Further, insubordinate Portuguese officials were acting as local sultans and lining their own pockets. To restore royal authority in India, João III brought Vasco da Gama, now in his mid-sixties, out of retirement and appointed him viceroy to replace Meneses. The admiral's prestige was legendary, and his wealth equally so. A fleet of fourteen ships sailed for India in April 1524 with the admiral, his two eldest sons, a personal guard of 200 men at arms and a vast entourage of administrators, pages and doormen, all dressed and bejeweled in a manner fitting a king's company, with a table of equal splendor. Two ships were lost crossing the Indian Ocean, but the viceroy landed safely at Goa and set to work dismissing or arresting those he found guilty of slovenliness, abuse of office or fraud, such as selling the king's arms or adding sand to pepper to increase its weight and quantity. The viceroy then descended on Cochin and arrested Duarte de Meneses, who was accused of owing the king a good deal of money that was not properly accounted for in his ledgers. He was ordered back to Portugal, where, still hoping to collect, the king refused to punish him and instead reinstated him as governor of Tanger.

Da Gama's methods, swift, firm and, according to some, cruel, such as the flogging of prostitutes, instilled fear, and those involved in administering the colony quickly mended their ways. But worn down by the debilitating climate and his duties, not least among which was the war he conducted against the Muslim pirates along the Malabar coast, Vasco da Gama died on Christmas Eve only three months after his arrival. The new appointee, Henrique de Meneses, a kinsman of Duarte, was honest and not afraid of a fight but was a poor diplomat and administrator. In a battle against the prince of Gujarat a leg wound proved fatal. His successor, Lopo Vaz de Sampaio, a captain of da Gama, was a capable and honest administrator. His major accomplishment was the destruction of the king of Cambay's fleet.

CONQUEST OF DIU

During the nine-year term of Nuno da Cunha as governor, Portugal returned to the offensive in the East. In command of a strong armada sent to India by João III, da Cunha first stopped in East Africa and seized Mombasa, whose rulers had not been friendly to Portugal. Arriving in India, he set about the conquest of Diu across the Gulf of Cambay (Gulf of Khambhat) from Damão. The city itself was in a state of internal conflict. The ruler had died, and his sons were engaged in a struggle among themselves and with the king of Cambay over who would rule.

In 1531 da Cunha attacked Diu, but the assault failed. Maintaining a blockade of the city, he occupied himself by taking other coastal towns, and three years later Diu was delivered into his hands without a fight. The Portuguese were allowed to construct a fortress there by an agreement with the then-raja of Gujarat, who requested their help in protecting his domains from the Mongols now firmly established in Delhi and expanding southward. The Portuguese were considered a nuisance but, unlike the Mongols, no threat to the existence of the state. Diu commanded the gateway to India from the Persian Gulf and guarded the shipping lanes of the Gulf of Cambay. It was a worthwhile prize.

The Mongol conquest diverted to the east relieved the pressure on Gujarat, while the Portuguese continued building solid walls around their stronghold at Diu. But antagonisms arose between them and the locals, and war erupted in 1537 between the raja and the Portuguese garrison. The raja was killed in battle. The Turks meanwhile constructed a large fleet of seventy-two ships in the Red Sea commanded by the terrible Sulaiman Pasha, and after subduing Aden, they descended on Diu. Pasha was joined by a Gujarati general, Ali Khan, and by Khwaja Safar, who was governor of the non-Portuguese part of the city. Their combined numbers of perhaps 30,000 against the Portuguese garrison of 800 seemed to augur certain disaster. Turkish artillery, some of the best available, knocked down one wall after another, forcing the Portuguese to withdraw into their inner sanctum. Just as a relief armada approached under command of da Cunha's successor, Garcia de Noronha, the Gujarati fell out with the Turks and ceased to supply them with provisions. The Turkish fleet weighed anchor and sailed away to Suez, never again to threaten Portuguese hegemony in India.

Estevão da Gama, son of Vasco and successor to Viceroy Noronha, set out at the head of some seventy vessels to search out and destroy the Ottoman navy in the Red Sea. Failing to tempt the Turks into a sea battle, the Portuguese commander sailed up the Red Sea and attempted a raid on the Suez dockyards where the Turkish fleet harbored. Bereft of surprise, the attack failed to do any significant damage and the fleet returned to India. This was the last attempt of the Portuguese to dominate the Red Sea, a failure that cost them dearly in their efforts to control the European spice trade.

THE FOUR HUNDRED

In 1537 a force of Portuguese volunteers went to the aid of the negus of Abyssinia under threat by a Muslim invasion from Somaliland. The news of the invasion reached Lisbon via João Bermudes, a Galician, who had remained behind when Rodrigo de Lima returned home. He claimed to be the ambassador of the new negus and patriarch of Abyssinia. He had escaped overland via Egypt and taken ship to Rome, while the Muslims, with Turkish support, slaughtered the Abyssinians, who were without firearms. João III sent him back to India with the volunteer soldiers known as the Four Hundred, but the governor of India, Estevão da Gama, gave command of the Four Hundred to his younger brother Cristóvão. Several years passed before they were assembled at Massawa on the Red Sea.

Setting out for Abyssinia, the volunteers encountered the enemy while the negus remained in hiding. After a series of small battles, including the capture of a village of black Jews, a wounded Cristóvão was captured and killed. Some of the Portuguese settled down in the country, while others returned home to tell the story, of which it is impossible to separate fact from fiction. João Bermudes with none of his self-proclaimed authority remained in Abyssinia keeping well clear of the negus and the Abyssinian court. He eventually fled with his slaves and considerable treasure to India, where he was welcomed by the Jesuits at the College of São Paulo before returning to Portugal. The Jesuits were just beginning to make inroads into Abyssinia, but they made few converts to Roman Catholicism.

JOÃO DE CASTRO

Raised at the court of King Manuel while his father was governor of Lisbon, João de Castro became a naval officer and explorer. At sea de Castro set himself the task of checking navigational theories. He may have been the first to discover that the magnetic needle was affected by iron such as that found in a cannon. By moving his compasses to other parts of the ship, he determined that the readings changed to truer indications. He appears to have also worked on a type of chart foreseeing that a ship's course might be charted on a straight line, a kind of forerunner of Mercator's Projection.

In 1545 he was called upon to take up the post of viceroy, replacing Martim Afonso de Sousa, where he distinguished himself by overthrowing the king of Gujarat and raising a second siege of Diu. De Castro completed the subjugation of Malacca and prepared the way for further conquest. The forty-eight-year-old de Castro died in 1548, a few weeks after the arrival of the messengers bringing the news of his second appointment.

By allying themselves with the successive rulers of Kotte, whom they protected from other island leaders, the Portuguese were able to gain political control of much of the island of Ceylon. All this changed in 1554, when King Rajasinha of the local kingdom of Sitawaka, taking his lessons from the Portuguese, trained an army, furnished it with modern weapons and defeated the Portuguese in some local battles. His newly constructed navy harassed Portuguese shipping. Before long he managed to subdue other island leaders, and at the height of his reign, which lasted until 1593, he controlled all of Ceylon with the exception of Colombo and Jaffna, a small island off the north coast. Rajasinha became a national champion acclaimed for defending the island against foreign invaders.

An incident, major in the eyes of the islanders, turned many of them against the Portuguese. A relic, sacred for most of the population—an alleged tooth of the Buddha and the most revered artifact on the island—was captured. When the Portuguese archbishop at Goa ordered it burned as a heathen talisman, the chances of the Portuguese recovering their previous influence in Ceylon evaporated. When the Dutch began to expand their international trade, Portuguese weakness in Ceylon made their takeover there easier.

CHINA TRADE, MACÃO AND JAPAN

Portuguese merchants reached China about 1516. The first attempts to establish trading centers on the south China coast had failed through the reluctance of the Chinese imperial bureaucracy to sanction barbarian intruders from the west. Their diffidence was, in part, due to the behavior of the Portuguese. Trying to do business with the Chinese without understanding their customs and attitudes led to numerous problems. If they were deeply offended, and it was not difficult for this to occur, it took years before they would deal with the Portuguese again. When Fernão Peres de Andrate reached Canton, he fired a booming salute to his hosts. The Chinese, believing guns should be discharged only in anger, were highly provoked. When his brother Simão arrived at the estuary of the Pearl River in the summer of 1519, without receiving permission from the authorities, he set to work building a fort impressing Chinese laborers into service. He then forcefully prevented other foreign traders such as Cambodians and Siamese from landing their cargoes until the Portuguese had sold all of theirs. He is said to have bought some Chinese children as slaves.

When Tomé Pires reached Peking after long and frustrating delays at the hands of Chinese officials, he was denied an audience with the emperor and instead faced charges concerning the Andrate brothers' misconduct. The letter he carried from King Manuel addressed the emperor as an equal and not as a superior and fermented more misunderstandings. Pires and his party returned to Canton in September 1521, where they were promptly arrested since an order had arrived from the imperial court that all Portuguese were to be expelled from China, but Pires died in captivity. Nevertheless, a smuggling trade developed among Chinese coastal officials, while the Portuguese kept a low profile, using Malays and other more acceptable nationals to man their ships and trade on shore until the political situation settled down. They continued to press the Chinese for a trading center of their own, and, eventually, in 1557, their wish was granted. They opted for a place called Amangao, "Bay of the Goddess Ama," which soon became Macão. From the beginning Macão was different from other Portuguese settlements in that it was occupied and administered by a pure trading class of merchants without the usual resident aristocratic captain-general looking out for the interests of his class and the court.

Portuguese ships exchanged spices in China for silks or porcelain, sold them to the Japanese for silver from their mines on Honshu and then exchanged the silver back in China (where there was little of it) for gold. Japanese businessmen welcomed the new arrivals and through trade between Japan and China, many Portuguese merchants became wealthy. Chinese traders who had enjoyed exclusive, if clandestine, trade with Japan (for it had been officially forbidden by the Chinese) made an effort to put an end to Portuguese interlopers and attacked their ships. European cannon proved decisive, and the Chinese junks that frequented Japanese harbors were seen no more. Impressed with Portuguese firepower, the Japanese had learned to manufacture their own firearms within a decade.

BRAZIL

When Cabral came across Brazil on his voyage to India, the original inhabitants were, for the most part, essentially seminomadic peoples who subsisted by hunting and gathering and simple agriculture. The widely scattered indigenous Indian population probably numbered no more than 1 million. Exploitation and colonization of Brazil made little progress during the reign of Manuel, who, intent on the Indies, all but ignored it. No Brazilian gold had yet been found, and only exotic animals and brasilwood were of any value. (The country takes its name from the red dye wood called brasil probably from *brasa*, a red-hot ember or glowing charcoal.) Nevertheless, rumor had it that silver mines did exist in the interior of the continent, and in 1524 Aleixo Garcia, a shipwrecked Portuguese sailor, led a party inland in search of a reputed land rich in minerals. Aleixo was murdered by his native porters for reason unknown, but stories of his exploits reached Europe. He may have learned that there were, indeed, mines in South America worked by the Inca peoples. When John Cabot made a voyage to South America between 1526 and 1530 and sailed up a great river, he found a few trinkets of silver among the Guaraní Indians and named it River of Silver (Rio de la Plata). The news generated much excitement in Lisbon, and the story went around that a mountain of silver lay somewhere up the river. Naturally, João III was anxious to obtain control of these lands and initiated a program of systematic Brazilian colonization in 1530. As a first step, he divided the coastal country into twelve districts or captaincies and granted each of them in perpetuity to a person prominent at the Portuguese court. The grantees, known as donatories, were obliged to found settlements and open up trade.

Because of French depredations along the coast, Brazil was placed under the rule of a governor-general. The first, Tomé de Sousa, arrived in Brazil in 1549, organized a central government with the newly founded city of Salvador (Bahia) as his capital and established a coastal defense system.

Colonists first forced the native Indian populations to work the land, but the Indians often ran away or simply did not survive under conditions of slavery. Africans were then brought to the American colonies, primarily because it was believed that they could endure forced labor in the enervating tropical climates. Large numbers of slaves were brought to Brazil especially for the growing sugarcane plantations—the first crop successfully exported—followed by tobacco. The latter appeared in Lisbon about 1550 (used for medicinal purposes on wounds or for smoking), where it was exported to France about 1560 by Jean Nicot, the French ambassador—hence, the word nicotine. Meanwhile, the French founded a colony on the shores of Rio de Janeiro Bay, but the Portuguese destroyed it in 1560 and in 1567 established on its site the city of Rio de Janeiro.

GUINEA-BISSAU, ANGOLA AND MOZAMBIQUE

Many of the slaves for the Brazilian plantations came from the region of present-day Guinea-Bissau, Angola and, to a much lesser extent, from Mozambique. The area of Guinea-Bissau was first visited by Portuguese explorers in 1446 and a post was established at Bissau, which became an important slave center. The Portuguese claim was disputed by the French and the British, but in 1879 the region was constituted a Portuguese colony and border disputes with the French were settled by treaty in 1886. Not until 1915, however, were the Portuguese able to exercise effective control over the country. The status of Guinea-Bissau was changed from colony to overseas province in 1951, but the native inhabitants reaped little benefit from Portuguese rule.

Soon afterward an African nationalist movement arose, led by the African Party for the Independence of Guinea-Bissau and the Cape Verde Islands. After sporadic violence, especially in the capital city of Bissau, the party launched a war of independence in the early 1960s. By September 1973 the rebels proclaimed an independent republic and sought international recognition. On 10 September 1974 Portugal formally granted Guinea-Bissau independence.

Portuguese explorers had first arrived in Angola in 1483 followed, a few years later, by traders and missionaries. Religious conversion was dramatic, if short-lived. When João II dispatched ships crowded with missionaries and artisans to the region in 1490, he hoped to convince the natives to adopt the Portuguese religion and way of life. One powerful ruler of the Congo basin was impressed enough to change his name from Nazinga Nkumm to João I, dress in European style, learn the catechism and fill his court with "counts" and "marquises."

The Portuguese were, however, generally more interested in profit from a booming trade in slaves than in either missionary work or spreading European civilization. The slave traffic, greedily aided by local chiefs, undermined the authority of the missionaries, and many natives disappeared into the bush to escape the slavers' clutches.

Meanwhile, the Portuguese had extended their reach southward to the area around present-day Luanda, which they founded in 1575 and over which they claimed colonial authority. Royal governors were appointed who tried to impose their will on the population, but foreign rule was stubbornly resisted. Prolonged warfare ensued, while slave raids helped to keep the country in continuous turmoil. Hence, few white settlements were attempted during this period. By 1845 there were still only 1,800 Europeans in all Angola. The slave trade went on almost uninterrupted throughout the nineteenth century, by which time an estimated 3 million slaves had been exported.

Portugal did not gain full control over the country's interior until the early twentieth century. After that, Angola was governed under a system of economic exploitation, educational neglect and political repression that remained in force until February 1961 when the first wave of violence erupted. In 1951 Angola's official status was changed from colony to overseas province and soon after, a policy of accelerated white settlement was adopted—the last futile attempt of the colonial power to ward off the inevitable. During the 1950s a nationalist movement grew rapidly, and in 1961 a guerrilla war against the Portuguese was initiated, culminating in independence fourteen years later.

Beginning with Vasco da Gama's visit in 1498, coastal East Africa, occupied by black city-states and ruled by Arabs, began to break up as Portugal came to dominate parts of the region with way stations and forts on the route to India. However, to maintain, let alone expand, its interests over such a vast territory so far from home was beyond the economic capabilities of Portugal. In less than a century Portugal retained only some of the coastal cities of present-day Mozambique. Exploiting the area for the slave trade, little money was invested in Mozambique, and only a few hundred Europeans settled there. A colonization scheme was begun in the late eighteenth century to lure settlers through large land grants, but it failed because the proprietors were more interested in the slave trade than land and farms.

In the twentieth century, with forced and contract native labor and harsh treatment, Portuguese rule undermined African life. While Portugal claimed that Africans could achieve equality with whites by assimilation into Portuguese culture, the system produced few converts and despite special incentives to whites, Portugal's colonization policy also failed. Relatively few whites were resident in Mozambique in 1964, the year revolt against Portuguese rule began. The ensuing war ended with Mozambique independence a decade later with only 10 percent of the native population literate.

MISSIONARIES

The church served as an extension of the Portuguese state in the vanguard of imperial expansion. The king endowed the churches and appointed the bishops, and the state sometimes used clergy on diplomatic missions and as administrators. The closeness of church and state was reflected in the laws that provided greater civil liberties and commercial privileges to Christians. A group of Franciscans, sailing with Cabral's expedition of 1500, were the first of the evangelizing missionaries to reach India, where they built a church at Cochin. Dominicans followed and were the first of the orders to enter China in 1556 but were forced to retire due to local hostility. Most success in gaining converts occurred among people of very different societies—the Japanese and the Amerindians. At the forefront of this proselytizing activity was the Society of Jesus, or Jesuits.

Saint Francis Xavier, a cofounder of the society, traveled to Lisbon at the invitation of João III and established a college at Coimbra, beginning two centuries of Jesuit influence in Portuguese education. Xavier then sailed for India in 1541, where he found sinful Goa in dire need of religious redemption. After organizing a college for the instruction of missionaries, he then set about preaching in more distant towns and villages, eventually reaching Malacca and the Spice Islands. As he ranged the steep terrain of the various islands in steaming heat with only an acolyte bearing a cross, singing hymns as they went, the natives generally hid in the bush, and he found little success. In 1548 he returned to Goa. That things were not progressing very well is clear from a letter he sent to João expressing his intention of going to Japan. Hindus, Muslims and Jews did not make good material for conversion. In Japan he expected to find civilized pagans open to the true word, and in a short time Xavier had made many converts there. He was so impressed with the character of the Japanese and their receptivity to Christianity that he envisaged converting the entire islands. On a visit to China he died in Sanchwang in 1552.

In Japan the undiplomatic destruction of Shinto and Buddhist temples by the small Christian minority, coupled with official fear of the Jesuits, a foreign power that may have been the vanguard of foreign armies, brought about a shift in attitude. In 1596 executions of Christians began. Some of the fathers renounced their beliefs to save their lives, and others were martyred. In one case the victims were crucified upside down in the tidal flats to await the incoming tide. Christian sects were eventually eliminated, but trade continued until well into the seventeenth century, however, when the Portuguese were expelled from the country.

In India the Portuguese had not tried to force their religion upon their non-Christian subjects apart from proscribing suttee, but that changed with the arrival of the inquisition in 1560, which tried to eradicate any vestige of Hinduism, even prohibiting converts to use their Hindu names and banning all Hindu ceremonies. Jesuits established their presence in the colony of Macão in 1565, but the Chinese would not tolerate religious persecution, and there was no question of interfering with the local temples.

Missionaries to the Congo were never enough to make a lasting impression. Many who went died of tropical diseases, while the association between missionary and slave trader did not entice many natives to Christianity. The general view was that the black natives were too savage to convert by love and kindness and had to be subdued by arms and the whip. Once defeated and broken, they would become servile Christians.

The Jesuits' most effective work was in Brazil and Paraguay, where they participated in laying the foundations of the Portuguese occupation and constructing their own communities. The first Jesuits reached Bahia in 1549, accompanying the governor-general, Tomé de Sousa, and immediately set about founding hermitages among the Indians. The city of São Paulo is said to have developed from a straw hut in which a Jesuit priest held religious classes for the natives. The priests had their hands full instilling a sense of decorum among the rough and avaricious colonists, who were often more truculent than the natives. Between the years 1549 and 1604, twenty-eight Jesuit missions sailed to Brazil, not to mention many Franciscans, Benedictines and Carmelites.

SEBASTIÃO

Lisbon, meanwhile, had become the third largest city in continental Europe after Naples and Paris, while other cities of Portugal declined in population and trade. Overseas commerce attracted foreign bankers and businessmen, who siphoned off an ever-growing amount of the incoming wealth. This was especially true of the Genoese, Florentines and Pisans, whose commercial interests shifted westward to Portugal as the Ottoman Turks embraced the eastern Mediterranean. The ill-advised Moroccan policy dissipated significant expenditures of money and men. Financially ruinous as these things were, there was more to come.

João III died in 1557, and his grandson Sebastião, aged three, inherited the throne. His grandmother, Catarina of Austria, acted as regent until the brother of João III, Cardinal Henrique, archbishop of Lisbon and inquisitor-general, took over the regency in 1562. This was the first time a priest directly governed the country. Legislation now had a definite religious orientation, with the creation of new bishoprics at home and overseas, the strengthening of the Inquisition and expansion of its powers in India, new bylaws granted to the religious-military orders and the establishment of the Jesuit university at Évora.

In January 1568 Sebastião reached the appointed age of fourteen, and the cardinal's administration terminated. The young king's ten-year reign was a disaster. Poorly educated, with little or no interest in affairs of state, he had two abiding passions: religion and warfare. The boy king was naturally drawn toward a synthesis of the two—a great crusade against the infidel. Where better to strike than in Muslim Morocco, where his grandfather had relinquished several outposts, which he intended to recover and then bring the entire country under his suzerainty. Willful and inept, Sebastião tried for ten years to prepare for this great adventure with Portugal's meager resources.

In 1574 the sultan of Morocco, Muley Muhammed, was unseated by his uncle Muley Abd al-Malik with a little help from Turkish forces, instigating a civil war. Sebastião grasped the opportunity to ally himself with the ousted nephew, who sought Portuguese assistance to restore his throne. In 1577 the port of Arzila, a little south of Tanger, gave itself over to Portuguese protection. Sebastião tried to enlist support from both the papacy and Castilla against what was termed the Turkish menace in Morocco. Muley Abd al-Malik meanwhile attempted to buy peace by offering to return the port of Larache to the Portuguese, but Sebastião ignored the offer in order to maintain his own plans unencumbered. Finally, in 1578, with financial assistance from the church, he was able to assemble an expeditionary force, which included numerous aristocrats, along with 4,000–5,000 mercenaries.

THE AFRICAN EXPEDITION

Sebastião named a cousin, António, the prior of Crato, governor of Tanger, who took up the post in July 1574. He then informed his grandmother, Catarina, and his great-uncle, the cardinal, of his plans to cross to Africa and to appoint the cardinal regent in his absence. Letters to nobles and city governments ordered men and horses to be sent to Tavira in the Algarve. When all had assembled, they crossed the strait to Ceuta, then proceeded on to Tanger. The king had no detailed plans for a campaign, behaved capriciously, spurned all advice and spent much time hunting. As winter approached, and the North African ports became more dangerous, he was urged to return to Portugal. Even Felipe II of Spain, his uncle, requested his return and refused to sell him grain and horses. The queen swore to go to Africa and bring him back or die trying. Sebastião gave in and returned home.

After some persuading and a meeting at Guadalupe, Felipe II agreed to support Sebastião. Felipe offered fifty galleys, men and the sale of supplies on condition that Sebastião could recruit at least 15,000 men and launch the expedition within eight months.

Sebastião immediately set to work gathering finances, arranging loans, demanding donations. The New Christians pledged 240,000 cruzados for the suspension of the inquisitorial rights of confiscation for ten years. Even the subject kings of India were asked for money. Some 3,000 German mercenaries were contracted, and an emissary in Rome was ordered to raise 6,000 German and Italian fighting men. The king prepared himself physically by sleeping outdoors, exercising and sailing out to sea on stormy nights. But in spite of the efforts to begin the campaign within the time frame set by Felipe II, the expedition was not ready on time, and Felipe withdrew support, using the revolt against the Spanish in Flanders as the excuse. The fact that he learned that Sebastião was to be his own general may have given him some misgivings. Catarina died in February, stilling a voice of reason that the headstrong Sebastião, surrounded by fawning sycophants, had not listened to in years.

Spurning all advice, except that which he deemed favorable, and with a mixed army of Portuguese, Spanish, Germans, English, Dutch and others, the king set sail on 14 June. Some 500 ships assembled at Cádiz and met again at Arzila. It was Sebastião's intention to march south on Larache, where he thought the Moors were weak and would desert to him as he approached. The fort at Ksar el Kebir, a little southeast of Larache, would fall like a ripe plum. Rough seas delayed supply ships, and rations were cut as news filtered in that Muley Abd al-Malik was nearby with a large force supported by cannon. The king was certain, however, that such reports were fabricated by spies.

Short on rations, undisciplined, skittish, many ready to flee at a moment's notice and subject to harsh punishment for minor infractions of military code, resulting in low morale, the king's troops set out on 29 July, accompanied by hundreds of ox-drawn supply wagons carrying biscuits, water, powder and the king's wardrobe and chapel. It has been estimated that they consisted of about 15,000 infantry and 1,500 cavalry. Camp followers numbered another 9,000 or so and were made up of lackeys, pages, ox-herds and women of various nationalities and virtues. The march southward toward Larache through parched land under a relentless sun had made little progress before supplies began to dwindle alarmingly. Bands of Moors fell upon the stragglers, and sickness, lack of food and sunstroke took their toll. Seemingly oblivious to the plight of his army and determined to fight a pitched battle and settle the issue for which he had come, Sebastião bypassed Larache. Against all advice he pressed on, slowed by the heavy cannon in tow and the famished, exhausted troops.

On 3 August, while scouting for a ford across the river Makhazen, east of Larache, several thousand Moorish horsemen were seen on a ridge. Scouts sent out to reconnoiter discovered many thousands more behind the hill. The Muslims had assembled a force of about 40,000.

The king now called a halt, and camp was made, but he scorned advice to retire on Larache or to maintain a defensive camp in their protected position at the junction of the rivers Makhazen and the Rur until his men were recovered from the grueling march. Knowledge that his opponent was mortally ill only prompted Sebastião to a greater desire for immediate battle before Muley Abd al-Malik died, but there were no signs forthcoming of the enemy desertions that the king had predicted.

The next day he commanded his army to do battle. The troops were lined up for the fight, and the king rode off for breakfast. By nine o'clock the Moorish army was seen advancing in a vast crescent formation whose ominous flanking horns seemed about to enfold the Portuguese army in a fatal embrace. The enemy cannon opened fire and the ill-trained recruits fell to the ground or panicked. When the Moorish harquebusiers (soldiers using a matchlock gun) fired into the Portuguese infantry, the king seemed stunned and speechless, failing to give orders. He finally did command the cavalry forward but apparently forgot to give orders to the rest of the line. Many troops were unsure what to do. The experienced mercenaries took matters into their own hands and charged, beating back the enemy. It is said that Muley Abd al-Malik, seeing the rout of his army, emerged from his litter, tried to draw his sword to stem the retreat and collapsed. He was quickly stuffed back into his curtained litter, where he lay dead from a heart attack, while an attendant, feigning orders from within, gave the commands. The Moors rallied and relentlessly counterattacked just as the Portuguese thought victory was theirs. After four hours of desperate conflict in ferocious heat, only the still-unrecognized king and a small band of followers remained on the field of battle. This little coterie, too, was soon swallowed up in the torrent of flashing Moorish steel.

Muley Mohammed, the deposed sultan who had fought on the side of the Portuguese, fled the carnage downriver but was thrown from his horse, landed on his head in the river and drowned. About 8,000 of the Portuguese and their allies were killed in the bloody battle, and thousands more were taken captive. The prisoners were herded to Ksar el Kebir and Fez to be sold into slavery or ransomed. Only about eighty managed to escape and make their way to Arzila or Tanger.

On that black day in Portuguese history most of the army and the cream of the Portuguese nobility were slaughtered in the rash and desperate battle, which took the lives of three sovereigns—Sebastião, the sultan and his deposed nephew. It also ushered in the end of Portuguese expansion in Morocco. Sebastião died without heirs, immediately giving rise to the problem of succession.

CARDINAL HENRIQUE

The reports of the disaster at Ksar el Kebir in the Moroccan desert began to reach Lisbon about a week after the event, but the whereabouts of Sebastião were then unknown. He was, in effect, missing in action. There was apprehension in what remained of the upper classes, which feared a lower-class revolt if the chaotic political situation was not righted and strong rule reinstated. The void left in high society offered little in the realm of leadership, and the late king's great-uncle, Cardinal Henrique, the last surviving son of King Manuel, was summoned from Alcobaça and proclaimed king. Ill and feeble, there was little chance of his producing an heir to continue the dynasty even if the solicited papal dispensation for marriage had come through (which it didn't).

6

Union with Spain, 1580–1640

About eighty surviving noblemen after the Battle of Ksar el Kebir required a collective payment of 400,000 cruzados for their freedom (gentlemen were generally ransomed at the standard price of 4,000 cruzados and servants at 100 cruzados). With the large number of prisoners in Muslim hands, the Portuguese government could find only a fraction of the money, so that contributions had to come from the families of the captives. Jewels, expensive garments, horses and saddles, anything of value was sold or traded in Ceuta to apply to the ransoms. The wealth of Portugal flowed into Morocco in vast quantities. When the money dried up, the organizer, Francisco da Costa, the Portuguese ambassador, remained in Fez as a pledge for the last prisoners. In the meantime, Felipe II of Spain ransomed a few nobles for his own future interest.

SUCCESSION CRISIS

For two years after the death of Sebastião and the decimation of the Portuguese nobility, the country was in a state of crisis. Contestants were not lacking for the immediate question of succession. Catarina, daughter of Duarte and married to the sixth duke of Bragança, was a candidate for the throne, as was Felipe II of Spain, who based his claim on his mother, daughter of King Manuel.

The duchess of Bragança had a strong claim, but she made a weak bid. Felipe II had ransomed her son from the Moors and could, if he wished, hold him in exchange for her loyalty. The most dangerous candidate from Felipe's point of view was António, prior of Crato, the illegitimate son of Luís, duke of Bejar. All three were grandchildren of King Manuel. The prior maintained that his out-of-wedlock birth was no bar to the throne since his father had legitimated him on his deathbed. The Spanish maintained that this had been done only to allow him to enter the Order of Malta, which required it, not with any view to succession to the Portuguese throne.

António's mother was a New Christian, a point not in his favor. He had participated in the Battle of Ksar el Kebir and was captured but successfully concealed his true identity. Pretending to be a lowly peasant-priest, he was ransomed for a minimal amount of money. This dishonest and ungentlemanly behavior along with other miscalculations would be a severe detriment to his regal ambitions. On his return to Portugal he did not present himself immediately to his uncle, deeply offending the cardinal-king, who already disliked him intensely.

In June 1579 Felipe sent his able Spanish lawyers, the duke of Osuna and the Portuguese Cristóvão de Moura, to Lisbon to present his claim to the throne. News accompanied them of a buildup of Spanish military forces on the frontier as Moura presented the king's demands to the Lisbon municipality. Both lawyers were well endowed with money for the appropriate bribes and distributed it generously. When the matter was presented in Lisbon, the only active opposition came from the prior of Crato and his followers, who, although favored by the commoners, were heartily disliked by the clergy and most of the nobility. Elizabeth, queen of England, sent gifts to António and to the duke of Bragança. It was clear where her sympathies lay.

First banished from court and later ordered arrested by his uncle, António fled north, to be warmly welcomed by the students of Coimbra and many of the common people. When the news reached the cardinal's ears that António had once again reentered Lisbon, he dispossessed him of his titles and favors and ordered penalties for all who sheltered him. The prior spent a short time in Spain but, fearing arrest by Felipe, returned to Portugal and moved secretly from place to place. A spokesman for the people, Febo Monis, demanded more consultation with the commoners over the matter of succession but to no avail. On 11 January 1580 the Cortes assembled at Santarém and Almeirim. The nobles, those who had survived the battle and clergy elected to the Cortes sitting at Almeirim began the selection of judges who would decide the succession. Several representatives in favor of António were dismissed by the cardinal-king. Two of the elected judges were supporters of the duchess of Bragança, and Moura and Osuna obtained their removal, possibly through bribery.

Under pressure from Felipe's delegates, Henrique advised the commoners at Santarém that the king of Spain's candidature was for the best. The clergy approved the succession of Felipe, while the nobles remained divided. Those in favor of Felipe saw in his reign advantages to themselves. He was rich and powerful, the frontier with Spain would be opened for commerce, the Spanish fleet would be available for trade to the Far East and Brazil and Spanish gold and silver from the Americas would also benefit Portugal. These nobles all saw in a strong king such as Felipe a guarantee against rebellion of their own people who might be disposed to abolish their privileges. Those against royal union with Spain were motivated primarily by the idea of the loss of independence, which could lead to the disappearance of Portugal as a country. Undaunted, the commoners declared their willingness to die rather than obey a Spanish king. Meanwhile, Osuna and Moura continued distributing their largesse, concentrating on the Cortes and even suggesting that commoners not be allowed to participate in the election of the next king. Febo Monis demanded an inquiry into cases of bribery by the Spanish court and an ambassador sent to Rome to ask the pope to restrain Felipe from any violence, knowing that Spanish troops were on the frontier, but he was ignored.

Worn down by duties of office and intrigues, Henrique slipped into a semicoma on 28 January 1580. As he lay dying, and the leaders of the cities and towns gathered to his bedside, he could only whisper that Felipe would be the best choice for king of Portugal. Three days later Henrique gave up the ghost and was promptly forgotten. It now fell to the five governors whom he had appointed earlier for just such an emergency to keep order in the country.

They dismissed the wavering Cortes in March 1580 with the agreement of the clergy and nobles, most of whom feared that António's popularity among the people would lead to disturbances and even revolts. The possible use of force had been considered even before the death of the cardinal by Felipe, who had prepared a fleet at Gibraltar to act in conjunction with the troops massed on the border and appointed the duke of Alba, his best general, to command the army.

To coax the Portuguese into a more welcoming attitude, Felipe let it be known that he would dismiss no one from his appointed office, he would take some Portuguese subjects into his own household and defend the country along with its Indian and African possessions and he would ransom the remaining prisoners in Morocco, supply grain to the people and have his son educated in Portugal. He promised not to change the currency, the language would remain Portuguese in all its functions, and only the Cortes could make the laws of the country. He also pledged to ease the problems caused by the plague (exactly how is not clear). Emissaries from the governors were sent to meet Felipe at Guadalupe, where they were kept waiting for an audience for over a fortnight and then were told that Felipe would allow no one to speak on the merits of his case. Well aware of delays and the opposition of the people of Portugal casting a shadow over his claim to the throne, he gave the governors one month in which to obey his wishes and decide in his favor. Fearing an uprising of the people should they decide for Felipe, the governors called the Cortes to meet again. They were walking a thin line, hoping to appease the commoners and make Felipe think his case was progressing satisfactorily. In the Cortes, indecision continued to reign.

On 18 June 1580 the threatened frontier town of Elvas with Spanish troops stationed just across the border declared for Felipe, provoking widespread agitation in the country. The following day António was proclaimed king at Santarém in a carnival atmosphere of popular enthusiasm. He departed for Lisbon, where he was greeted with warmth and celebrations. The governors fled to Setúbal and from there by ship to a Spanish port where, under duress from Felipe, they declared that António was illegitimate, a usurper, traitor and rebel and that Felipe was the rightful heir.

WAR WITH SPAIN

Felipe finally lost patience and ordered the invasion of Portugal. On 27 June 1580 the Spanish army, over 20,000 strong under the duke of Alba, crossed the frontier and entered Évora. Arraiolos and Montemór fell next. Setúbal showed some resistance, but the Spaniards were let into the city during the night by well-placed, grateful Portuguese whom Felipe had ransomed in Morocco. The local fortress of Outão held out for only three days. Alba then embarked his soldiers with the aid of the Spanish fleet and sailed north to Cascais at the mouth of the Tejo estuary west of Lisbon, avoiding in the process what could have proved a difficult crossing of the Tejo River if Lisbon had resisted.

At Cascais his cannon fire dispersed the ill-supplied Portuguese force, and the battered fortress there hoisted the white flag after two days of shelling. Known for his cruelty, Alba instantly created an atmosphere of anxiety by hanging the governor of Cascais, beheading a Portuguese general and even executing some common soldiers before he moved on to Lisbon. The brutal behavior had the desired effect, and he met little opposition as he approached Lisbon.

When Alba met António on the western outskirts of the capital at the Alcántara bridge, the latter with about 5,000 ill-trained citizenry (many of them liberated black slaves), short of officers and arms, the fight was brief and decisive. Alba was a master of warfare. António departed hastily into the city, while the council sent the Spanish general the keys and offered submission. The prior of Crato fled to Santarém and finally to Coimbra, where he still enjoyed support from the majority of the students. Pursued, he fled again to Oporto, but, not able to hold the city as the Spanish force approached, he disappeared into the bosom of the common people. After seven months in hiding, he finally took a ship to France in May 1581.

FELIPE I OF PORTUGAL

In December 1580 Felipe himself crossed the frontier into Portugal, received the homage of the chief nobles and churchmen and the representatives of the duchess of Bragança and assumed authority over the country. He issued letters summoning the Cortes and directed the towns to elect no one who had been in sympathy with António. On 25 March 1581 the king of Spain was confirmed as king of Portugal under the name of Felipe I. He had his coronation in Lisbon. The Spanish were now masters in Portugal, and only the Azores remained faithful to António.

Felipe established his government in Lisbon. He swore not to meddle in the customs and laws of his new acquisition, to maintain the current system of government and not to appoint Spaniards to high office in Portugal, and, in general, this pledge was kept. The overseas empires of both nations remained separate. He issued pardons for those who had supported António but with exceptions. On 12 November 1582 he issued a charter that confirmed the rights and privileges of the nobility and guaranteed the retention of all civil, military and ecclesiastical offices by Portuguese. Despite the economic and military decline, the country still maintained a powerful oceangoing fleet. He refused the request of the Cortes to withdraw Spanish troops and to reduce taxation. Felipe's choice for governor of Portugal fell on his nephew, the cardinal-archduke Albert, twenty-three years of age. To assist him, the king selected a council of regency comprising three prominent Portuguese. In 1583 he departed the country for home.

Unification with Spain ended centuries of border warfare that had drained the country financially; it also helped protect the vast waterbound empire and allowed the Portuguese nobility and the clergy more opportunity for advancement in a larger framework. Merchants would have more commercial opportunity with open borders, and Spanish possessions in the Mediterranean would become more accessible to trade along with the vast overseas Spanish territory in the New World. Only the peasant would not benefit and might even be worse off, deprived of the small profits from smuggling, of a career in the army guarding the border or of selling produce in the border towns, where competition would now increase. While the peasant had little to look forward to from a predominant foreign power, the upper classes could envisage more opportunities from the spice-rich Far East, to the silver and gold mines in the largely uncharted Western Hemisphere.

THE AZORES

Since the Azores had held out for António, a Spanish fleet was dispatched from Lisbon to reduce the rebels there. The assault on Terceira with 600 men turned into a disaster for the Spanish, who were overwhelmed first by a stampede of half-wild bulls into their midst as they came ashore and then by the ferocious locals who cut them down as they ran for their ships.

António, meanwhile, reached England, where he nearly secured English support for his cause (Queen Elizabeth, unwilling to make war on Felipe, finally turned him down). Returning to France, he found Catherine de Medici more receptive. In return for the future cession to her of Brazil, she sent 800 soldiers to defend Terceira, and fifty more ships and 5,000 men were made ready to face the Spanish. In a naval engagement off the Azores the French were defeated, their commander killed, numerous ships lost and captured sailors over seventeen put to death for piracy.

A French military contingent destined for Terceira, nevertheless, reached the island along with António, who supervised the defense and then sailed back to France to try to recruit more men. Another 1,500 French troops arrived in June 1583. After only one day of battle, the Spanish with ninety-six ships and about 10,000 fighting men took the island. The pretender, António, now a fugitive, fled to La Rochelle, from which he made further attempts to win over the English.

Meanwhile, in the year 1581 the Netherlands, a possession of the Habsburgs under the leadership of the House of Orange, declared itself independent of Spain. England supported the Dutch, sent an army to Holland and carried out piratical acts against Spanish shipping. The prohibition of the use of Portuguese ports by English ships promulgated by Felipe in 1583 had serious repercussions. The geography and history of Portugal had long favored the development of Atlantic coastal towns, where most of the population lived. Attempting to ruin English trade, Felipe devastated the commerce and livelihood of these towns and of many inhabitants.

Dragging Portugal into Spanish conflicts, Felipe assembled the invincible armada, much of it in Lisbon harbor. It finally sailed in 1588 to conquer England. Most of the 130 ships, some Portuguese and 30,000 men were lost without ever coming close to achieving their objective. Success almost came to António, the would-be king, when, after the defeat of the Spanish armada the queen of England countenanced a raid on mainland Portugal. She sent thirty warships under the command of Francis Drake with 11,000 men-at-arms to accompany António home, where, he assured the English, the populace would rise up in his support and eject the Spanish from the country. After attacking Coruña in May 1589, the fleet sailed south to subdue the castle at Peniche and approached Lisbon. The city was prepared. Lacking siege equipment and losing men through attrition and disease, Drake withdrew. As the English carried on their war with Spain, Portugal became the primary recipient of their attacks. One took place in the Azores in 1591 commanded by Cumberland; another under Essex not only attacked Spanish Cádiz but sacked Faro and barely failed to take Lagos.

Archduke Albert left Portugal in 1593, and five governors, strong supporters of Felipe, were appointed in his place. In 1594, to punish the Netherlands for its rebellion against Spanish rule but compounding the economic problems of the Portuguese, Felipe ordered the fifty Dutch vessels in Lisbon harbor seized and all further commerce with the Lowlanders prohibited. Back again in France, the tenacious António began to organize another expedition against Felipe, but in August 1595 death intervened before much was accomplished. A third attack by the English in 1597 on São Miguel, again in the Azores, failed, as did the attempt to waylay the Spanish treasure fleet from the New World.

THE DUTCH

Deprived of their lucrative commerce in spices that they purchased in Lisbon and distributed throughout Europe, the Dutch were driven to seek this trade at its source. The government was quick to enlist a disgruntled Dutch resident of Lisbon, Cornelius Hautman, who had sailed in Portuguese ships to the East and now offered to guide his countrymen to the fabled land of riches. Before long a fleet of eight Dutch ships brought back spices, followed by forty more in 1600. Within two more years the Dutch East India Company was founded. From its base on Java it soon overran much of Southeast Asia, and the company flourished. The English were also becoming active in Eastern trade with the establishment of an East India Company in 1600 and laying the foundations, like the Dutch, for an Eastern empire. These were followed by Swedish, Danish and French East Indian companies.

Peace with England was achieved in 1605, and in 1609 the Netherlands and Spain signed a twelve-year truce reestablishing Dutch commerce in Spanish territory in Europe but also allowing the Dutch to negotiate trade agreements outside Europe. This clause gave them the right, which they were quick to exploit, to make agreements with peoples of the Portuguese empire.

Dutch and English involvement in the spice trade and the loss of English markets greatly deprived Portugal of an income. The situation was compounded by other problems for the Portuguese. There was resentment throughout the empire, especially among Hindus and Muslims, against proselytizing by missionaries, and the Dutch, with little or no interest in promoting Christianity, were less obtrusive and more welcome in foreign societies. The Dutch and English organized their trade better through their East Indian trading companies than had Portugal, and widespread circulation of the formerly secret maps further cut the ground from under the Portuguese empire. Decline became more pronounced in the reign of the next Spanish monarch.

FELIPE II OF PORTUGAL

Felipe I of Portugal was succeeded by Felipe II in 1598, and the agreement with Spain allowing Portugal to mainly conduct its own affairs was soon broken, first with the arrival of three Spaniards in Lisbon to audit the books of the treasury and then with the installation of five Spaniards to the Council of Portugal. In spite of protests and growing unrest, Spaniards were appointed to keep check on the finances of the Casa da India. This second Felipe had not bothered to sanction his reign by calling the Portuguese Cortes on his accession, nor did he visit the country until near the end of his rule. Portuguese affairs were handled in Madrid, and when he did come calling for a mere five months in 1619, the treasury coughed up some half million cruzados to pay for his lavish recreation, entertainment and lodgings. When he died in 1621, few Portuguese mourned.

FELIPE III OF PORTUGAL

Relations between the Portuguese people and Spain became strained to the breaking point as Felipe III succeeded to the throne in 1621. Spain was in financial trouble, the silver mines in Peru were played out, attacks on overseas trading posts disrupted commerce, the truce with the Netherlands expired and the powerful Spanish minister, Olivares, the count-duke who headed the government in the name of the king, coordinated the finances and defense of both countries so that the Portuguese could better accompany the Spanish into a renewed war with Holland. Commerce with Holland again ceased, and a Dutch West India Company began operations in the Americas. Fortresses were established by the company on the west coast of Africa, from which black slaves were shipped across the Atlantic. To compound matters the English captured Ormuz in 1623.

Dutch privateering gave way to building colonies in Brazil. In 1624 the company seized Bahia, although the city was recaptured two years later. In another Dutch attack in 1630, an expedition sponsored by the Dutch West India Company captured Pernambuco (now Recife) in north-eastern Brazil, which they occupied until 1654. Between 1623 and 1638 Dutch squadrons had captured over 500 Portuguese and Spanish ships, a problem intensified by the disappearance of ships plying the Indian trade—victims of storms and pirates, some carrying cargoes estimated at 1 million or more cruzados.

Olivares and his pleasure-seeking king tried to offset losses by raising taxes. In 1628 Portugal was obliged to provide a loan for its defense over six years. The news caused a popular demonstration in Oporto. In the following year, the clergy, by papal order, were told to contribute, whereby many priests joined the growing army of the discontented.

Desperate for money, the crown imposed a tax in 1631 by which all persons obtaining any lay office for a period of over three years would be taxed at the rate of half their first year's salary. A salt monopoly was also introduced, forcing the industry (and one of Portugal's best exports) into decline. Reduction in trade and excessive taxes, coupled with the obligation of the Portuguese army and navy to help fight Spain's wars, were almost more than the little country could bear.

THE PEASANTS AND SEBASTIÃO

The Portuguese peasants, the most ignorant and backward on the peninsula, cherished a messianic hope known as Sebastianism, which surmised that the young king was not really dead and would return to lead Portugal back into prosperity and greatness. It brought forth four major pretenders: the first, a Portuguese, appeared in 1584. He managed to gather a small entourage of believers who were soon rounded up by Spanish troops in Penamacor, where he was sentenced to the galleys. He managed to escape to France, however, where he disappeared. Another, with some resemblance to Sebastião, collected a force in Ericeira, but Felipe had him hanged and quartered for his efforts. Two others then appeared outside the country: in Spain a pastry cook convinced a local nun of some influence that he was the dead king. With her support, he gained a following, which resulted in her solitary confinement for four years, while he was put to death for his trouble. The last pretender surfaced in Venice, where a number of supporters of the prior of Crato had found refuge. Although he spoke no Portuguese and had no resemblance whatever to Sebastião, he managed to acquire a following, which included members of the church and others in high places. However, the net result was the same, and after a series of adventures, he and his associates were executed. The willingness of the people to believe almost any story that involved the reappearance of the deceased king indicates the strong desire to cast off Spanish authority and return to a sovereign Portuguese state.

INDEPENDENCE MOVEMENTS

The appointment of a cousin of the king, Margaret (widow of the duke of Mantua), as governor of Portugal and her secretary, Miguel de Vasconcelos, considered a tool of Olivares, was much resented. In 1637 a riot against heavy taxation in Évora was the first taste of defiance. It quickly spread to other localities but after some months was repressed by the Spanish army. The next year Cardinal Richelieu of France, seeing an opportunity to humble Spain through the disintegration of its possessions, sent an emissary to sound out the possibility of insurrection in Lisbon, offering men and ships to aid the rebels along with further collaboration with France in a subsequent struggle. The French even offered to produce a king if the duke of Bragança should decline the offer.

The duke of Bragança, with huge holdings and overlord of some 80,000 Portuguese, was the logical choice for king. Hitherto he had shown no interest in such matters and had declared his loyalty to Felipe III. Olivares, never slow to detect trouble, now ordered the recruitment of large levies in Portugal to serve Spain against its enemies, thus depleting the country of its own defenses. Spanish captains were put aboard Portuguese ships, and four trained regiments plus two more of volunteers were demanded along with 1,000 men from the duke of Bragança. The duke's objections were dismissed, and he began collecting the force while paying no attention to the conspirators. He was then elevated in 1639 to governor of the arms of Portugal. Olivares may well have chosen the duke to keep him close to the fold and, as a servant of Felipe III, undesirable as a potential king of the country.

In 1640 the Catalans rebelled against the Spanish crown. Olivares saw the opportunity to use Portuguese soldiers to put down the insurrection and accordingly demanded new taxation. The number of adherents to the conspiracy in Portugal grew by bounds, and it became urgent to find a leader. When approached again, the duke of Bragança this time agreed to assume the throne.

After a number of clandestine meetings in Lisbon the conspirators were ready to act. The time set was nine o'clock on the morning of Saturday, 1 December 1640 to shed the sixty-year-long Spanish yoke. The duke's job was to incite and raise troops in the Alentejo from his estates at Vila Viçosa. Near the appointed hour the conspirators and a crowd of citizens gathered before the royal palace in Lisbon, which stood on the left side of Praça do Comércio. When the cathedral clock struck nine, they swarmed up the palace stairs, dispersing the Spanish garrison with a few wild shots. Vasconcelos was found hiding in a cupboard, dragged out, shot and hurled from a window. The duchess of Mantua was dragged from the palace window where she was screaming for help and arrested. Three governors were selected to take charge of the city of Lisbon until the duke should appear.

7

House of Bragança, 1640–1910

João, the eighth duke of Bragança, arrived in Lisbon on 6 December 1640 to take charge of the insurrection and begin a new dynasty. The personality of this mild and amiable man, with a fondness for hunting and musical composition and a lack of interest in military affairs, alarmed some of his followers and contrasted sharply with that of his willful and dynamic Andalucían wife, Luísa de Gusmão, sister of the duke of Medina Sidonia, the leading nobleman of Andalucía. She was no friend of Olivares, and with queenly aspirations, she may have been instrumental in convincing the hesitant João to do his duty to Portugal.

JOÃO IV

João IV had already been acclaimed king in the major cities of the country as the last towns garrisoned by Spanish troops such as Sétubal and Viana surrendered to Portuguese officials. The city of Ceuta across the Strait of Gibraltar cast its lot with Spain.

The change in dynasty took place without great disturbance. Most of the nobles still loyal to Spain departed the country, a cabal that developed around the archbishop of Braga, who maintained pro-Castillian sentiments, was brought under control and the conspirators, about ten in all, were imprisoned or executed. The archbishop died in custody.

Of greater significance was the crafty, ambitious Olivares. A council of war was created a few days after the dynastic changeover to coordinate preparations for the struggle that was bound to come. Governors and staff were appointed for each province with authority to conscript all able-bodied men between the ages of fifteen and seventy. The defense of each province was allocated to its own recruits to help prevent desertions and inspire patriotism. Concentrating his forces on the reduction of rebellious Cataluña, however, Olivares made no immediate moves against Portugal, and the first six months of João IV's reign experienced no threats from that quarter. The Cortes assembling in Lisbon at the end of January 1641, nevertheless, recommended the construction of new warships, raising of levies, refurbishment of fortifications and improvements in municipal defenses. To pay for all this a 10 percent property tax was instituted for all classes save the church, which paid a lump sum based on the resources of each diocese. Taxes on business and public offices were instituted, and the town council of Lisbon allowed increased duties on meat and wine.

IN SEARCH OF ALLIES

Meanwhile, diplomatic negotiations were begun to solicit support from erstwhile, present and possible future enemies of Spain. Envoys were dispatched to Barcelona, France, Holland, England, Sweden, Denmark and Rome. From the Catalans Portugal obtained a treaty of alliance and assistance for the supply of arms. The French under the leadership of the wily Richelieu were careful to avoid a firm future commitment but did send twenty-two fighting ships and ten auxiliary vessels to Lisbon in early August 1641, which later in the month, joined by nineteen Portuguese ships, made an abortive attack on Cádiz. The surprise they had hoped for did not materialize, and the heavily reinforced garrison of the port proved too formidable to attempt a landing by the 4,000 soldiers aboard. The French fleet sailed for home, and the Portuguese returned to their ports.

Diplomatic maneuvering with the Dutch called for a truce, which was agreed upon for a period of ten years, and the Dutch were to resume their commercial privileges in trading with Portugal. In return they would help attend to the recruitment of officers and men-at-arms in Holland for use in Portugal and allow the Portuguese to purchase supplies and munitions. Both the fleets would engage in the common purpose of attacking Spanish ships. The Hollanders denied requests for the return of overseas colonies they had taken from Portugal and continued to hold the territory they had seized in India, Africa and America. On 10 September 1641 a Dutch fleet comprising twenty ships, accompanied by twelve more that the Portuguese had contracted in Holland, arrived in Lisbon harbor. With them came 1,000 infantry, officers, horses, arms and munitions. Having arrived too late for the attack on Cádiz, the Dutch ships were content to search for the Spanish treasure galleons arriving from the New World, but when, after a month, they found no trace of the expected treasure fleet, they returned to Lisbon and remained there until the following January.

When news arrived that Hollanders had invaded Maranhão in Brazil and Angola in Africa, João IV refused advice to seize their ships lying in the Tejo, desiring to keep the conflict away from home soil. The admiral, grateful that his ships remained unmolested, offered to join the Portuguese in an expedition being prepared against the Spanish in the Azores, where some of their forces still held out. On 6 January the fleet crossed the bar of the Tejo, but once in the open sea the admiral directed his ships north and returned to Holland, forsaking his promise of assistance.

The embassy sent to England in February 1641 found a friendly reception. The ambassador had little difficulty in persuading the English to accredit the new government. It was readily agreed in London that there would be mutual friendship between the two thrones and that neither country would aid the enemies of the other and, in case of need, would provide ships and arms. The ports of both countries would be opened to ships of the other for trade.

Problems arose when the English demanded the same privileges accorded to their rivals, the Dutch. The exclusive hire or purchase of Dutch ships to which the Portuguese had committed themselves could not be undone, but a compromise was reached. Commissioners were appointed to look into the problem within two years, and before the time was up it had resolved itself. Relationships with the Dutch grew steadily worse, and in the end the Portuguese were more than pleased to contract English ships in their place. A clause in the negotiations with Holland that allowed the exercise of the Protestant religion in Dutch houses or ships in Portugal was similarly demanded by the English for their merchants and sailors. To resolve this issue, a commission was established, presided over by the archbishop of Lisbon, which decided that liberty of conscience could not be condoned, though there could be no objection to Englishmen receiving the same treatment as other foreigners. With this evasion the matter was settled.

A Portuguese envoy arrived in Copenhagen in April 1641, but the Danes refused him a royal interview, not wishing to offend Spain. After waiting around for five weeks without result, the envoy took a ship to Sweden, where he was received on 10 June, and concluded a treaty of peace, friendship and freedom of trade. The Swedes sent several warships to the Tejo with considerable supplies of arms and sailed home loaded with sugar, salt, spices and coin in payment. The following spring Swedish ships brought a consignment of iron, copper and ships' masts to Lisbon.

Due to Spanish control of northern Italy and considerable naval power in the Mediterranean the Portuguese envoy to Rome, the bishop of Lamego, had to find a roundabout way of reaching the Vatican. The journey took six months, followed by a seven-month delay waiting for an audience with the pope, who refused to recognize the embassy. Olivares had instructed his Vatican representative to demand a condemnation by the pope of Portuguese independence along with the excommunication of the duke of Bragança. If the opportunity arose, the Spanish representative was to kidnap the Portuguese bishop. A committee of cardinals was appointed to settle the matter but would not see the envoy until it had been established that he represented an independent state.

The Portuguese representative in Rome defended before the cardinals João IV's right to sit on the throne of Portugal. As the representative appeared to be making some progress in his justification of events, the Spanish ambassador took steps to prevent the reception of the bishop of Lamego. Ambushed on a dark street on his way home from the French Embassy by Spanish ruffians, the bishop scarcely managed to escape. In the exchange of gunfire a dozen or so people were killed. The pope still refused to see him in his official capacity, the stipulated year of the Portuguese Embassy expired and the bishop departed Rome in December, having accomplished nothing.

WAR WITH SPAIN

The first shots of the inevitable war were fired on 9 June 1641 in a skirmish between the frontier towns of Elvas and Badajoz. While Portugal had been stripped of cannon by the Spaniards, efforts had been made to shore up the defenses along the most obvious invasion routes.

Elvas, Olivença and Campo Major were fortified, although the garrison troops were not numerous or well trained compared to the enemy. Other vulnerable points along the Galician border, in the Algarve and in Beira improved their defenses, as did the key forts defending Lisbon. A full-scale attack came on 16 September as 8,000 Spanish troops besieged Olivença in a surprise night attack. The intruders were repulsed, and the Portuguese retaliated by striking at Valverde, but with no better results. The following year, as improvements in fortifications continued, the supply of money dwindled, and revenues fell well short of requirements. Border raids increased, and the countryside was plundered on both sides of the frontier. The king never attended the meetings of the Council of War and generally left this business to a small group of ministers who were not military men and had a poor grasp of the problems facing the nation. The Cortes met in September 1642 in Lisbon, when the three estates met in three separate monasteries to tackle the problem of finances to cover the costs of defense. João IV proposed an increase in taxes, but the third estate, the commoners who would have to carry the tax burden, proposed that the required amount of money be shared equally. The representatives of the people lost the dispute and were forced to pay.

In July 1643 a large Portuguese force consisting of 2,000 cavalry and 12,000 infantry was assembled at Elvas under the command of the count of Obidos for an attack. The troops then marched on Badajoz, but Obidos, fearing his forces were not sufficient to capture the town, retired. The king had him arrested for his timidity, and he was replaced by Matias de Albuquerque. Meanwhile, in Galicia the Portuguese had some minor successes defeating two Spanish generals in limited engagements. When the 1643 campaigning season closed, no decisive action had yet been fought. However, the Spanish had suffered a major defeat at Rocroi in northern France, Olivares, hated by the Spanish nobility, was forced from office and the country, in desperate need of finances, found it difficult to raise an army large enough to vanquish Portugal.

BATTLE OF MONTIJO

In May 1644 Matias de Albuquerque captured the town of Montijo east of Badajoz with about 7,000 troops. On the morning of 26 May Spanish forces totaling 2,500 cavalry and 8,000 infantry crossed the Guadiana River and faced the Portuguese in the town. The first attack of cavalry raised havoc on one of the Portuguese flanks sweeping through to threaten the rear of the Portuguese army. When the attack lost some of its momentum, Albuquerque rallied his men, who with great determination drove the Spanish back over the river. The Spanish reversal was the occasion for great celebrations in Lisbon, but in Madrid the government ordered their general, Torrecusa, to make up the loss by taking some Portuguese territory and sent additional troops. With an army 17,000 strong, the largest so far in the war, he attacked Elvas. After ten days of heroic resistance by the small Portuguese garrison, the Spanish withdrew with nothing to show for their efforts.

In spite of these minor successes, the cost of the war and its prolonged duration took a toll on Portuguese morale. When the Cortes met in 1645, the third estate complained about the arrogant and immoderate behavior of officers, the lack of discipline and plundering forays of the rank and file, causing alarm in town and country, the imprisonment of the parents of deserters, the billeting of troops among the people, requisitioning of food and fodder and conscription.

While the desultory war dragged on, the Spanish maintained pressure on the pope to prevent his recognition of João IV as king of Portugal. Another emissary, Nicolau Monteiro, dispatched to the Vatican in 1645, received no better treatment than had the bishop of Lamego four years before. Attacked on the streets of Rome in full daylight, he barely managed to escape with his life. Many sees in Portugal became vacant as relations with the papacy deteriorated. João IV's younger brother, Duarte, was also a victim of Spanish intrigues. In the service of Emperor Ferdinand III he had pursued a military career but was arrested in 1641 at the instigation of the ambassador of Felipe IV of Spain at Donauwörth in Germany. Attempts to gain his release proved fruitless, and the unfortunate brother was sold by the emperor to Felipe for a considerable sum of money. His fate was to die in prison. In 1647 a Portuguese expatriate, Leite, living in Madrid, was paid to assassinate the king of Portugal and sent to Lisbon with a plan to shoot João IV as he passed along the narrow street in the Corpus Christi parade. The plan failed for unknown reasons, and the would-be assassin went back to Madrid for fresh instructions. Upon returning to Lisbon a second time, the plot was given away by an assistant, and Leite was arrested and hanged.

AFONSO VI

João had for some time suffered from gout, and the queen, Luísa, often took his place in affairs of state when he was confined to bed. When he died on 5 November 1656, she assumed the regency. Three of their children were still living: Catherine, a future queen of England, and Afonso and Pedro, successive kings of Portugal. Afonso, still a minor, was proclaimed king by the Cortes nine days after the demise of his father in spite of the effects of a childhood disease that had left him somewhat retarded and his right arm and leg partially paralyzed. Under a tutor he had learned to read and write but little else and was generally ungovernable. Luísa ruled as regent and pursued the search for allies, hoping for a league with France and a dynastic alliance by marrying Catherine to Louis XIV.

The war between Spain and France was now winding down. When João da Costa, count of Soure, arrived in Paris to seek military aid, he learned that peace talks had already begun. Louis XIV would not wed Catherine of Bragança but instead would marry a Spanish princess, Maria Teresa, daughter of Felipe IV. A secret article in the treaty required France to break off relations with Portugal and leave the country at the mercy of Spain. Da Costa offered, Mazarin the French statesman and cardinal, who controlled the French government during the minority of Louis XIV, 1 million cruzados and the lucrative archbishopric of Évora if Portugal were included in the peace arrangements, but it was too late. Spain and France signed the Peace of the Pyrenees, which ended twenty-four years of warfare, on 7 November 1659.

Disappointed in her efforts to form an understanding with France, Luísa now made arrangements for the marriage of her daughter to King Charles II and for the renewal of the English alliance through the Portuguese ambassador in London, Francisco de Melo. In spite of the efforts of the Spanish ambassador there to prevent the marriage, the wedding took place on 23 June 1661. The English bound themselves to defend Portugal, but the price was high. Charles received as a dowry 2 million cruzados (the highest yet paid anywhere), Tanger and Bombay, free trade at Goa, Cochin and Diu and in Brazil at Bahia, Pernambuco and Rio de Janeiro. If Ceylon could be recovered from the Dutch, England would receive Galé, while Portugal retained Colombo. The object of relinquishing Tanger was to make it easier for the English to assist and protect Portugal, but in the end it proved too costly and was given up just over two decades later. Catherine of Bragança sailed from Lisbon to Falmouth, and the ships on the return voyage brought 2,000 English foot soldiers and 700 cavalry in time to help stem a Spanish invasion.

In May 1663 a Spanish army under command of Felipe IV's son, Juan José, attacked and took Évora in the worst reversal of the war so far for

Portugal. Portuguese troops were rapidly moved south from Beira to face the enemy. Under their commander, the German duke Schomberg, who had been given the task of reforming the Portuguese army, they met the Spanish at Ameixial, near Estremóz, won a decisive victory on 8 June 1663 and recaptured Évora.

The Spanish made a final effort in June 1665, when they attacked Vila Viçosa a little southwest of Elvas. Schomberg sallied forth from Estremóz to meet the advance, and the armies met at Montes Claros. With 4,000 men dead, 6,000 taken prisoner along with 3,500 captured horses, the Spanish commander limped back across the frontier, his offensive capacity crippled for some time to come. Three months later Felipe IV died, and his widow made peace, recognizing the independence of Portugal.

King Afonso VI remained a problem at court. He fell into a friendship with a young shopkeeper of Italian descent named Antonio Conti de Ventimiglia. The queen tried to break off the relationship, but Afonso became so unmanageable that attendants allowed Conti into the palace. At night the pair roamed the streets attacking citizens and frequenting taverns in the city. Afonso's tutor found little to interest the king, not even riding. When he turned sixteen in 1659, the queen gave him a household attended by young nobles, and Conti assumed the airs of a royal favorite. Eventually, the queen called Afonso to a meeting with her while her attendants removed Conti from the house and put him on a ship for Brazil. A fit of rage over the loss of his friend prompted Afonso VI to set out for the royal estates at Alcántara, where he gathered some 400 men and then returned to inform his mother that her regency was terminated, sending her off to a convent. The king's attendant, count of Castelo Melhor, now appointed secretary to the king, purged the court of his enemies and took over the reigns of government, which he held for five years. Afonso VI married Marie-Françoise-Isabelle of Savoy in February 1666, and in the same month Queen Luísa died.

The new queen from Savoy found that she was excluded from the inner circles of policy making at court and that her husband was little better than a slave to Castelo Melhor, but she soon changed that and demanded and received admission to meetings of the Council of State. As her influence over the king grew, Castelo Melhor's waned. He was dismissed from service under a dark cloud and fled to the monastery at Buçaco, but, pursued by royal troops, he hid in the forest and managed to make his escape to England, where he became adviser to Catherine of Bragança.

PEDRO II

Afonso now fell under the sway of both the queen and his brother Pedro, who took up residence in the palace. The city of Lisbon petitioned for a meeting of the Cortes with a view to making Pedro regent. After threatening to withhold taxes, the city fathers received permission to hold the Cortes on 1 January 1668. (Only the king could summon and dismiss the Cortes.) About this time Queen Marie decided to have her marriage annulled and return to France. Afonso had been incapable of producing an offspring, and the annulment proceeded without reference to Rome, where contact hardly existed. He agreed to turn over the government to his brother Pedro, keeping for himself the estates of the duchy of Bragança and an annual income. The Cortes supported the deposition of Afonso and the transfer of power to Pedro, who was entitled prince regent. He was asked not to allow Queen Marie to leave the country, as it would be necessary to refund her dowry. Instead, Pedro married her.

Afonso was dispatched to the Azores, where he was confined to three rooms in the governor's house and remained a virtual prisoner. A plot to rescue him by the Spanish ambassador in Lisbon and a plan to take him to Spain, where he might marry the queen mother, creating untold problems for Portugal, failed. The conspirators were executed, and Pedro considered it prudent to have his brother closer to home. In August 1574 Afonso was conveyed to Sintra, where he passed the remaining nine years of his life confined to an apartment. He died in 1683, and his younger brother became King Pedro II. Queen Marie died just a few months later. Pedro II married again, this time to Maria-Sophia-Elizabeth, daughter of Philip William of Neuberg, who gave birth to Pedro's successor, the future João V. She passed away in 1699, followed by Pedro in December 1706.

JOÃO V AND THE SPANISH WAR OF SUCCESSION

João was seventeen when he succeeded to the throne upon the death of his father. He appears to have been excessively extravagant and excessively pious. For the first five years or so he wisely left the functioning of government to a Council of State.

Although the king was theoretically extremely rich, there was a chronic shortage of money. His substantial income from the colonies was generally drained away through fraud and embezzlement (public finances were never audited), and only about one-quarter of his revenue was said to reach his treasury. Numerous individuals had the right to claim annuities, dividends and salaries from the customhouses, the tobacco monopoly or other royal enterprises. The war with Spain left many areas devastated, and supplies issued to troops in 1706 remained unpaid. By 1709 the army itself had not been paid for eleven months, and it became necessary to sell some of the major offices such as the Casa da India.

Carlos II of Spain had died in 1700. Although he had named the Bourbon Felipe, duke of Anjou and grandson of Louis XIV of France, as his heir, this was unacceptable to the Habsburg and Holy Roman Emperor Leopold I, whose wife was a daughter of Carlos II. Not only was Felipe's legitimacy in question, but his accession to the Spanish throne would make possible an enormous increase in the power of France, threatening to upset the European balance of power. A coalition was formed by the emperor, England, the Netherlands and Denmark to nullify the accession that would place both France and Spain under Bourbon rule. The alliance was subsequently joined by Prussia, Portugal and Savoy, and the ensuing conflict inherited by by JoãoV became known as the War of the Spanish Succession.

Portugal entered the war due to British influence and the offer of two slices of Spanish territory on its frontiers in return for support of the pro-Habsburg, anti-Bourbon forces. In 1706 an Anglo-Portuguese army entered Madrid, where one of Leopold's sons, Archduke Charles III, was proclaimed king. This army was defeated soon after at Almansa, and Portuguese forces played little part in the war thereafter. The Treaty of Utrecht brought the conflict to an end in 1714 with the Bourbon Felipe V on the throne. It was a costly enterprise from which Portugal derived little benefit.

After the conclusion of the war Portugal remained at peace except for a naval campaign in aid of Venice against Turkey in 1717. In the ensuing battle off Cape Matapan in which the Portuguese bore the brunt of the fight, the Turkish navy suffered defeat. This victorious engagement served to heighten João V's prestige at home and abroad, but generally he carefully stayed out of European conflicts.

Meantime, gold and, later, diamonds from Brazil gave the king the necessary income to finance much new building. He spent lavishly on construction, the chief example being the luxurious palace, monastery and library of Mafra thirty miles northwest of Lisbon, begun in 1717 in fulfillment of a vow if he were granted a son. Prince José, his heir, was born in June 1714. During his reign the great aqueduct with 109 arches bringing water to Lisbon over a distance of about eleven miles was built, as was the hospital at Caldas da Rainha.

The king was given the epithet "the magnanimous" that was no doubt derived from his benevolent nature. He generously endowed the arts and sciences, sponsoring various publications, such as Manuel Caetano de Sousa's *Genealogical History of the Royal House*, and founded various institutes, among which was the Royal Academy of History. Students were sent abroad for further studies in astronomy, mathematics and economics, while the Academy of Portugal was founded in Rome for Portuguese artists. Destruction of antiquities in the country from the time of the Phoenicians down to the Arabs was officially prohibited. His emissaries on missions to Rome or Madrid went with large amounts of coin, gold and diamonds to distribute where needed to demonstrate the wealth of the king. On hearing that the queen mother of Spain was having difficulty collecting her pension, he sent her a huge sum of money. Diamonds were lavished on cardinals, gold on nobles and cruzados on assistants or attendants and artists who served him well. Not in all cases was the wealth confined to the upper classes. In 1735 the king sent 2,000 measures of grain to the peasants in the Alentejo who lacked seed.

He spent enormous sums to beautify Lisbon, while in Coimbra he ordered the construction of the grand ornate library. During his reign the crown continued to centralize power, and he ruled with increasing absolutism. He has been criticized for subservience to the church, from which he drew most of his ministers, especially in later years.

RICHES FROM BRAZIL, DEMISE OF THE CORTES AND RISE OF ABSOLUTISM

Successive kings since João IV had urged prospectors to intensify their efforts in the search for the elusive mineral wealth in Brazil. In the last decade of the seventeenth century significant gold strikes promised a bonanza. This soon materialized, as large deposits were found in Mato Grosso and Minas Gerais. The rush was on. All ages and classes—nobles, monks, women, sailors and farmers—set out for the goldfields. For a time emigration from Portugal had to be stopped to keep families on the farms and prevent the total ruin of agriculture.

In 1728 diamonds were discovered in the gold-bearing region of Minas

Gerais. While João's share in all this wealth was supposed to be one-fifth of everything mined, he saw only a fraction of this. Yet the riches that flowed into Portugal were enough to contrast sharply with the penury of times past. It was no longer necessary for the king to raise money to pay for royal extravagance. The incoming gold and gems from Brazil relieved him of any dependence on the Cortes for finances, and it was not called into session. Having recognized João V as heir to the throne, the Cortes disappeared from the political arena, and from João V's reign until 1820, absolutism based on the principle of divine right prevailed. The model of this absolutism in many eighteenth-century European courts, including Portugal, was the French court at Versailles presided over by Louis XIV.

STAGNATION AND REGRESSION

Near the end of João V's reign amid lavish spending and waste, the revival of the distinction between New Christians and old and a decline in agriculture and commerce began to set in, and a general lethargy seemed to grip the nation. The government and economy stagnated, the institutions, unchanged for centuries, were overloaded and lacked imagination and flexibility and the people, in dire poverty, saw little of the incoming wealth. The bureaucratic machinery of state ground down in the hands of the secretary of state, António de Azevedo Coutinho, and upon his death in 1749 the government passed to Frei Gaspar da Encarnacão, whose only interest seemed to be in promoting claims of his family to titles or property that lay vacant. By the end of the reign little had been done to promote and develop national industries. Many farms lay deserted, and repair of the roads over which goods had to pass was a thing of the past. Even the silk industry, which had once looked so promising, was starved for raw material, which was shipped directly to France. The inquisitor general, Nuno da Cunha, exercised as much power as that of the first minister. The Jesuits still controlled education, adhering to routines unchanged for two centuries.

With attention focused on Brazil, Asia and Africa were somewhat neglected. The last stronghold in North Africa, Mazagão, was abandoned in 1769, when the inhabitants were transported to Brazil to found a town of the same name. Valuable primarily for the Brazilian slave trade, towns in West Africa made little progress in development and colonization. The Cape Verde Islands and Guinea, with Bissau as the main station, along with Angola, became colonial backwaters of decline where the residents were too engrossed in slave traffic to do much else. In East Africa also, without renewal from settlers and investments, control was lost over much of the coastal regions. Mozambique on the route to Goa shared in the latter's prosperity, but with the shift of emphasis to Brazil, Mozambique became a rundown, isolated outback whose prospects were not helped by convicts deported from Portugal. Lack of military resources to maintain law and order did not help against the constant attacks by English and French privateers. In India and the Sunda Islands the wars with the Dutch sapped the strength of the already declining Portuguese strongholds.

JOSÉ I AND THE MARQUES DE POMBAL

João V had been ill for about eight years before his death. He succumbed on 31 July 1750 and was succeeded by his son José I, indolent, middle-aged and deficient in experience, talent and energy. The government was in paralytic crisis from the end of the last reign and suffered from the decline in trade revenues. José appointed some new ministers who were dissatisfied with the breakdown of state machinery and were determined to institute administrative and economic reforms. Chief among them was the fifty-one-year-old sometime diplomat Sebastião José de Carvalho e Melo, son of a cavalry officer of the lesser nobility, later created the marques de Pombal.

As he gathered in the reins of power, Pombal dedicated himself to reforms to make the government more efficient. Brazilian gold was on the decline, and it was important to make sure the crown's share was not siphoned away. Private export of gold was prohibited. Steps were taken to curb the power and privileges of the upper classes, even the richest families, and of the church. The jurisdiction of the Inquisition was constrained, and the influence of the Jesuits at court and in Brazil was curtailed. At the time the church owned nearly one-third of all cultivated land in Portugal. There was one cleric for thirty-six inhabitants—the highest ratio in Europe.

Pombal is best known for his program to rebuild Lisbon after the devastating earthquake, fire and tidal wave of 1755, in which much of the city was destroyed. The buildings erected by order of João V such as the opera house (finished only a few months before) were destroyed in the disaster, along with the royal palace and chapel, and most of the palaces of the upper aristocracy were consumed in flames. The working-class districts disappeared under a mountain of rubble. Pombal took total charge of the reconstruction of the city, hiring his own architects, who set to work laying out the city on a rectilinear plan with the same design applied to buildings of private use. He forbade the rebuilding of partly destroyed palaces, no outward manifestations of dwellings were allowed that indicated the occupant's social status and the height of church façades could not exceed that of the surrounding buildings. On the site of the ruined royal palace, government offices were constructed above shops around three sides of Praça do Comércio.

Pombal was made chief minister in 1756, and from then on his powers were close to absolute. His state mercantile program was designed to squeeze out, or control, the inefficient trader, mostly small businesses, by the establishment of monopolistic trading associations such as the one for the Douro wine trade, where prices were in decline as a result of overproduction. Among other things, Pombal intended to make the sale of wine, diamonds and tobacco more profitable. To this end the government established a Junta do Comércio. Pombal's authoritarian acts eventually galvanized a strong reaction, and a five-day riot in Oporto in 1757 against the government wine monopoly led to equally strong government countermeasures resulting in nine executions and seventy-eight deportations. The following year, when an attempt was made on the life of the king, Pombal managed to implicate both the Jesuits (who were banished in 1759) and the nobility, some of whom were tortured to death.

The country was now faced with a severe colonial commercial slump. Apart from the nearly exhausted gold mines in Brazil, sugar and other export commodities dropped by 40 percent due to invigorated foreign competition. The slave trade also fell off. The government set up a central tax and treasury system to more efficiently collect its due. By 1769 the depression was so severe that the government tried to develop domestic industries to produce what could no longer be imported. The Junta do Comércio established some seventy manufacturing centers, mostly in Lisbon or Oporto, to produce textiles, ceramics, clothing, paper and glass and to refine sugar. Most of the new companies fared poorly.

Pombal abolished slavery in Portugal in 1761 and reorganized the university curriculum with more emphasis on the natural and physical sciences, while streamlining the organizational system. He published a new code of laws and improved the system of schools for the upper and middle classes, and literacy improved, but the peasants and urban lower classes remained untouched by all this. In addition he effected the reorganization of the army and the introduction of new colonists into the

Portuguese settlements. At the same time he suppressed freedom of discussion of liberal political ideas of the Enlightenment by setting up a government censorship board in 1768. Works by Voltaire and Rousseau, for example, were prohibited.

His reforms encountered much opposition, and his power encountered much enmity, especially among ecclesiastics and the nobles. Those who objected to his methods were locked up for an indefinite term. Pombal's career ended with the death of King José in 1777, and he was later brought to public trial, declared guilty of abuse of power and banished from court but allowed to live out the rest of his life in disgrace on his rural estates. Upon his resignation some 800 political prisoners were released from their cells by exuberant crowds.

In foreign affairs Portugal ranged itself on the British side during the American Revolution but soon established a position of neutrality. Conflicts with Spain over borders in Brazil were settled by negotiation in 1778.

MARIA I AND PEDRO III

Maria, daughter of José I and heir to the throne, married her uncle (her father's brother), who was given the courtesy title of King Pedro III. Her senior by seventeen years, he spent most of his time at prayer and attending mass, taking little or no interest in running the country. Maria was also devout. She desired to make amends for Pombal's offenses to the church by permitting clerical influence to again become strong, although the Jesuits were not reinstated. Pombal's old enemies found places again in government. To restrict expenditures many people lost their jobs at the arsenal, bullfighting was banned for a time and the animals were sold off along with royal carriages and horses and mules in the royal stables. Public works were suspended, many unfinished. Unemployment grew, and people became disenchanted with her rule, but her policies were not necessarily reactionary: educational reform continued in her reign, and a decree of 1790 abolished separate seigneurial justice throughout the country, incorporating such functions under standard royal jurisdiction. The Academy of Science and the Royal Orphanage were founded, a new road was begun from Lisbon to Oporto and the first regular stage coach service began in 1798 between the two points.

After the death of her husband in 1786, the queen became greatly depressed, and in spite of medical treatment her melancholy worsened.

She ceased to govern in 1792, when her son, João, began to rule in her name. He was officially proclaimed prince regent in 1799.

Of significance during the latter half of the eighteenth century was the rise of a strong mercantile upper-middle class not dependent on the aristocracy. Small businesses, traders and shopkeepers once again began to prosper with the demise of the great monopolies imposed by Pombal.

THE FRENCH REVOLUTION, INVASION, DEPARTURE OF THE ROYAL FAMILY

The governments of Europe were shocked by the outbreak of the French Revolution in 1789 and appalled by the execution of Louis XVI in 1793, but Portugal remained mostly unperturbed. The illiterate peasant class was stable, the middle class was prospering, Catholicism continued strong, the weak and uncritical intelligentsia made few waves and all were presided over by the relatively considerate government of Maria I.

Far-reaching decisions had to be made, however. Portugal joined England and Spain in 1793 as European states geared up to mount an offensive against the revolutionary armies of France. When France declared war on Spain, the French sent a representative to Lisbon to open diplomatic relations and secure Portugal's promise of neutrality. They were particularly concerned with keeping Lisbon neutral as a port of call for French ships trading with the Americas, but the envoy's credentials were rejected, and he was sent away. Portugal then signed separate peace treaties with England and Spain and entered the war on their side. Portuguese troops disembarked for Cataluña to fight with the Spanish in Roussillon as they invaded France, but, faring poorly, Spain sued for peace and allied itself with France. Except for its treaty with England, Portugal would have followed suit. Little Portugal had to perform a juggling act to appease and maintain peaceful relations with France, Spain and England.

In 1801 a Spanish army under French influence seized the district of Olivença in what has been termed the War of the Oranges since an orange branch was sent to the queen of Spain as a symbol of the conquest. It was a bloodless affair. While the Portuguese crown was forced to pay an indemnity to Spain and make commercial concessions to France, the region remained in Spanish hands. Nevertheless, Portugal endeavored to maintain neutrality and was the only state in continental Europe outside Napoleon's control.

When Napoleon declared a blockade of English trade, and the English responded with a continental blockade, the so-called neutral Portuguese ports became vital to both France and England if they were to effectively close off all enemy shipping. The French insisted that the Portuguese close their ports to the English, open them to Spanish and French ships and arrest all Englishmen in the country and confiscate their property. Not to meet these demands would result in an invasion. The Portuguese government procrastinated.

In the autumn of 1807 the country was invaded by a French army. The government abandoned any expectation of holding off the French and ordered resistance stopped and the invaders welcomed. The royal family, the government and many citizens packed up their wealth and sailed to Brazil in late November, leaving a regency behind, departing Lisbon harbor the very day French advance units entered the city. The French commander, Junot, assured the people of Lisbon that he had come to liberate them from the English. He confiscated the property of those who had left for Brazil, the regency of five members presided over by the marques de Abrantes was quickly ousted, and a military government of occupation was established. About 50,000 French and Spanish troops roved the countryside arresting, killing, plundering and raping as they pleased. The Portuguese army was partly disbanded and partly converted into a legion to fight in foreign lands wherever Napoleon wished.

DUKE OF WELLINGTON

On 2 May 1808, when Napoleon put his brother, Joseph, on the throne of Spain, riots in Madrid spread into a national revolt sweeping Portugal up in its embrace. Junot was forced to send troops to subdue the Spanish rebels, leaving Portugal less guarded. This was a signal for the British to send General Arthur Wellesley, later to become the duke of Wellington, to the peninsula in aid of the insurrectionists and deal a blow to the French. Landing at Mondego Bay, Wellington advanced on Lisbon and defeated the French forces in two battles, at Roliça and Vimeiro in upper Estremadura. Junot then agreed to allow the English to transport the French army back to France in English ships. They were even permitted to take their booty with them.

The reinstated Regency Council, now under the marques de Minas, governed the country in the name of Maria I and the prince regent. Defense against a renewed French effort was begun under the command of the English general William Beresford, who was promoted to field marshal in the Portuguese army and given extreme powers, with which he practically ruled the country.

A second French invasion began in February 1809 under the command of Marshal Soult. His army entered the country via Trás-os-Montes in the north and conquered the territory down to the river Douro. Napoleon had promised Soult the kingship of this land, to be called Northern Lusitania. The French dream faded as Soult was driven back to Spain by combined English and Portuguese forces in May of that year. Wellington then led an Anglo-Portuguese army into Spain, but as opposition stiffened, he withdrew back to Portugal to prepare defenses and await the massive attack that he knew would come. In August 1810 he was defeated at the frontier fortress of Almeida some nine miles from the Spanish border, and his forces retired to Buçaco near Coimbra, where he occupied the heights. On 27 September Messéna, the French commander, attacked but was repulsed with the loss of some 4,500 men. Wellington then withdrew to prepared positions at Torres Vedras.

DEFENSES OF TORRES VEDRAS

Some months before, the British commander had visited the Torres Vedras region to study the topography and subsequently gave instructions for the building of defensive lines to his chief engineer, Lieutenant Colonel Fletcher, assisted by Captain Luís Maximo de Sousa Bellegard, while Beresford organized and trained the Portuguese army. Unknown to the French, work on the line was actually begun in mid-November 1809 with local labor and two regimental militias.

The defenses consisted of three fortified lines around the city of Lisbon to about twenty miles. The first ran from the mouth of the river Sizandro west of Torres Vedras to the river Tejo at Alhandra; a second from Ribamar on the coast southwest of Torres Vedras went to Póvoa de Santa Iria on the Tejo estuary just north of Lisbon; the third defended São Julião da Barra a little west of Lisbon, the chosen evacuation point in case of a French victory.

Torres Vedras was an important agricultural town from which supplies of food could easily be transported to other forts in the chain. The garrison here consisted of 2,200 troops and was protected by forty cannon and its hilltop position. Most soldiers were armed with muskets, but some had the more recent, faster loading and more accurate Baker rifle, which took about thirty seconds to load and fire. Survival rate was low for severe wounds, as casualties were treated by field surgeons with the usual method of amputation in the open air with unwashed instruments.

The forts, constructed mainly by Portuguese laborers, came to number 152 and were manned by 40,000 Portuguese troops along with 427 guns. Communication between the forts was either by semaphore or a system of balls and flags from a shiplike mast and observed by telescope.

Wellington's army of about 60,000 men was deployed behind the lines ready to shore up any breach. The French army in Portugal and Spain greatly outnumbered the allied forces, but they were at a disadvantage as food supplies had to be gathered from a hostile population whose harvests were already in and hidden or destroyed by the British. The English controlled the sea-lanes, facilitating their supply capacity, and the French, to their surprise, faced massive fortification from the Atlantic to the Tejo. Many of the villages in the area derived their names from the military activity of the time, for example, Sapataria (boots), Caixaria (coffins), and Perna da Pau (wooden leg).

For five months the two armies surveyed each other, but the French could not penetrate the Torres Vedras lines and ended up starving in front of them. Early in March 1811 they pulled back, beginning a full-scale retreat. Pursued by Wellington, they were again defeated at the Battle of Redinha and forced back into Spain. Here, confronted by English, Portuguese and Spanish irregulars, Messéna retreated all the way to Toulouse, which was reached in the spring of 1814.

CONSTITUTIONAL MONARCHY

The Napoleonic War had devastated the country, especially north of the Tejo. Agriculture, industry and trade were at rock bottom. Destruction had been wanton and rampant—monasteries, churches, palaces and even the houses of the peasants had been looted by English and French alike—and paintings, jewelry, furniture, sculpture, books and other sundry items were taken from the country. Much was destroyed such as libraries, archives and museums, and trade went from bad to worse as the English gobbled up the Brazilian commerce, and the country's expenditures increased as three-quarters of the revenue was spent on the army.

From 1808 to 1821 Portugal was both an English protectorate and a kind of colony of Brazil as the government was still in Rio de Janeiro. The aftermath of the war, coupled with the influence of the American and French Revolutions and discontent with the absolutism, brought about the rise of liberalism in the major cities, especially Oporto and Lisbon. In the forefront of liberal views were the Masonic lodges, which, composed of many army officers, had developed and spread during the period of foreign occupation when the officers were in contact with English and French Masons. General Gomes Freire de Andrade, known for his liberal views, became grand master of the Portuguese Freemasons. He was opposed to the return of absolute monarchy and vocal in his criticism of the Council of Regency. He especially disliked Beresford, the politically obtuse commander in chief of the army who ruled the country with a heavy hand. Arrested for a liberal conspiracy in 1817 that hoped to expel the British from the country, he was executed on the orders of Beresford, an act that earned the commander eternal detestation in the Portuguese army—one commanded by high-ranking British officers but more and more imbued with liberal ideas and in a perpetual state of discontent.

REVOLUTION OF 1820

A movement begun in Oporto in 1818 and organized by a liberal clandestine organization called the Sinédrio (from a Greek word for assembly) soon gained the support of local military units and high-ranking officers. In March 1820 Beresford left the country for Brazil to consult with the king and raise money to pay the army. On 24 August the movement rose in revolt and was joined by military units in Lisbon. A junta took over the government and called a provisional Cortes, the first representative assembly in Portugal in over a century, and a committee was assembled to draw up a constitution. The members of the committee were men disposed to liberal ideology who saw the state governed by a parliament with the king relegated to a subordinate role.

Returning to Portugal from Brazil, Beresford was denied permission to land and went on to England. The first deputies assembled in Lisbon on 24 January 1821 and began drafting Portugal's first modern constitution, which established a hereditary monarchy responsible to a unicameral parliament to be elected by all literate males. Their base of support came mostly from the middle class, about 9 percent of the population, and was concentrated mainly in Lisbon and Oporto. The constitutionalists wanted the king to return from Brazil but considered that the nation's sovereign should have a veto only to delay legislation, not curtail it. They wanted greater civil liberties and desired that Catholicism should be the religion of the state but that others should be allowed. The cardinal-patriarch protested and was driven into exile.

JOÃO VI, PEDRO IV AND MIGUEL I

João VI, who was promoted from prince regent to king on the death of his mother, Maria, in 1816, after fourteen years in Brazil, indicated no desire to return home. His sons, the princes, were more Brazilian than Portuguese, the eldest, Pedro, having left Lisbon at the age of nine and Miguel at five, but the king was ordered back to Lisbon by the Cortes, and it was either return or forfeit Portugal. He disembarked in Lisbon on 4 June 1821 and swore to uphold the new forthcoming constitution, which was completed in 1822. Queen Carlotta-Joaquina, her royal dignity insulted, refused to swear the oath and was sent off to confinement in the convent of Ramalhão near Sintra. She was a highly ambitious woman who had earlier encouraged her father, Carlos IV of Spain, to invade Portugal and place her in total charge. To the same end, she had also unsuccessfully attempted to have her husband declared insane. Obviously, they were not a happy couple.

Prince Pedro, heir to the throne, remained in Brazil, and he, too, was summoned home but ignored the call, and on 7 September 1822 he did the unthinkable. In a famous declaration given on the banks of the river and known as the Cry of Ipiranga, "Independence or Death," he broke off with the mother country. A month later he was proclaimed emperor of an independent Brazil.

On 23 May 1823 the second son of João VI, Prince Miguel (the favorite of his ultraconservative mother), who had also returned to Portugal and refused to swear allegiance to the constitution, joined a pro-absolutist uprising in Vila Franca de Xira. The new Cortes did not have the support it needed to carry out its radical ideas. João VI seized the moment to declare the new constitution of 1822 abolished, and there was no opposition to this bold stroke. Most of the landowning nobility and the traditional core of the Catholic Church were still the most influential components of society and interested in maintaining the status quo.

The following April, Miguel with the connivance of his mother plotted against his father. On 30 April 1824 the garrison of Lisbon came out to hail him as king, and Miguel took charge of the revolt. He arrested opponents and placed supporters in high military positions. João VI signed a decree on 3 May sanctioning Miguel's action but then changed his mind three days later. He went aboard a British vessel lying in the harbor and from this secure position summoned Miguel and relieved him of all authority, sending him off into exile on an extended journey throughout Europe.

On 10 March 1826 João VI died, and his eldest son, Pedro, emperor of Brazil, succeeded him. Pedro then submitted a constitutional charter for Portugal and abdicated in favor of his seven-year-old daughter, Maria da Glória, on condition that his charter was accepted and his brother Miguel married her and acted as regent until she came of age.

The charter itself advocated firm monarchical rule, with the right of the sovereign to dissolve parliament at any time, veto its decisions and appoint or dismiss governments. It attempted, however, to appease both liberals and absolutists, allowing both participation in government, dividing the Cortes into an upper chamber of nobles and clergy appointed by the king and a lower chamber of deputies elected to four-year terms by indirect suffrage from local town assemblies.

In February 1828 Miguel returned to Lisbon from his foreign "holiday" to swear an oath of allegiance to the charter. Once in power, he appointed an absolutist ministry, nullified the charter and dissolved the Chamber of Deputies. Anyone suspected of liberal tendencies was abused or imprisoned. Orders were sent to all city and town councils to send in petitions in favor of Miguel as king. Refusal to do so resulted in their dismissal. The next month Miguel called the traditional Cortes of the three estates and, applying the required pressure, was appointed king in July. Maria da Glória had meanwhile been sent to Portugal from Brazil by her father, Pedro, but when her ship reached Gibraltar, and news was received of Miguel's usurpation of the throne, she went on to England. Miguel soon completed his authority over the entire country with the exception of the Azores, which remained faithful to Pedro.

After uprisings in Coimbra and Oporto met stout resistance from Miguel's supporters, liberal forces fled the country. Some 3,000 émigrés found refuge in Plymouth, where they formed the nucleus of a liberal army, but Terceira in the Azores was the chosen place of exile of many, where in 1830 the duke of Palmela established a Council of Regency that was sanctioned by Emperor Pedro in Brazil. Liberals soon occupied most of the Azorean archipelago.

Having problems in Brazil, Pedro abdicated his imperial throne in favor of his son in 1831 and arrived in the Azores on 3 March 1832, where, now known simply as the duke of Bragança, he reestablished constitutional government under his charter of 1826 and proclaimed the rights of his daughter to the throne. His new minister of justice and finance, Mousinho da Silveira, proceeded to draft the laws of the new government, which swept away dues and tributes, church tithes and hereditary offices. The abolition of entailment of estates was begun, monopolies were prohibited and taxes and duties were reduced. Equality before the law of all citizens was established, and the jury system was proposed. But Miguel and his growing, albeit poorly trained, army occupied Portugal. Preparations for an invasion of the mainland were begun.

CIVIL WAR 1832

On 8 July 1832 about 7,500 men landed near Oporto and entered the city the following day as the Miguelite soldiers fled, but they were soon back with a stronger force of some 23,000 and besieged the city. With the aid of British volunteers the Miguelites were beaten back in their initial attack, losing 4,000 men and then held in check. As the impasse went on for ten months, over which time the liberal army increased in strength, the adherents of Miguel finally departed. A direct attack on Lisbon by sea was ruled out by Marshal Saldanha, commander in chief of the liberal forces. Instead, it was decided to land a contingent in the Algarve and march on the capital. Vila Flor, who had recently been made duke of Terceira, commanded the landing force, while the duke of Palmela was to become governor of any captured territory. Landing near Tavira, they soon took Olhão and Faro, while Miguel's fleet, sent out to interdict the attack, was destroyed by ships loyal to the liberal cause. The Miguelite defenders of Lisbon abandoned the city in the midst of a liberal uprising as the enemy approached, and Terceira and Palmela took command. Miguel regrouped his forces and attacked but was beaten off.

The demoralized followers of Miguel, defeated in several more skirmishes, finally signed an agreement 26 May 1834 at Évoramonte ending the hostilities as well as the old Portuguese regime. Miguel abandoned all future claims to the throne and went off into exile. The little princess, Maria da Glória, arrived in Portugal from England while bands of partisans ranged the countryside raiding, looting and settling scores with one another.

MARIA II

Meanwhile, Pedro, who had entered Lisbon in July 1833, restored the charter in the name of his daughter and dismissed from office Miguel's supporters, including bishops, which caused an immediate breach with the Vatican. To reduce the enormous debt accumulated during the civil war, Pedro decreed the abolition of monasteries and convents. The land was seized and sold to his supporters. A new landed class now had a vested interest in the continuation of liberal policies.

Pedro died of consumption on 24 September 1834 at age thirty-six. Maria, only fifteen, who had already been declared of age by the Cortes summoned earlier by Pedro, assumed the throne. She inherited a turbulent land. Trade and industry were at a standstill, and regular government income was nearly nonexistent. Demobilization of about 100,000 men from both sides returning to their homes found themselves without employment and forced to live as best they could. Many blamed the government for the country's lamentable condition.

Three factions seethed throughout the country: the absolutists and the liberals, the latter split into moderates (conservatives) and radicals (progressives), each with institutional preferences. All were monarchists, but absolutists wanted the traditional Cortes of the three estates to be summoned and not elected, and the moderates adhered to the charter of 1826 and a parliament of two houses, the lower elected, while the radicals were for the constitution of 1822 and a parliament of a single chamber with power over the king.

Under the charter Maria II's government consisted of six ministers of the various departments, including a head, while the Cortes was composed of two houses, that of the peers and that of the Chamber of Deputies, in which each member represented 25,000 inhabitants divided between the moderates (in the majority) and the radicals. Her first ministry was headed by Palmela, but over financial disagreements it fell in May 1835, replaced by one headed by Saldanha. It, too, soon fell. After a three-month marriage and the death of her husband she again married in 1836, this time a cousin, Ferdinand of Saxe-Coburg-Gotha.

In elections of July 1836 the radicals made a strong showing in Oporto, and when the deputies from that town arrived in Lisbon in September, they were met with sympathetic antigovernment demonstrations in favor of the 1822 constitution. When the national guard was brought out to disperse them, the soldiers joined the movement, and the government toppled.

The new government headed by the radical Manuel Passos suspended the charter and introduced a dictatorship that ruled by decree and lasted for two years until a new constitution was prepared. Some enlightened legislation was passed. To provide for a broader base of education for the middle class, grammar schools were founded, and a National Academy of Fine Arts was instituted.

CHARTISTS (MODERATES) AND SEPTEMBRISTS (RADICALS)

The radicals who favored the constitution of 1822 came to be called Septembrists after the September revolt. Those who opposed them and favored the charter became known as Chartists. The Septembrists embarked on a revision of the 1822 constitution that brought about a violent reaction from the Chartists, and a compromise was reached in which the constitution and the charter were to be modified to reflect a constitutional monarchy in accordance with some of the wishes of both groups.

The new constitution, the third, was duly promulgated in April 1838. It divided power between an executive, legislative and judicial branch of government, reaffirmed that sovereignty rested with the nation and abolished the Chamber of Peers, substituting a Chamber of Senators composed of nobles, and established the direct election of the Chamber of Deputies under a restrictive franchise. Four years of inept Septembrist government led to a rejection of the 1838 constitution and to the restoration of the charter in 1842 in a bloodless coup inspired by the authoritarian António da Costa Cabral, then minister of justice, and, it was widely believed, by the queen. Among the many new measures put into affect by Costa Cabral, who was the power behind the government, were fiscal reform, a new code centralizing administration, judiciary reform, revision of the public education system, a resumption of relations with the papacy, the establishment of a register of rural property and the banning of burials in churches. The last two caused a wave of unrest among the peasantry in the north of the country.

MARIA DA FONTE

In the year 1846 a rebellion broke out that primarily involved women. It was named after Maria (who may have been a mythical heroine to conceal the identity of those responsible) from the hamlet of Fonte. For sanitary purposes, a prohibition on churchyard cemeteries demanded that burials be allocated to public cemeteries away from villages and towns. Priests and many of their following, mostly women, objected. From the north the revolt spread rapidly, and troops were called out. Furious peasants repelled the troops with anything at hand. Soldiers from the countryside frequently went over to the insurgents, and a revolutionary junta was set up in Coimbra. Rebels closed in on Lisbon from north and south. They were joined by Septembrists, Miguelites and others who detested Costa Cabral and his brother, José da Silva Cabral, who had been elevated in government circles. The alarmed queen, Maria II, realizing that Cabral was finished, named a ministry headed by the influential duke of Palmela, who thought it best to recall the troops and allow the matter to fade away. Cabral, who now styled himself count of Tomar, went into exile.

A revolt in Oporto produced a local provisional Septembrist government opposed to Maria II, and both sides took up arms in another civil war lasting ten months and known as the *patuleia*, or rabble (the name given to the popular Oporto junta). Troops approached Lisbon, and the British government decided to intervene in aid of the queen, whose throne and perhaps life seemed in danger. They blockaded the mouth of the Douro River. A Spanish division then entered the country and reinstituted royal authority in Oporto. Peace was achieved 24 June 1847, when representatives of Spain and Great Britain, Queen Maria and the insurgent junta signed the Convention of Gramido, by which the junta dissolved itself, and a general amnesty was proclaimed terminating the war.

REGENERATORS, HISTORICALS AND PEDRO V

Palmela died in 1850, and the duke of Saldanha seized power in 1851 and changed the name of his party from Chartists to Regenerators, broadening its base by including conservative ex-Septembrists and amending the charter by "Additional Acts" introducing direct elections on the basis of broader, but still limited, suffrage, increasing the powers of parliament and abolishing the death penalty for civil crimes. He hoped with the new name to dilute the old bitter animosities and begin a new approach to the problems of the country.

In 1853 Maria II died in childbirth, her ninth, at age thirty-four and was survived by her consort King Ferdinand and eight children. Her eldest son, the studious Pedro, succeeded to the throne at age sixteen, although his father exercised the regency until he was eighteen. Saldahna, whose Regenerators were still in office, placed Fontes Pereira de Melo in charge of the treasury. Fontes established a new ministry of public works and undertook the construction of roads, completed the first telegraphs and opened the first section of railway in 1856. In a dispute with the king, Saldanha resigned in June 1856 and was sent off as ambassador to Rome.

The opposition Septembrist Party now styled itself the Historicals under the leadership of Sá da Bandeira. They succeeded the Regenerators in 1856, when the young king called on the duke of Loulé to form a government of Historicals along with Sá da Bandeira. Loulé was a genuine liberal or Progressive (as his party began to call itself).

In 1857 a French ship carrying slaves was taken by the Portuguese off Mozambique and brought to Lisbon. The French protested with the story that the many blacks on board were volunteer workmen heading for French Réunion Island near Madagascar. They sent a threatening squadron to anchor in the Tejo estuary. Portugal was forced to return the ship and pay a humiliating indemnity to the French. Europe had already agreed to stop slave traffic, and now the Portuguese government, endorsed by the young king, decreed in 1858 the abolition of slavery in the Portuguese colonies within twenty years. In part due to the French incident the Loulé government fell in 1859, the Regenerators won the election and the duke of Terceira headed the next government, but he soon expired, followed by King Pedro and his brother, who both died in November 1861 of typhoid fever after a hunting trip. Two other brothers traveling in Europe returned home immediately; one soon died, while the other, Luís, inherited the throne. The large Bragança family had been suddenly drastically reduced.

LUIS I

The new king came to the throne at age twenty-three. To continue the line Luís married Maria Pia, daughter of King Victor Emmanuel of Italy, and she soon gave birth to a son, Carlos. As a good constitutional monarch Luís left the running of government to the political leaders. A Reformist Party was founded under Sá da Bandeira, and in 1876 it united with the Historicals to form a new Progressive Party under Anselmo José Braancamp. The leaders agreed to the rotation system of government in which conservative (Regenerators) and liberal parties (Progressives) took turns in power.

Each faction would govern as long as it comfortably could and then step down for the other. Both parties were monarchists, and there were only minor differences between them. The alternating system with the king as arbitrator led to a period of stability in which the country gradually improved its communications infrastructure, the civil service and education and saw an expansion among the middle classes. The system began in 1879 and persisted until the first decade of the twentieth century but did not solve the country's underlying problems. The government was in perpetual deficit, forced to borrow from abroad for public works, while foreign investment was not readily forthcoming.

With a largely illiterate rural population controlled by local agents known as Caciques, whom the party leaders supported by favors and who on their behalf turned out the vote, the masses were in no position to participate in political activities or party affairs.

Near the end of the century socialist organizations—socialists, Marxists, Anarchists—began to emerge along with a small, but, vocal urban, lower-to-middle-class Republican Party. Both were especially interested in abolishing the monarchy and further limiting the power of the church. A further appeal to Republicanism, especially among the middle class, was enhanced by its emphasis on nationalism, promoting universal suffrage and abolition of aristocratic titles.

CARLOS I

Luís died in October 1889 at the age of fifty-one and was succeeded by Carlos, aged twenty-six. In 1890 Portuguese and British interests clashed in Africa. A proposed railroad link from Cairo to Capetown, north to south, conflicted with Portuguese intentions to link up their colonies of Mozambique and Angola, east to west. In present-day Malawi the two nations had opposed interests: the British issued an ultimatum, and the Portuguese withdrew. Back home the Republicans led a movement denouncing the government and the king as responsible for the national humiliation, the resurgence of clerical influence and corruption in high places. The party primarily consisted of city dwellers, and its influence was greatly enhanced as new members flocked to it during the crisis. A Republican rising in Oporto, while quelled by the municipal police, left an impression throughout the country. Fed by the press, agitation continued with street riots and bomb throwing. Inquiries were then made in parliament about the money from the public treasury going to support the royal family.

In 1901 the Regenerators developed a splinter group called the Liberal Regenerating Party under the guidance of pro-monarchist João Franco, and by 1905 there were five principal groups: the older Regenerators, the Liberal Regenerators, the Progressives, the socialists and the Republicans.

ASSASSINATION OF THE KING

By 1906 the system of rotation between Regenerators and Historicals had collapsed, and neither party could now obtain a parliamentary majority. King Carlos, fearful of what appeared to be a movement toward a republic, dissolved the parliament and invited the anti-Republican João Franco to govern by decree. In 1908 an attempted military coup supported by the Republicans engendered a crackdown on the party and cancellation of the elections. The principal leaders were arrested and about to be exiled when on 2 February 1908 two Republican activists, a teacher, Manuel Buiça, and a clerk, Alfredo Costa, gunned down the king and his eldest son, Luís Felipe, in their carriage on a Lisbon street. The king's younger son Manuel escaped with only a slight wound.

8

Monarchy to Republic to Dictatorship

The sudden death of the king and his heir brought to the throne a prince who was ill trained to rule. A council of state was summoned, and the dictatorial João Franco was dismissed and sent into exile. He was replaced by Admiral Ferreira do Amaral, who formed a cabinet that included both Regenerators and Progressives. The partnership did not last, much to the benefit of the Republican Party.

MANUEL II AND THE FIRST REPUBLIC

The government tried for the next two and a half years of Manuel's brief reign to reconcile the country. It failed. Several ministries came and went, but they were no longer labeled Regenerators or Historicals. On 3 October 1910 significant units from the Lisbon garrison supported by armed civilians and navy warships in the harbor revolted and joined the Republican cause. Manuel II abdicated and went off to exile in England. After nearly eight centuries of monarchical rule, the republic was proclaimed in Lisbon from the balcony of the city hall, and a provisional government was established of the top leaders of the Republican Party (PRP) and the interim presidency of Teófilo Braga. His anticlerical minister of justice, Afonso Costa, published decrees dissolving all religious orders (their property being given over to the state) and forbidding religious instruction in schools and in the army. Elections were held six months later in which the Republicans gained an overwhelming victory.

The Republican constitution of 1911 provided for a four-year presidency and a bicameral legislature consisting of a Senate and a Chamber of Deputies, separated church from state, legalized the right to strike and provided for full civil liberties (except for the Catholic Church) and the right of habeus corpus. Manuel José de Arriaga became the first elected president of the Portuguese Republic. The strong man in the government, Afonso Costa, leader of the radical Republicans and a new Democratic Party, became prime minister but was forced from power in 1914. The Republican government, in spite of some progressive legislation, did not live up to expectations. No economic improvements in the standard of living had occurred. The primary rise in statistics related to the number of those now emigrating. The anticlerical stance of the government upset the conservatives, while promised freedoms failed to materialize. Manuel de Arriaga dismissed the Democratic government and appointed General Pimenta de Castro as prime minister in 1915 in an attempt to bring some conservative influence into the arena of decision making. The Democratic Party, not to be thwarted, resorted to arms to regain power, and several hundred casualties resulted from the confrontation. Teófilo Braga replaced Arriaga for a few months, followed by Bernardino Machado. In the meantime World War I had broken out.

WORLD WAR I

When Germany and Great Britain went to war in August 1914, the Anglo-Portuguese alliance was still operative, but Britain did not insist that Portugal fulfill its obligations since there was little immediate help the country could give. Opinions also differed with regard to the war. The Republican conservatives were generally in favor of maintaining neutrality, while the Democratic Party was for entering on the side of the Allies.

The Portuguese government worried about Angola and Mozambique, which lie adjacent to German territories in Africa. Some fighting flared up on both the colonial frontiers as a result of German intrusions and the mistaken German intelligence in Africa that the two countries were at war. When the error was corrected, German penetrations ceased. England then asked Portugal for active participation of men and arms on the Western Front. Also, England coveted the many German cargo ships that had been interned in Lisbon harbor when war broke out. If the Portuguese would commandeer the ships, the British would buy them and have them refitted in Portuguese shipyards. The government complied, taking command of the ships on 24 February 1916, and Germany, followed by Austria-Hungary, declared war on Portugal. A Franco-English military mission came to Lisbon and helped with stepped-up training of the army. In January 1917, 25,000 Portuguese troops were ready to be sent to France under General Fernando Tamagnini de Abreu e Silva; the number was later increased to 40,000. Simultaneously, Portugal reinforced its troop contingents in Africa, where fighting again broke out.

Volatile discontent with the war and with the government remained high, and disorderly disturbances in Lisbon throughout 1917 were brutally repressed, often with the loss of life. A particular issue of unrest was the poorly managed distribution of food that left many cities close to famine.

On 5 December 1917 a military coup placed General Sidónio Pais in charge, and elections confirmed him in the office of president. He promptly maneuvered a change in the constitution to give the presidency more power and called the regime the New Republic. His support was derived from Conservatives, Catholics, Monarchists, military men who had opposed entry into the world war, and many of the lower-middle class who had been frightened by all the turmoil of the last few years. He modified some of the anticlerical decrees and resumed relations with the Vatican that had been severely disrupted. About this time the German spring offensive of 1918 caught the poorly trained Portuguese army at Lys in France by surprise and overran their positions, endangering the entire front. The Portuguese took little part in the remainder of the war.

The New Republic ended along with Sidónio Pais, who was assassinated in December 1918 by a pistol shot while boarding a train in Lisbon. The Democratic Party again came to the fore, but Afonso Costa, tired of the game of politics, left the country. An uprising in the north led by Paiva Couciero attempted to restore the monarchy. Parliamentary squabbles and the forming and dissolving of factions continued unabated. In the year 1920 there were four ministries, one lasting only twenty-four hours. In the election of 1921 a conservative wing of the Republican Party came out well ahead in seats compared to the radical Democratic Party, and on 19 November of the same year, another military rebellion brought down the government. The prime minister, António Granja, and several other ministers were subsequently assassinated. In 1922 the president, António de Almeida, had to flee to Cascais until troops could restore order in the capital. President for a second time in 1925, Machado found himself in the middle of one of the great scandals of all time. In 1922 the Bank of Portugal had employed Waterlow and Sons Limited of London to print its banknotes. Two years later a group of Portuguese led by a Dutchman with forged credentials and a bogus letter from the director of the Bank of Portugal convinced the gullible Mr. Waterlow to print 100 million escudos using the old plates. With the money the conspirators started their own bank, which opened in Oporto in July 1925. It remained in business for five months before the fraud was detected. The inept government fell.

MILITARY DICTATORSHIP

The state of the republic was chaotic. Workers organized into anarchosyndicalist unions, bourgeois groups demanded strong leadership to control terrorist activities among the labor force and Republicans and Monarchists fought each other. In three attempts to overthrow the regime during the last thirteen months of the republic, the last proved successful. On 25 May 1926 General Gomes da Costa, selected to lead a coup by fellow officers, announced his intention from Braga to lead a march on Lisbon. Before he reached the city, President Bernardino Machado, aged seventy-five and serving again as president, invited a staunch Republican and naval commandant, Mendes Cabeçadas, to form a ministry that reflected the aspirations of the military and not those of Gomes da Costa, who was offered the ministries of war, overseas territories and agriculture. With no interest in potatoes, as he put it, he accepted only the first two. On 29 May the unpopular prime minister, Maria da Silva, resigned, and the First Republic, lasting sixteen years, came to an end. On 17 June Gomes da Costa ousted Mendes Cabeçadas and assumed power, but on 9 July he, too, was overthrown by General Oscar Carmona and packed off to the Azores. General Carmona was named head of the military government or acting president, later confirmed as president.

The army officers in the north demanded and got the replacement of the multiparty system by a national nonparty government. The new revolutionary government had no real modus operandi for solving the nation's problems apart from maintaining law and order and on 3 February 1927 a rebellion broke out in Oporto fomented by politicians and pro-parliamentary army units fearful that a restoration of the monarchy was in the making. After six days of fighting in which the government employed heavy artillery, and Oporto was in danger of being leveled, the rebels, with 120 dead, surrendered. Some 600 of the perpetrators were exiled to the Azores and Cape Verde. Others fled before arrest and organized dissident groups abroad. The military dictatorship remained in power. The financial crisis that had plagued all the governments continued unabated, and President Carmona asked António de Oliveira Salazar, a professor of economics at Coimbra University, to help solve the fiscal problems. Salazar had served briefly as finance minister in 1926 but had resigned because he was not given full veto power over all expenditures. Now, two years later, he was given the mandate he desired.

The Great Depression of the early 1930s aggravated a worsening economic and social situation. The currency was devalued, wages went down and workers aspired to protect themselves by joining trade unions. They pursued their rights by strikes, arson and setting off bombs. The Russian Revolution of 1917 frightened the bourgeoisie in many countries, and Portugal was no exception. A forceful hand was demanded to quell subversive and terrorist activity among the workers and bring back social harmony and economic stability. Judging from past experiments in democracy, that could come only from a totalitarian government.

The dictatorship navigated the ship of state through troubled waters until 1933. By this time Salazar was trusted enough by the military to be asked to form a government. He received virtual dictatorial powers, drafted a new constitution and submitted it to a plebiscite, in which it was approved. Salazar, an austere and pious bachelor, shunned publicity and devoted all his time to state affairs. A balanced budget, his primary aim in 1928, became sacrosanct policy thereafter. Meanwhile, the Portuguese people remained the poorest and least educated in Western Europe.

The constitution of 1933 was antiparliamentary and anticommunist and emphasized the power of the executive. It subjected the market economy to state control and united the state and society into a corporate unit. This Second Republic, referred to as the Estado Novo (New State), dominated by one man, Salazar, gave the country stability at a high cost. It quickly evolved into a completely authoritarian state with political police to punish any form of dissidence. Primary targets of the PIDE (Polícia Internacional e de Defensa do Estado) were communists or those affiliated with workers' organizations, both of which were forbidden.

Secret societies, including the Freemasons, to which many Portuguese intellectuals and politicians belonged, were banned, and working-class opposition to the regime, controlled mostly by the Communist Party, went underground.

PORTUGAL AND THE SPANISH CIVIL WAR

The fall of the Spanish general and dictator Primo de Rivera in 1930 and the dissolution of the monarchy in 1931, leading to the proclamation of the Second Spanish Republic, encouraged the Portuguese Left and the labor organizations but, apprehensive of events in neighboring Spain, the government reacted by clamping down on left-wing groups. Salazar's New State reaffirmed the ban on strikes in 1933 and formed workers into official syndicates, their activities strictly regulated.

The government had less cause for alarm during the conservative period of the Spanish Republic in 1934–1935, when center and right-wing parties came to power, but in February 1936 the Spanish Popular Front of leftist parties won the parliamentary elections. The Portuguese government now viewed its neighbor with much disquiet as public order in Spain dissolved and was replaced by a wave of general strikes, church burning and factional murders. Relations between the authoritarian Portuguese state and the Spanish Republic were formal and correct during these troublesome times in spite of the fact that the Spanish government supported left-wing groups in Portugal, and Portugal allowed Spanish rightists, such as General Sanjurjo, who found refuge there after an attempted coup in 1932, to live in, and operate from, its territory.

On 17 July 1936 a military uprising initiated the long civil war in Spain, and Salazar faced his first major problem in foreign affairs, but in just over a week he arranged to cooperate with the right-wing insurgents. On 1 August he gave notice that he proposed to aid the rebels with all available means, including the Portuguese army if necessary. Then, on 13 August, Portugal accepted the idea of nonintervention in principle (proposed by France and England), so long as its borders were not threatened. Early in September the crews of two Portuguese warships in Lisbon harbor confined their officers and prepared to sail to Spain in aid of the republic. Salazar ordered the ships destroyed by gunfire. On 10 September he issued a decree requiring all service personnel and public servants to declare alliance to the social order of his New State and to repudiate communism and all revolutionary ideas. He created the Legião Portuguesa to defend (in his words) the spiritual heritage of the nation from Bolsheviks and the Mocidade Portuguesa, a military youth organization (complete with the fascist salute) compulsory for children between eleven and fourteen.

The foreign supporter and major arms supplier to the Spanish Republic, the Soviet Union, accused Portugal at a meeting of the nonintervention committee in London of allowing its territory to be used as an insurgent base of military operations. The charges detailed a number of incidents of arms and supplies transported from Lisbon to the Spanish frontier. The Russian diplomat, Maisky, demanded a commission to patrol the Portuguese-Spanish border. The Portuguese representative walked out of the discussion, and later the foreign minister, Monteiro, refuted all accusations and blamed the Russians and their propaganda for the war in the first place. Relations with the Republican government in Madrid were suspended in October, and Salazar continued to ostensibly subscribe to the international nonintervention agreement as a convenient way to avoid foreign complications.

The Portuguese government feared an invasion if the Left should win the war in Spain, and it was through Portugal that much German aid to Franco was arranged. Germany, a signatory to the nonintervention agreement, did not comply with the rules. The aid Salazar himself could offer the insurgents was not great, but he gave them a place of refuge, if needed, and the means of communicating between their separate forces in the north and south of Spain at the beginning of the war. Franco's older brother Nicolás was allowed to establish his headquarters for the purchase of foreign arms at Lisbon. Spanish Republicans who escaped Franco's insurgents into Portugal were quickly returned to face his firing squads. Salazar personally facilitated the movement of German arms from ships at Lisbon to the rebels. He also allowed Portuguese volunteers, numbering several thousand, to fight on the side of the Spanish insurgents.

Among international leftist groups the ill feelings against Salazar soon ran as high as those against Franco. When the Spanish civil war came to a conclusion in 1939 with victory for Franco, the Portuguese government signed on 17 March a treaty of friendship and nonaggression known as the Iberian Pact.

WORLD WAR II

Germany relied on Portugal for reexports of produce from Portuguese African colonies and elsewhere and for its domestic tin, wool, sardines, olive oil and, above all, tungsten. The principal uses of tungsten (previous name wolfram) are as filaments in incandescent lamps and wires in electric furnaces, in the manufacture of spark plugs, electrical contact points and cutting tools and in the production of hard alloys of steel. For a nation going to war it was an essential product. Sweden produced only about one-tenth of that produced by Portugal, and Korean supplies were no longer available after the rupture of the trans-Siberian route.

In the years prior to World War II, Salazar's government sought to extend the country's international friendships, maintain its close alliance with Britain, consolidate links with Brazil and Spain and patch up disagreements with the Vatican. The latter led to the Concordat of 1940, in which the state restored nearly all the privileges of the church enjoyed under the monarchy. This included financial support and educational jurisdiction. It more or less reversed the anticlerical trend of the last century and a half.

As World War II loomed on the horizon, Salazar's primary concern was to preserve the neutrality, independence and integrity of Portugal, at the same time cementing strong relations with countries that could help in this effort. Too strong a commitment to one or the other opposing nations could tip the balance and ruin the prospect of neutrality. For example, the Allies also needed tungsten but hoped that none would reach the Germans and Italians. Salazar sold to both sides, shipping it out of the neutral port of Lisbon.

From the beginning of the war, when Germany invaded Poland on 1 September 1939, and France fell nine months later, Salazar stood nearly alone among European statesmen in his estimate that the war would be long, that England would be bloodied but unbowed, that the United States would be drawn in and that the war would be won by the Allies. In 1942, when everything seemed to favor the Axis, Salazar insisted to Franco, at a meeting in Sevilla, that the Allies would eventually win. His views may have helped persuade Franco to resist Hitler's desire to bring Spain into the Axis orbit. Later, in 1943, he allowed England and the United States to establish air bases in the Azores when it became obvious that the Axis powers might lose.

After the fall of Holland, Belgium, and France in 1940, refugees flooded into Portugal, especially Jews escaping the Nazi tyranny, many wishing to go to America. Salazar had issued orders that Jews escaping the Nazis not be permitted to enter the country, but the Portuguese consul general in Bordeaux, Aristides de Sousa Mendes, defied the decree and in 1940 issued in three nights 30,000 visas, about one-third of them to Jews. He was abruptly dismissed and died in poverty and ignominy in 1954. Not until 1987 was his bravery recognized, when President Soares visited the United States and presented a medal in his memory to some of his sons and daughters living there. In 1995 Soares honored Sousa Mendes in a ceremony in Lisbon, where he apologized for Portugal's past persecution of Jews.

Portugal's neutrality was useful to both sides, and Lisbon became a hotbed of intrigue and espionage—a terminus for Atlantic clippers and ships from New York, planes from England, Germany, Italy and Spain, as well as a Portuguese air service to Tanger. It was also the primary distribution center for the Red Cross and its relief supplies. Official German limousines circulated throughout the city, and well-organized networks of spies, German, Italian and English, mingled with reporters crowding the hotel lobbies and bars on the lookout for information. The magnificent old Palace Hotel at Estoril and the nearby casino welcomed a steady stream of characters, from Russian countesses and German barons, to English lords. The Germans mostly occupied the Hotel Parque, established their high-profile propaganda machine, a more discreet fifth column (in case Portugal was to be incorporated into the Third Reich) and business contacts in an attempt to displace British traders from their old markets. The rich and famous, such as the duke and duchess of Windsor, moved into surrounding villas and maintained their lifestyle of luxurious self-indulgence.

All European nationalities crowded into Lisbon to escape the Nazis. Charities helped many survive as they waited for visas and steamship tickets to America or elsewhere. The Lisbon human marshaling-yard also attracted a steady stream of diplomats and officials as a stopover between England and the United States. Rumors, lies, propaganda, fears and hopes, sometimes intertwined with facts, were mingled together in hushed tones in the alleyways and back rooms of the hotels. Press censorship prevented a clear picture of events. Wendell Willkie, who in 1940 ran as the Republican nominee against President Roosevelt (FDR) and lost, traveled abroad as Roosevelt's semiofficial envoy and passed through Lisbon on his way to London. Other distinguished Americans came, such as A. Drexel Biddle, the U.S. ambassador in London to the occupied countries; J. G. Winant, the U.S. ambassador to England; and Captain Jimmy Roosevelt (FDR's son) on his way from Egypt. Dorothy Thompson, one of America's outstanding columnists, also stopped on her way to London and picked up stories for her readers. Crowds of reporters surrounded the celebrities as they disembarked from clipper or ship, demanding their views on the war, but when the noted novelist H. G. Wells stopped off after a sojourn in America, he would allow an interview only at so much per word. When the United States came into the war at the end of 1941, shipping lines abandoned their voyages to Lisbon for fear of German U-boats. As trade and imports to Portugal sagged, gasoline became nearly nonexistent, food was scarce and life in the city became much less animated.

PORTUGAL AT THE UNITED NATIONS AND NATO

In September 1946, Salazar applied for admission to the United Nations (UN). A document signed by eleven members of an antifascist movement in Portugal was sent to the UN declaring that only under a democratic government had Portugal any right to join. The eleven were arrested and brought to trial but were pardoned with only the loss of their jobs when things became embarrassing for the government. Salazar got his way, however, despite opposition from some member states, and Portugal was admitted to the UN in 1955 and subsequently to the International Monetary Fund (IMF), the World Bank, the World Health Organization (WHO) and the World Trade Organization (WTO). Colonial problems occupied the regime and the UN in the 1950s, with Portugal maintaining the position, against UN opposition and concern for the self-governing and independence of oppressed peoples, that its overseas territories were an integral part of the mother country and not colonies. The debate continued for two decades.

The country lists nine historical sites with the United Nations Educational, Scientific and Cultural Organization's (UNESCO) World Heritage Organization, including the monasteries of Batalha, Alcobaça and Jerónimos. Portugal also committed itself to the European Free Trade Association (EFTA) in 1960 and to the General Agreement on Tariffs and Trade (GATT) two years later. In 1995 the country sent troops to Bosnia as peacekeepers under the UN.

Portugal joined the North Atlantic Treaty Organization (NATO) in 1949, and the armed services participate regularly in training exercises for nuclear, biological and chemical warfare. Portugal produces its own small arms, but other equipment is generally supplied by more wealthy NATO member countries. For example, the United States recently supplied twenty latest-model F-16 jet fighters to bolster the aging air force, and Germany handed over advanced Alpha-Jet training aircraft and financed three frigates built in Hamburg for Portugal's modest fleet. They are equipped with British-built Sea Lynx helicopters.

DELGADO AND THE PRESIDENCY

One of the remaining pretenses to democracy left in Portugal after years of authoritarian rule was the elected office of the president, largely a figurehead but, nevertheless, subject to a vote on a limited suffrage every seven years. The elections offered the opportunity for a brief display of political activity for the world to see that Portugal was not suppressed under an autocratic regime. For PIDE, Salazar's secret police, the occasion was useful to determine who opposed the dictator. In 1958 Portugal's delegate to NATO, General Humberto Delgado, returned to run against Salazar's candidate, Admiral Tomás. His slogan, "We are tired of being treated like sheep," attracted huge audiences on the campaign trail. His answer to the problem was to become president and exercise the constitutional right of the office to dismiss the prime minister, that is, Salazar, and dismantle the New State. With the government controlling the entire electoral system and limited suffrage, Delgado lost, polling only a third of the vote. Salazar then abolished direct suffrage for the presidency, firmly closing the constitutional loophole. The elections had clearly been fixed, and the Portuguese army was not pleased to see one of their own humiliated.

Delgado then wrote a letter to four senior generals criticizing the military for its apathy toward the regime that allowed Salazar and Santos Costa (the minister of defense) as well as the secret police, PIDE, to remain in power. He accused the army of acting as the dictator's praetorian guard and urged them to refuse to recognize the elections, to protest the transfer of several officers who had voted for Delgado and to resign their ranks to show their displeasure with the regime. The honor and pride of the army were at stake.

The response to his frank and bold declaration was not favorable, but some officers and Delgado continued to plot during the summer of 1958. Meanwhile, illegal strikes occurred, and Alvaro Cunhal, general secretary of the underground Communist Party, escaped from prison, to the profound embarrassment of PIDE, and fled to Prague, where he waited for more propitious times to return home. Delgado formed an independent military movement and enlisted such men as Captain Vasco Gonçalves, an engineer of clear left-wing views; Captain Varela Gomes, a spirited infantry officer; a young naval officer, Manuel Serra, a socialist; and a politically minded lawyer, Mário Soares, who lent them his Lisbon offices for their headquarters. In March 1959, Delgado, Serra and Gonçalves attempted to seize key centers in Lisbon as a prelude to a coup, but the attempt failed, as loyalist forces had warning. Delgado fled the country.

ANGOLA

The first wave of violence began in February 1961. Luanda felt the full brunt of the anger with attacks on police stations and prisons, followed by rioting and then by the massacre of settlers near the border of the Republic of the Congo. Portuguese officers on the scene wrote their reports on the situation and sent them back to Francisco da Costa Gomes, then a forty-six-year-old colonel working in the General Staff. The prevailing opinion was that in the event of widespread guerrilla warfare in the African colonies there would, by necessity, have to be negotiations with independence movements. A military solution in territories so large and diverse would simply be beyond the capabilities of Portugal. Costa Gomes agreed with this consensus and prepared a document to that effect. It was passed on to General Botelho Moniz, who agreed with it, but it finished up in the hands of Salazar, who did not. Moniz was dismissed from his post, and Costa Gomes was packed off to a sinecure administrative position in Beja. Salazar went on television to state his determination to maintain the Portuguese empire in Africa in the defense of Western and Christian civilization.

Also in February 1961, with the intention of publicizing the plight of the Portuguese under Salazar, Captain Henrique Galvão, a fellow conspirator of Delgado, along with some Spanish exiles, hijacked a cruise ship in the Mediterranean, the *Santa Maria*, and renamed it the *Santa Liberdade*, in order to bring world attention to the dictatorial Portuguese regime. They intended to sail to the island of Fernando Po and set up rival governments to Portugal and Spain. Shadowed by U.S. warships for thirteen days, they wound up surrendering in Brazil to the authorities.

By the end of the year, Portugal had sent 50,000 troops to Angola, the most troublesome of the colonies. The tiny nation of Portugal of 9 million-plus maintained an army that at times numbered 200,000 men and sustained a defense budget that amounted to 40 percent of the total public expenditure. Many army officers felt the African wars were not only losing causes but morally wrong.

On 1 January 1962 Varela Gomes masterminded an attack on the military garrison at Beja, and Delgado returned from Brazil to perhaps take the office of president. The attack failed when the commander shot Varela Gomes when he came to ask for the surrender of the garrison and had to be taken to hospital by his fellow rebels. Delgado fled again, roving the planet in search of support to overthrow Salazar, but in 1968 the PIDE cunningly lured him into a trap and murdered him in a field near Badajoz.

GOA

Late in 1961 the Portuguese enclave of Goa, on the west coast of India, with a population of about 555,000 inhabitants and a Portuguese garrison of 3,500 troops, suddenly faced 30,000 Indian troops approaching from land, sea and air. The 1943 rifles and dried-up powder of the Portuguese artillery were more apt to misfire than to discharge. The story is told that just before the invasion the commander urgently sent a message to Lisbon asking for more artillery shells and using the code word for them, *chouriços*, or "sausages." The Ministry of Defense in Lisbon, which had long forgotten the code word, complied and sent thousands of sausages!

As far back as 1954 the Nehru government of India had asked Salazar to enter into negotiations with a view to decolonizing Goa and its outposts of Damião and Diu, but the dictator had refused. Further attempts to change his mind failed; Goa was Portuguese and would remain so. At four in the morning on 18 December 1961 the Indians attacked. On the eve of the battle Salazar had cabled General Vassalo e Silva, the military commander at Goa, demanding that the Portuguese soldiers and sailors fight to the last man. There would be no surrender. It was conquer or die, but although a few fought bravely against impossible odds, the rest surrendered. The struggle lasted thirty-six hours, ending four centuries of Portuguese occupation.

The loss of Goa was a shattering blow to the dictator, who henceforth regarded the enclave as merely occupied by a foreign power, and until 1974 the representative continued to sit in the National Assembly for the province of Goa. Salazar's court-martial proceedings against Vassalo e Silva were finally dropped after an outcry from the military. Soon afterward, the three African colonies rebelled: first Angola in 1961, then Guinea in 1963, and finally Mozambique in 1964.

RELATIONS WITH ENGLAND

Portugal's relationship with England, its oldest ally, whose cooperation dates back to 1386 and the Treaty of Windsor, has been strained at
times: Britain refused Portugal the use of its air bases in India when Goa
was overrun by Indian troops, and when Portugal supported the uni-
lateral declaration of Rhodesia for independence from Britain in 1964,
British warships blockaded the port of Beira (Mozambique) to keep petroleum from reaching the rebel regime of Ian Smith. In addition, Britain
became increasingly dissatisfied with Portugal's insistence on maintaining its colonial empire. Trade has always continued, however, and the
close economic alliance was partly embodied in British participation in
Portuguese wine producing, especially port, and investments in transportation and telecommunications.

POLITICAL AND SOCIAL CLIMATE UNDER SALAZAR

Salazar's thirty-six-year term of office was inspired by fascism and its
hold in Italy under Mussolini, who came to power in 1922. Salazar made
his corporate state totalitarian, and all national activities were controlled
by centralized bodies. Only one political party was allowed—National
Action, which was really a civic association. There were to be only national trade unions or syndicates whose leaders had been approved by
the government, and employers and employees were expected to work
in harmony, but in the case of disputes, the state arbitrated through
government-appointed labor courts, whose decisions were final.

The National Assembly functioned as a deliberative chamber, but as
only National Action could put up candidates, it was a rubber-stamp
organization of the government. Salazar paid little attention to it and, in
fact, held legislative bodies in high contempt. He once predicted their
disappearance from all European countries within twenty years.

To protect his corporate state, the unsupported allegations of the secret
police were sufficient to convict. It had the power to detain people without charge for six months. For the regime the fact that many people were
poor was not considered an economic matter but a moral and psycho-
logical characteristic of the person—a form of vice.

Salazar added to the usual dictatorial policies another law peculiar to
Portugal. This Law of Control of Industry provided for the growth of
private monopolies clustered around a few wealthy families. It prohibited the creation of any new factories or the start of new industries or

even the extension of existing enterprises without government approval. Salazar used the law to encourage a few large private enterprises, protecting them from small businessmen and from the encroachment of foreign investment. In return they gave him total support for his policies both domestic and colonial.

On the other side of life more than one-third of adults remained illiterate, numerous villages lacked electricity, Portugal was the least industrialized of European countries and those who found jobs in the factories received Europe's lowest wages (roughly ten dollars a week in 1960). In general, compared to earlier years, the political, economic and social order of the country was stable, the colonies yielded up profits and foreign competition was minimal. Even the Coca-Cola company was excluded from Portuguese markets.

COLONIAL WARS AND DECLINE OF THE DICTATORSHIP

The revolt in Angola spread to Guinea in 1963 and to Mozambique. Assailed on three distant fronts, the Portuguese government was forced to mobilize large-scale forces and extend the length of service. As expenses rose to support the war, consuming much of the budget and investments, the economy slowed. University students and intellectuals protested against military service in far-off dangerous places and because their conscription interrupted their education and delayed their careers, sometimes for years. The prolonged struggle in Africa wearied the army, and many officers realized that they were engaged in a futile war and that political negotiations were inevitable. However, pro-Salazarists believed resoluteness and inflexibility toward the colonies would triumph.

During the last decade of the dictatorship more than 1 million people, or nearly one-tenth of the population, emigrated. Prompted by low wages in Portugal and lack of jobs or to escape military service, most went to France or Germany to seek employment. Remittances from abroad brought in needed foreign currency and helped finance the country's high trade deficit. The regime did not object to this large emigration, preferring to have foreign currency to help finance the African wars than to have long unemployment lines in the towns at home.

Many of the restrictions inhibiting the inflow of foreign capital into Portugal were lifted in the 1960s, and links were forged between the Portuguese wealthy families who owned most of the industry and foreign companies bringing in welcome capital and keeping the economy buoyant. Wages rose somewhat between 1963 and 1970, and prices were kept down. In the country, oxen, still in common usage in 1960, were mostly replaced by tractors by 1970. With much of the land in the hands of the wealthy, however, modernization in agriculture did not greatly benefit the peasant. The growth of the tourist trade in the decade of the 1960s, especially in the Algarve, yielded a new source of seasonable employment and income.

Salazar's tight fiscal policy allowed for some public works programs; a few neglected roads were modernized, bridges were built, and many museums, libraries, hospitals and post offices were removed from disused churches and given new buildings. Sports grounds and airports were laid out. Dams and power stations were constructed, and harbor installations were refurbished. Low wages allowed industry to grow, and production rose steadily. Urbanization increased, and Portugal ceased to be an essentially rural country as the urban middle class expanded.

When Salazar suffered a stroke on 15 September 1968, the council of state met a few days later and nominated Marcelo Caetano, an old associate of Salazar's, as the new prime minister. More liberal than Salazar, he recognized the need for agricultural reforms, the problems and impatience of students, and the need for greater freedom of expression. He released a number of political prisoners and allowed the socialist Mário Soares, exiled to São Tomé in 1968, back into the country. Hoping for a change in the image of PIDE, he renamed it Direcção Geral de Segurança (DGS).

Caetano, like Salazar, continued to support the colonial war effort in Africa. As the new prime minister remarked: "Portugal was a small nation without Africa; with it, Portugal was a big power," but the burden of the wars continued to bring unrest to the nation. With a liberalization of oppressive decrees various organizations began to show increased antiregime activity. The Salazarist syndicates were undermined by the elections of antigovernment majorities to the executive councils, and factory committees began to appear, threatening the cohesion of the national union system. In October 1970 these committees formed themselves into an organization called Intersindical. Caetano allowed Intersindical to operate legally to avoid the inevitable backlash that would follow if it were banned. The organization pushed for various union freedoms such as the right to strike and ran ads to make its point.

Squabbles between Intersindical and the Caetano government became increasingly bitter until, having had enough, Caetano issued a decree banning the labor organization and forcing it back underground. Illegal strikes continued, however, and the more the riot police tried to suppress them and the more leaders who were arrested by DGS, the bigger and more widespread they became. In the past the government had employed the riot police to put down industrial action, the secret police to arrest the leaders and the media censors to make sure the public did not learn about them. This policy had worked when strikes were isolated and minor. But things had changed by the early 1970s as clandestine socialist, communist and trade union strength grew. Strike leaders asked for improved conditions in the workplace and a doubling of wages. During 1973 over forty strikes took place, mainly in textiles and engineering and against foreign subsidiaries. A few foreign companies met the demands of the workers by doubling their wages, which had the effect of increasing militant action in other sectors since Portuguese businesses did not follow suit.

Inflation climbed to about 30 percent, the highest in Europe, unemployment was on an upward curve and the balance of trade was the worst in many years. Even the civil servants who had never voiced strong opposition to the government complained about the slow march of progress and their paltry wages. They demanded a substantial pay increase, and the Ministry of Finance advised the government to pay it and not engage in a struggle they might not win. It was clear to most employees that the state had lost some of its authoritarian clout and that the time was ripe to challenge it.

The African wars continued to deplete the country of resources, and companies began to lose money on their African interests as rebel forces made headway. France and Germany tightened up on their immigration controls as the boom years began to dissipate in the early 1970s. Remittances from abroad slowed down, while companies, intentionally overstaffed during Salazar's time to give better employment numbers, now began layoffs to become more efficient, resulting in more unemployment. The world energy crisis came to Portugal, causing enormous inflationary increases. Workers became worse off and more determined for industrial action. Prime Minister Caetano was besieged on every front—economic, political and social. Industrial conglomerates were turning against the colonial wars, student unrest revolved around military obligations and lack of scholarships and students generally sided with the workers. Besides the public sector, Caetano was only too aware of the unrest in the army, whose sympathy he required to maintain the power that had been in effect for forty-eight years.

THE ARMY

Until the 1960s the army had not seen battle since World War I, and as a peacetime army it had become a stratified, class-oriented institution. The officer hierarchy was closely linked to professional and financial organizations. Generals sat on the boards of large companies, and middle-ranking officers boosted their pay in a number of different consultancy jobs such as engineering, which they learned in the service. Within the rank and file pay was poor, and morale was low. With the beginning of three colonial wars, admissions to the military academies fell by 50 percent; by 1973 they had fallen to a quarter of what they had been in 1958. Aristocratic and upper-class families preferred to send their sons to university or professional schools rather than to the once-prestigious military institutions.

The regular officers corps was desperately short of manpower in the lower and middle ranks. To solve this problem the government decided to make up the shortfall by recruiting university graduates who had done their military service. They could enter the service and attend a one-year course at the military academy, and their seniority would date from their initial conscription. This angered those who had spent four years at the academy and had slowly worked their way up to the rank of captain or major. The new officers could soon outrank them. This source of discontent was one of several as guerrilla warfare in Africa intensified. Young officers who, along with their men, fought in the swamps and jungles of Africa against guerrilla insurgents gradually became disenchanted with the dictatorial regime and its intransigence in promoting the wars in which the men might fight for two years in Angola, return to Portugal and then be immediately sent to Mozambique for a another stretch of service. Junior military officers were also unhappy with the political aspects of the army whereby a man might be promoted because of his political affiliations regardless of his competence. They were not alone in their disillusionment with the dictatorship. Under the Caetano government the country, protected for years, was opened up still further to foreign investment, and social benefits were extended to rural communities and to domestics. However, the mechanism for the reestablishment of political parties that the more liberal segments of society hoped for was not forthcoming. Also, by April 1974, in anticipation of May Day, the traditional worker's day, industrial militancy was preparing to show its strength.

9

Revolution and Democracy

Colonial policy took two opposed approaches. General Arriaga, a Salazarist officer who had made his name in the jungles and bushland of Mozambique, was convinced that the colonial wars could be won in a short period of time with determination and highly mobile offensive units combined with air support. His views mirrored those of his friend the American general Westmoreland on Vietnam.

In Guinea, on the other hand, the strategy under the leadership of General António de Spínola was of a different nature. Marcelo Caetano heard Spínola's report reiterating that the war in Guinea was already lost and that the only way to avoid another humiliating defeat as in Goa was to negotiate with the rebels. To maintain the colonies a political solution had to be found. Spínola advocated a radical change from all-out war to a campaign to "win the hearts and minds" of the colonial peoples. Caetano did not approve of this approach but went along with it, not with a view to independence of the territory but to prevent it. To the liberation movement in Guinea with the acronym PAIGC, Spínola offered a partnership in governing the country.

He employed his troops there in community service, encouraged local businessmen to construct schools and hospitals and made sure his plans and projects were heard back in Lisbon, where they received an enormous amount of press coverage. He won great respect in Guinea and returned to Portugal in 1972 to a hero's welcome. PAIGC, on the other hand, was not impressed.

On 24 September 1973 PAIGC declared Guinea-Bissau an independent nation, and within a few weeks sixty countries had recognized this declaration, even though about one-third of the country and its major cities were occupied by the Portuguese army. Meanwhile, the struggle continued, growing in ferocity in Angola and Mozambique, and by the early years of the 1970s guerrillas had wrested considerable territory from Portuguese control. With the introduction of SAM-7 ground-to-air missiles by the rebels, the Portuguese began to lose heavily in the air and, with diminishing air cover, on the ground.

REVOLT OF THE JUNIOR OFFICERS

On Sunday, 9 September 1973 a group of 140 junior officers gathered at a farmhouse about thirty kilometers from Évora for what could be considered under the current law an illegal assembly. The farmhouse was owned by a cousin of Captain Diniz Almeida. They called themselves the Armed Forces Movement (MFA).

The purpose of the clandestine meeting was to discuss unfair practices of promotions, and the men who attended ranged in their political views from Marxists to Conservatives, but all were agreed on the problems in the military.

A document of protest was drawn up and delivered to Marcello Caetano's office. The army chief of staff, General Costa Gomes, was in agreement with the young officers, but in this he had little support from other senior officers and none from Caetano. On 6 October a second meeting of MFA took place in a private house near Lisbon, this time also attended by delegates from the navy and air force. The discussion ended with a decision to submit personal resignations to Silva Cunha, the minister of defense, if the government refused to repeal the decree of unfair promotions. The MFA was run by a coordinating committee of eight officers, including a full colonel, Vasco Gonçalves, who had joined the protests. From a political point of view, left-wing officers were in the majority on the committee.

Another unofficial topic of conversation among MFA members was the wars being waged in Africa and the hardships encountered by many officers and their families, and most of them also bitterly remembered that the loss of Goa was blamed on the army, and the government would presumably blame them again for the inevitable loss of the colonies in Africa. Many of the left-wing officers were in favor of granting independence immediately.

Lieutenant Colonel Ataide Banazol, who until then had played no role in the MFA, suddenly turned up at a further meeting in São Pedro do Estoril, interrupted the discussions on resignations and announced his dissatisfaction with the paper protests against the government. He suggested action—a coup d'etat. He himself would occupy the military garrison at Évora with his battalion and declare a military junta. As his bold proposal was too much to absorb on the spot, it was placed on the agenda for the next meeting, which took place 10 December 1973 at Obidos, where eighty delegates arrived for the chestnut-eating session. On each occasion a special event had been planned to give the meetings the appearance of a defined, nonpolitical character to circumvent the laws on illegal assembly. Of the various options discussed, including a coup, the conservative point of view to protest entirely within the law was duly adopted. This did not satisfy many of the young officers, who proceeded to determine who among the top brass was sympathetic to a government takeover. Costa Gomes was sympathetic, but what of Spínola, his deputy, or Arriaga? General Arriaga had returned from Mozambique still convinced that his hard-line policies were best, but he had always considered the prime minister, Caetano, too soft. A coup appealed to him. His plan was to seize power while Caetano was away at meetings in Madrid and at the same time dispose of Costa Gomes and Spínola, whose colonial views he deplored. But promotion of the colonial wars was not what the officers were seeking. Vasco Lourenço, an MFA officer, warned Costa Gomes and Spínola of Arriaga's plans, and the plot was foiled.

Aware that something was in the air, the government reacted by transferring officers around the country, punishing some for spurious and trifling reasons with a few days under house arrest. Then, through a book written by General Spínola, published in Portugal, in which he destroyed the Salazarian myth that the colonial wars were necessary to save Western civilization, he became a popular hero of the young captains and majors of MFA. The ruling establishment considered his views verging on treason.

A house in the fishing village of Cascais, thirty kilometers west of Lisbon, was chosen as the location for the next meeting of MFA on 5 March 1974. Of the 176 officers present most now agreed that the current regime must be toppled, and they argued into the night about what kind of regime should replace it. Agreement was reached on one main point: the revolt must involve an alliance with the people. Contacts with communists, socialists and other labor organizations had been nonexistent. Infiltrated by the secret police, liaison with such groups would have been dangerous to MFA's own security. Now informal steps were taken to advise civilian groups that they could expect a change toward a democratic government, although its political orientation was still under debate.

Caetano made the first move. On 8 March some of the leaders were given notice that they were being posted overseas. Among them was Melo Antunes, a committed Marxist who had joined MFA late but was one of their political theoreticians. Two other members then were arrested and imprisoned. Next, the prime minister convoked his generals and asked them to endorse the government's colonial policy. Costa Gomes, Spínola and Admiral Tierno Bagulho refused to attend. The two generals were sacked, and the officer corps both within and outside MFA seethed with anger at the dismissal of the two most senior men in the army. The hard-line conservative commander from Angola, General Luz Cunha, replaced Costa Gomes, which further heightened the tension. On 16 March the Fifth Infantry Battalion headquartered at Caldas da Rainha, about fifty miles north of Lisbon, rose in revolt. Two hundred men led by a major locked up the commander and his staff after rousing them from bed at three in the morning and then set off for the capital in ten armored vehicles. They intended to win over to their cause the Seventh Cavalry, which was stationed in Lisbon, and seize the city. Instead, they were met and stopped by the Seventh, still loyal to the government and supported by the paramilitary Republican Guards at Vila Franca de Xira, on the road ten miles north of the city. In a bloodless encounter the Fifth Battalion returned to its barracks. The plan had gone very wrong. Other groups that were supposed to join the insurrection failed in their support and did not leave their barracks. The men from Caldas were soon arrested by the secret police, adding further fuel to the conflagration devouring the military, especially when it was reported that the police had broken into the house of one of them at five in the morning and had beaten up his wife and children.

The nineteen-man coordinating committee of MFA met again in Oeiras, determined to try once more to overthrow the government. Melo Antunes finished the draft of the new political program drawn up for the government-to-be and immediately departed for his new posting in the Azores. The preamble stated the reasons for the coming coup, which included the inability of the ruling government to determine a policy that would bring peace after thirteen years of fighting in Africa. The document went on to reiterate the commitments of the new regime guaranteeing all the traditional liberties and freedoms and its intention to seek peace in Africa, recognizing the rights of the Africans to self-determination. It also promised free elections, after which the military junta would be dissolved.

The panicky Caetano regime meanwhile was losing its grip, arresting people on false charges and claiming they were only precautions against the coming traditional May Day unrest. The prime minister himself vacillated between a severe clampdown on dissidents, leniency and a studied attempt to ignore the overheated cauldron of the military.

COUP OF 25 APRIL 1974

After the Caldas uprising the officers of MFA knew that the secret police, DGS, would double its surveillance of the army and that they must act quickly to carry out the coup before plans were revealed to the government. Otelo Carvalho coordinated the military operation, while others worked on the political agenda to present to the people afterward. Carvalho divided the country into three regions, north, south, and central, and discreetly sounded out the army units stationed in each as to their loyalty to the regime. He chose about a dozen to participate directly in the insurrection. The primary target was Lisbon, for it was the key to the entire enterprise. The city had to be sealed off, police and military units neutralized and the prime minister arrested. Surprise was essential to secure the roads and bridges and catch the government off-balance. Airports had to be blocked to prevent the escape of key personnel who might later rally forces against them.

Having established the date and time of 3:00 A.M. on 25 April, the prearranged signal to begin the insurrection was sent out over the radio in the form of a popular song some hours before giving units throughout the country time to prepare and begin to move. The engineering building at Pontinha, outside Lisbon, was chosen as the headquarters for the operation. To the cavalry school at Santarém was assigned the essential role of advancing on Lisbon at the appointed time with 240 men in American M47 Patton tanks, scout cars and armored personnel carriers. Their firepower was essential.

In the dark hours of the morning, military units began to move. Under the command of twenty-nine-year-old Captain Salgueiro Maia, government ministries in the Praça do Comércio and other key points in the city were occupied. The bridges over the Tejo were taken and held, sealing off the city from any help from the south. A unit from the officers' training school at Mafra captured and closed the international airport on the north side of the city. The public woke up to the rumble of tanks and armored cars in the streets and a fait accompli as more units moved into the capital, although the situation was still tense. Loyal forces were still in the area, and a naval ship patrolled the harbor, its guns directed toward the city. The officers on board, disobeying the captain's orders, refused to fire on the rebel soldiers, however. Tanks of the loyalist forces finally appeared, and a standoff ensued in the streets of the city. In spite of the order to fire given by pro-government Brigadier Reis in charge of the unit, no shots were exchanged. The soldiers would not fire on each other. After some negotiations the brigadier surrendered to Captain Maia.

By noon the first phase of the operation was over, and Maia was ordered to move on to phase two, the DGS headquarters, the Portuguese Legion, and the national guard—the guardians of the old order despised by the army. When it was learned that the prime minister was at the Carmo barracks of the national guard, Maia divided his forces and headed for Carmo on the top of the hill in central Lisbon. Crowds of civilians helped push his lumbering vehicles up the hill over the slippery cobblestones. The national guard units held their fire, being informed by Maia, a bluff, that the area was surrounded. After a tense delay the young captain finally entered the building to talk to Caetano. The prime minister agreed to surrender his power to General Spínola when the latter made an appearance. Eventually, Spínola turned up at Carmo and accepted the surrender of the prime minister and the transfer of power to himself. The coup was complete. Spínola was the new provisional head of Portugal. Caetano and President Américo Tomás, the latter arrested later in the day at home, were flown away the following morning to temporary exile in Madeira.

At Oporto, in the early hours, two MFA officers turned up at the garrison, put a pistol to the head of the commandant and ordered his surrender. There was a flurry of other activity on 25 April besides military operations. Political opposition parties were also ready and waiting, although they had not known the precise military plans. The Communist Party had kept their intentions to themselves in the event of a coup, but when it happened, they urged their members onto the streets to back the armed forces. The communist newspaper emerged from its clandestine presses and began publishing in the open almost immediately. Students from the university and colleges came forth in great numbers to support the military, most having been radicalized by the hated and ceaseless activity of the secret police among their ranks.

Sporadic military activity continued into the night in some parts of the country, as in Évora, where the garrison held out against the rebels for many hours before surrendering. In Lisbon the political police fired on crowds from their headquarters, killing five people and wounding many more. This constituted the only major bloodshed of the entire coup.

During the day, as soon as the success of the uprising was apparent, the MFA met at Pontinha barracks, and Spínola announced the formation of a board of National Salvation comprising himself and six other high-ranking officers from the army, navy and air force. Spínola was chosen as interim president of the republic. To the annoyance of many members of MFA he was not willing to accept independence of the African colonies and agreed only to military disengagement. The general went on television at 1:20 A.M., 26 April to read the MFA program.

AFTERMATH OF THE COUP

The new military junta eventually took up residence in the Belém Palace. Unrest in industry and business as a result of the coup had to be addressed. The civilian police had to be reorganized, the borders protected and airports reopened. Many top brass, generals and admirals who had been loyal to the dictatorship were retired. Similar purges went on in the trade unions. Political prisoners were released, including the communist José Magro, who had been inside for twenty years; censorship was mostly abolished, but the names of people arrested were forbidden to appear in print; and Labor Day was made a national holiday. Import controls were introduced on many items, other emergency measures controlled the flight of money out of the country and limits were set on the amount of money that could be withdrawn from personal bank accounts.

The rejoicing that took place on 1 May was quickly followed by rampant industrial agitation. More pay and better conditions were demanded, and Salazar managers were purged. Companies conceded extravagant demands that they would not even have discussed a few weeks earlier. In order not to be labeled fascists by the new government, they doubled salaries, although the junta was displeased with these settlements, as they generated more unrest in the labor unions, where employers were not so generous. On 6 May the workers at the Lisnave shipyard across the estuary from Lisbon staged one of the largest strikes ever, demanding the exorbitant higher wages paid elsewhere and proclaiming their allegiance to the Communist Party. Other strikes soon followed in all the major industries (textiles, chemicals, electronics, banking) and even among the Lisbon bus workers. Manifesting support for the MFA, prostitutes demanded legality and a union and offered a 50 percent discount to soldiers below the rank of lieutenant. Administration was in chaos, food in short supply and transportation and services erratic at best.

Spínola proved inept as a politician and began to alienate supporters. His style was not to convince but to impose his views. The people in the streets knew little of the bitter wrangling behind the scenes, however, and exulted in their new freedoms. Carnations became the symbol of the revolution and were seen everywhere, including in the barrels of the soldiers' rifles.

In schools and colleges students drew up lists of teachers suspected of fascist sympathies, organized committees to oversee exams and opted to discontinue school attendance lists, and the teachers were allowed no more rights than the pupils. With no direction from Lisbon, student committees ran the schools and the universities. The public school system throughout the country collapsed. Many students returned home to denounce their parents as fascists.

Squatters from shantytowns on the outskirts of Lisbon took over luxury flats that had not yet been occupied, beginning a more general seizure of empty buildings by unauthorized people. The government was quick to assure foreigners, especially those with property in the Algarve, that they would be protected. The international airport also became a focus of attention as exiles poured back into the country to take advantage of the amnesty given draft dodgers by the new government on condition they reported for duty within a fortnight of their return, while soldiers at the airport bound for Africa became the center of demonstrations against what many now considered a hopeless war. Other returnees were political exiles who had fled the dictatorship. One of the first to return (by train) was Mário Soares, leader of the Socialist Party, who had been lecturing in Paris since 1970. Another was the communist leader Alvaro Cunhal, who had been living in Prague. He was met by the conservative member of the junta, Galvão de Melo, and asked if he would like to make a television speech that night. Such freedom he could scarcely believe! Like Soares he was taken immediately to see Spínola.

MFA AND SPÍNOLA

The officers of the MFA coordinating committee who had engineered the coup were being left behind in the power game. Suspicious of Spínola's intentions, they drew closer to the civilian politicians. The first major gathering of the emerging civilian political party leaders occurred on 4 May in the presidential palace at Belém, where they met the entire MFA coordinating committee.

Rightist politicians tainted by the old regime found it difficult to build up strength. Their chief blessing lay in the north of the country, where the Catholic Church lent its support. The parties of the Left supplied most of the stimulus for the first meeting. The socialists at this stage lacked a coherent national organization and were well behind their rivals, the communists, in appeal to working-class voters. The communists were the best-organized party in the country through intersindical, the umbrella organization overseeing all union activity. Spínola could not afford to form a government without their inclusion and invited them to participate. Cunhal's acceptance was a radical break with previous communist policy as, since the 1920s, the party had affirmed that it would never share power in a coalition government with bourgeois politicians. Now it would do just that, certain that independent proletarian power would eventually come.

On 15 May 1974 General Spínola became president of the Portuguese Republic. The ceremony performed by General Costa Gomes took place in the palace of Queluz about six miles west of Lisbon. His position was weak; selected by the junta, he exercised power only by its consent. No provisions had been made for future elections. Spínola now chose sixty-nine-year-old Adelino Palma Carlos, a friend and professor at the Faculty of Law, for the post of prime minister and asked him to form a provisional government. It included fourteen ministers but only one military man, who held the portfolio of defense. None of the men chosen had much experience, and some had spent years in exile or prison. They were briefed by their departments, by the civil servants who remained after the purge, and met for the first time, with the prime minister presiding. The agenda dealt with briefing the new colonial secretary on negotiating with African guerrillas, appointing new colonial governors, nationalizing some of the banks, taking measures to deal with strikes, the educational system and the purging of local governments.

When the 35,000 postal workers again struck on 17 June, demanding 6,000 escudos a month, they rejected the government offer of 4,300. They ignored the appeal of the Communist Party to go back to work, and the government threatened to call in the army to deliver the mail. It was willing to take the gamble that the soldiers would act as strikebreakers and not join the strikers. The postal workers capitulated and called off the industrial action. The provisional government then tried to achieve peace in the industrial sector by bringing into the government the old leaders who had for so long worked underground or had been exiled or imprisoned. Then it offered a package of somewhat radical changes in economic policies, and finally it relied on the army to carry out its will. In just two months it had moved from forbearance to authoritarianism.

Adelino Palma Carlos was unable to develop a coherent policy and resigned on 10 July after less than two months in office, and Spínola chose the minister of defense, Mário Firmino Miguel, for the post of prime minister. His choice was rejected by the MFA, and he was forced to select Colonel Vasco Gonçalves, an old member of the Communist Party and still sympathetic to its orientation. The MFA still controlled the power behind the scenes, but distrusting Spínola, whose imperious and paternalistic style of leadership was too reminiscent of the Salazar state, and to give itself more leeway in controlling events, the MFA organized a special military strike force, COPCON (or military units of Operational Command for the Continent—meaning mainland Portugal). This 5,000-man, handpicked elite force was placed under the command of Otelo de Carvalho, now a brigadier. Spínola found he had little power over MFA or his own government.

Mário Soares, his foreign minister, had begun negotiations with liberation movements of the African colonies on his own initiative. He had first made contact with PAIGC in Guinea and established official independence from Portugal for the colony on 10 September. He had also opened negotiations with FRELIMO. The date for independence of Mozambique was set for June 1975, but a few hours after signing the accord, nearly 200,000 white settlers broke out in revolt. A black counterrevolt left many dead and wounded. Spínola was forced to recognize the right of the people of Guinea-Bissau, Mozambique and Angola to self-determination, even though he and other conservatives considered this a mistake.

The president tried to assert authority by appealing to the people of Portugal, the Silent Majority (borrowing a phrase from American politics). He hoped a popular mandate would give him the support he needed to reorganize the government, disband the MFA and proceed at a slower pace toward decolonization. The appropriation of large estates in the Alentejo by anarchists and communists and the resultant reaction in the north where villagers, exhorted by the church, drove radicals and communists from the villages with shotguns and pitchforks, played into Spínola's hands. He hoped to rally the people to his side by a massive demonstration in Lisbon and set the date for 28 September 1974.

Lisbon was tense, with violence expected. Some of those who came to demonstrate would be armed. The Praça do Imperio in front of Belém Place, the site of the demonstration, was lined with police and soldiers to maintain order between left and right political factions. COPCON guarded the radio and television stations. Air force helicopters stood by. Supporters converged on Lisbon from all parts of the country, and their opponents organized barricades to block their way. The Council of Ministers had gathered at São Bonito palace the day before in a bitter meeting. Vasco Gonçalves, supported by MFA, had wanted Spínola to call off the dangerous demonstration or at least allow COPCON to search arrivals in the city for weapons, but the president, with few allies in the group, refused.

Radio stations appealed to left-wing supporters to man the barricades. Spínola had the COPCON guards at the stations replaced with Republican Guards, whom he felt he could trust. Then he ordered the stations to cease transmission and all newspapers closed. Only one station remained on the air under the direct command of Spínola's loyal information minister, broadcasting demands for the barricades to be removed and the demonstration to proceed in an orderly fashion. Communication between Belém Palace and the military units in the field were becoming chaotic. Telephone lines were clogged. Eventually, COPCON troops moved in and took over the barricades and began turning back all cars, buses and trucks trying to enter the city.

Radicals and their leftist supporters in Lisbon blocked the roads into the city from the north. The prime minister, Vasco Gonçalves and Carvalho, commander of COPCON, were ordered to appear at the presidential palace at Belém, where they were placed under house arrest. Spínola then directed Carvalho to issue orders to COPCON to remove the barricades. Carvalho gave the orders by telephone, but suspecting that they were given under duress, the officer who received them did not carry them out. Instead, COPCON announced that it would march on the presidential palace if Carvalho were not freed. Spínola conceded defeat and called off the demonstration.

The gamble had failed. Spínola resigned on 30 September 1974, and General Costa Gomes, chief of the General Staff, was announced as his successor. Of leftist persuasion, he undertook to carry out the program of the MFA. Vasco Gonçalves was retained as prime minister, and the next provisional government was installed. Unlike his predecessor, Costa Gomes was committed to rapid decolonization.

Over the next few months agreements were signed with all the colonial territories for independence except Angola, which was finally negotiated for 11 November 1975, with the colony to be ruled until then by Portugal and the three rival independence movements. About 600,000 embittered and often destitute Portuguese returned home from Africa.

Meanwhile, talk among the MFA and the government was now about socialization. Colonel Varela Gomes, a Marxist, was given the task of communicating to the people the socialist ideas of MFA, especially to the communities of the north, where the peasants were not well endowed with revolutionary zeal and ideals. The prime minister aligned government policies with those of the Communist Party and supported the communist monopoly over the labor unions, opposed by the moderates and socialists. Rural workers in the south continued to occupy more estate land; in Oporto and Lisbon squatters continued to take over unoccupied houses; and neighborhood committees sprang up, usurping the authority of city and town councils.

Spínola made another bid for power on 11 March 1975, but the poorly planned coup, known to MFA and COPCON in advance, failed miserably, and the general fled the country by helicopter to Spain. Vasco Gonçalves and the radicals purged Spínola's followers from office, and the Left reasserted itself. On 14 March the Board of National Salvation was abolished, and governing power was vested in a new organ, the Council of the Revolution, or CR. This organization included the president, prime minister, the heads of the three branches of the armed forces and other officers appointed by MFA. The CR was made responsible to a newly organized Assembly of the Armed Forces, whose 240 members were elected from the ranks of the three services.

Among the first actions to be undertaken by the CR were the nationalization of certain heavy industries, private banks and insurance companies and the expropriation and redistribution of large agricultural holdings. Then another provisional government was proclaimed, Gonçalves remaining as prime minister, with nearly half of his twenty-one ministers from the military and the remainder from the Left. The Communist Party encouraged employees of large industries such as the United Fiber Company to take them over. In the Alentejo farmworkers who appropriated the large estates were aided by the communists to turn them into collective farms.

The MFA then agreed to elections of a Constituent Assembly on the condition that the assembly would produce a constitution institutionalizing the MFA and make it the prominent guarantor of the transition to socialism.

ELECTIONS 1975

On 25 April 1975, the anniversary of the overthrow of the Caetano regime, a general election was held for the Constituent Assembly. Twelve parties contested the seats. The Socialist Party (PS) won the lion's share, 37.9 percent of the votes, winning 116 of the then-250 seats. Turnout was high, 91.7 percent of the eligible voters going to the polls. The communists (PCP) pulled in only 12.5 percent, beaten by the Social Democrat Party (PSD), which polled 26.4 percent. The others were divided up among marginal groups.

The communists and MFA as well as others of the extreme Left claimed that the election results signified nothing. A mere election was not going to stand in the way of the revolution. The communists refused to align with the other parties and reaffirmed their support for their ally MFA. Meanwhile the PS, the PSD and the Christian Democratic Party of the center (CDS), which had won 7.7 percent of the vote, withdrew from the government and announced that they were launching a campaign against encroaching communism in Portugal. On 13 July Catholics marched in Aveiro against the MFA, and farmers burned the communist headquarters in Rio Maior. By the end of the "Hot Summer" of 1975, the offices of a large number of leftist parties in the north were burned. Conservative farmers in the archipelagoes of Madeira and the Azores also sacked and destroyed Communist Party headquarters. Some of these people were returnees from Africa who felt they had been sold out by the Left; others were ex-members of PIDE and the Portuguese Legion. Arms were smuggled into the country from Spain. Portugal was on the verge of civil war.

THE FLEDGLING DEMOCRACY

A moderate group in the MFA, including Major Melo Antunes, published a paper on 7 August 1975 calling for a nonaligned socialism in

Portugal and asking for an end to disturbances and respect for the election results of 25 April 1975. The group criticized the government as incompetent to rule and made plans to resist any attempts by the communists or the Left to exploit the unstable conditions and take power. On 29 August Vasco Gonçalves resigned under fire and was replaced by Admiral José Baptista Pinheiro de Azevedo, who unlike Gonçalves, was not firmly attached to the communists.

Under the Azevedo government relative stability was restored, allowing the Constituent Assembly to finish its work on the new constitution, which was duly drawn up and approved, taking effect in early April 1976. It received the endorsement of all parties except the CDS, which found it too socialistic. It promulgated the basic rights and freedoms of the citizen and had as its political objective the transition toward socialism through the democratic exercise of power by the working class. It recognized the role of MFA in this transition and advocated nationalization of the means of production, declaring that such programs carried out after 25 April 1974 were irreversible. In addition, Portuguese subjects were guaranteed rights to employment, health care, housing and a clean environment. The document enshrined the right to create trade unions, agrarian reform and regional development. Devolution was granted to the Azores, Madeira and the only remaining overseas colony of Macão. It envisaged a central role for political parties, universal suffrage and separation of powers.

The popularly elected president selected the prime minister after consultation with the parties represented in the duly elected single-chambered Assembly, and the prime minister selected his Council of Ministers or cabinet to head the various ministries. The cabinet was required to submit to the Assembly its program for governing. If it was rejected, a new cabinet had to be formed. If no agreement was reached on its makeup, the president could dissolve the Assembly and call for new elections.

The function of the military was established in the CR, which advised the president and watched over government to ensure its faithfulness to the principles of the revolution. With the task of writing the constitution completed, the way was open for general elections.

RELATIONS WITH THE UNITED STATES

When Portugal joined NATO, it won the admiration of Dean Acheson and President Eisenhower, who met Salazar at Queluz. The United States changed its policy toward Portugal during the administration of President Kennedy, who, more sympathetic to the demands for liberation movements, instructed the UN ambassador, Adlai Stevenson, to remind Portugal of its obligations under the UN Charter, voting against Portugal's stance to retain its colonies in Africa. In retaliation, Salazar hinted that the treaty for the Lajes air base facility in the Azores under American jurisdiction might not be renewed. The Kennedy administration then began to abstain from, or veto, major UN resolutions condemning Portuguese colonialism.

The Americans had reacted to the 25 April 1974 coup with nervous agitation. The American ambassador, Stuart Scott, had arrived only in January but advised the State Department that the new government of Portugal should be supported during the difficult time of African disengagement and passage to democracy. The view was not accepted by the CIA or by Henry Kissinger, the American Secretary of State, who had visited Caetano in Lisbon the previous winter. Although American economic interests in Portugal were not great—some $150 million mostly belonging to the ITT company, and the air bases in the Azores were no longer crucial with the development of long-range aircraft and in-flight refueling—there were, nevertheless, fears that the CIA might try to oust the new anti-right-wing government. There were precedents, as in Chile.

Throughout the summer of 1975, the State Department debated the Portuguese issue, with Ambassador Scott failing to convince Kissinger to aid the insurgents. Kissinger, fearful of a communist takeover, instead denied Portugal access to confidential NATO briefings and files in Brussels, allowing Portuguese delegates to attend only routine NATO meetings. An embargo was placed on American military assistance. Only two months after the coup, Scott was abruptly dismissed from his job, and Kissinger sent a four-man fact-finding commission to Lisbon to review the situation. The mission vindicated Ambassador Scott's views and resulted in a reversal of American policy.

When Spínola, along with Sá Carneiro and the conservative air force member of the junta, Diogo Neto, flew to the island of Terceira to meet Nixon, the president was convinced that Spínola was no dangerous left-wing revolutionary. Portugal had no desire to leave NATO or the Western Alliance. After a visit to Washington by President Costa Gomes in October, telling both President Ford and Kissinger the same thing, on 13 December 1975 the U.S. government suddenly changed its position of hostility and announced $20 million in government-backed credits to Portugal. The new American ambassador, Frank Carlucci, spent some time in his Senate confirmation hearing denying allegations that there had been CIA involvement in Portugal. By this time, however, the Portuguese army had complete access to the DGS files showing extensive contact of the Portuguese secret police with the CIA.

In early 1988 Portugal announced that it would review the terms of the agreement permitting the continued use of the American air base at Lajes in return for economic and military aid. During a visit to Washington that year, the prime minister expressed his disappointment at the decline in the level of U.S. aid since 1983, when the last agreement was signed, but also made clear that he did not intend to reduce the facilities at Lajes. In 1989 the United States agreed to increase its level of compensation for use of the base. In 1990 Cavaco Silva reiterated his desire to negotiate a new treaty, and discussions began on the renewal of the treaty in June 1995, the two countries signing a five-year accord in which the United States undertook to supply Portugal with weapons and military equipment worth $173 million.

ELECTIONS 1976

On 25 April 1976 elections for the Assembly resulted in the Socialist Party's winning 34.9 percent of the vote, which translated into 107 seats out of the then 262. The Communist Party picked up 40 seats.

A further election was held on 27 June, for the presidency of the republic. General Ramalho Eanes, the army chief of staff, a nonparty candidate, became president, supported by the PS, the CDS and the Peoples Democratic Party (PPD). He replaced Costa Gomes, winning 61.5 percent of the vote.

President Eanes called upon the socialist Mário Soares to form the first freely elected government in nearly fifty years. Internally, the Socialist Party was weakened by splinter groups that disagreed with some of Soares' policies and by the communists, who accused the government of not being in tune with the spirit of the revolution. In the end, however, dire economic difficulties faced by the socialists brought down the government.

ECONOMIC REPERCUSSIONS OF THE REVOLUTION

The gap that had widened in the past 150 years between the economy of Portugal and that of the industrialized countries began to narrow in the 1960s. From then until 1973 the economy grew the fastest yet in the history of the nation as the country opened up to external enterprises. Nevertheless, along with Greece and Turkey, Portugal remained one of the poorest nations in Europe.

The economic ramifications of the 1974 revolution were immediate, and from 1974 to 1985 many problems arose. The growth that the country had been experiencing since the 1960s was stopped short by the loss of markets in the newly independent African colonies, while nationalization of certain enterprises and labor turmoil frightened off investment. Some wealthy industrialists, along with their money, left the country. The sudden worldwide energy crises—the first in 1973 to 1974—brought on a sharp increase in the prices of petroleum products, high inflation and recession, loss of remittances from abroad as jobs dried up and a downturn in tourism. This, coupled with newly instituted welfare policies, caused the government to experience a severe budget deficit. Decolonization led to returnees from Mozambique and Angola swelling the labor market and causing a further burden on the treasury when they were granted cash subsidies and accommodations.

The continuing drift from the farm to the city became more pronounced at this time. The primary economic sector of agriculture was still declining as peasants moved into the towns to participate in the commercial and service sectors of the economy, but as employment became scarce, they, too, added a further burden to public expenditure. Unemployment was running at 25 percent of the workforce, and balance of payments remained in deficit. To forestall bankruptcy, Soares was forced to negotiate a loan from the International Monetary Fund. The IMF terms were harsh and included devaluation of the escudo by 25 percent, public spending cut by 20 percent and taxes raised by 38 percent. Other parties were unhappy with this arrangement, and the coalition government that Soares had adroitly arranged fell apart. In December 1977 the government fell. A second socialist government fared no better, and in August 1978 Eanes dismissed Soares as prime minister. President Eanes then with limited success organized several nonparty governments of technocrats, but the first was rejected immediately by the Assembly, which resented the attempt to govern without them, and the second endured only a short time. Then, while scheduling an interim election, Eanes appointed a caretaker government headed by Maria de Lourdes Pintasilgo, the first woman prime minister, who was at the time Portugal's delegate to UNESCO.

SOCIAL REPERCUSSIONS OF THE REVOLUTION

Unlike many countries Portugal had no serious interethnic or linguistic problems, no cultural conflicts and no crisis in national unity as it passed from authoritarian centralization to democratic decentralization and from a colonial-oriented state to European regionalism.

It had, however, long been a hierarchical and elitist society with institutions a century behind the times. Social structure was considered immutable, and one simply accepted one's station in life. Few opportunities existed for upward mobility. The revolution of 1974 undermined this concept, blurring the distinctions as the society became more egalitarian, pluralistic and democratic. The revolutionary leadership undercut the economic base of the elite (nobility, landowners, high-ranking military officers and heads of large enterprises) by nationalizing big businesses, expropriating landed estates in the central and southern regions and decolonizing the overseas empire. A most significant change was the growth of a stable middle class, which came to dominate the many social and political institutions.

The sedentary rural population, mostly of the lower class, began a migration to the cities and to foreign countries, primarily France, Germany and Brazil in the late 1950s in search of better jobs and pay. This accelerated in the 1960s as industry and tourism grew, requiring workers, and as the economies of European countries expanded and needed labor. At the same time many young men were being sent off to fight the colonial wars in Africa. The exodus left the rural areas bereft of young people, farms decaying, and only an aging population remained in the villages. These movements began to break up the family structure and curtail the authority of the church, where it had traditionally been the strongest.

Social conditions in the major cities since the revolution have changed drastically. Family size has diminished on average; large families have become much fewer. Women, who had much to gain from the revolution, have found equality with men in all walks of life and can lead an independent existence. More children are born out of wedlock, and often women are having children later in life, enabling women to become better educated and begin a career. Marriages outside the church are now on the increase, with some 9 percent in 1960 to 30 percent in 1994. Divorces, even if marriage took place within the church, are available. In short, the rigid and reactionary social confines of prerevolutionary days are rapidly disintegrating as Portugal closes ranks with other modern European countries.

CONSTITUTIONAL REVISION AND FURTHER POLITICAL UNREST

At the expense of the socialists, the conservative Democratic Alliance (AD), headed by Francisco Manuel de Sá Carneiro, won a clear majority in parliamentary elections held in December 1979 with 45.2 percent of the vote. Sá Carneiro took office as premier in January 1980 but was killed in a plane crash the following December. He was succeeded in January 1981 by Francisco Pinto Balsemão, another conservative, as party leader and then prime minister. On his initiative, the constitution of the republic was revised in 1982, when it was purged of leftist ideological elements, and the CR was abolished, thus completing the transfer to full civilian government. The army was sent back to the barracks.

Following divisions within the PSD and losses in local elections, Balsemão resigned. The general elections held in April resulted in the victory of the Socialist Party, led by the former prime minister Mário Soares. It won 101 seats of the Assembly's 250. Soares formed a coalition government with the PSD (AD having been dissolved), which took office in June.

Soares' government introduced an austerity program and conducted negotiations leading toward Portugal's entry into the European Community, but open disagreements between Eanes and the prime minister led to friction. In April 1984 tensions between the trade unions and the government increased following an unauthorized demonstration by unpaid employees of state industries, which resulted in hundreds of arrests. This was followed by acts of urban terrorism, for which the radical left-wing group, Forças Populares de 25 Abril (FP-25), claimed responsibility. More than forty suspects were arrested, including Otelo de Carvalho, the former revolutionary commander.

In January 1985 relations between the president and the prime minister were further strained when the president was openly critical of the government's performance. The Social Democrats, now led by the conservative economist Aníbal Cavaco Silva, withdrew party support from the coalition. In June 1985 the PS-PSD coalition dissolved following disagreements over labor and agricultural reforms, and Soares resigned as prime minister. President Eanes was obliged to call a premature general election for October in which the PSD won eighty-eight seats in the Assembly, the PS won fifty-seven seats, and the new Democratic Renewal Party (PRD), founded in early 1985 by supporters of President Eanes, won forty-five seats. Aníbal Cavaco Silva formed a minority government, which replaced Soares and the socialists, becoming the tenth administration since 1976.

On 1 January 1986, after nine years of negotiations, Portugal formally became the eleventh member state of the European Economic Community (EEC), now the European Union (EU), which opened up new opportunities, and the economy entered a phase with characteristics markedly different from those of the previous ten years.

Money poured in from the EU—some $320 million in 1986, Portugal's first year of membership, and a staggering $23.5 billion in 1996. It was spent on roads, railroads, dams, irrigation, agriculture and job training, among other things. Low-interest loans were available from the European Investment Bank.

The 1986 presidential elections were narrowly won by Mário Soares, who was installed as the first civilian head of state in some sixty years. Outgoing president Eanes took over the leadership of the PRD, which had obtained a fifth of the vote in the 1985 elections. Soares retained Cavaco Silva as prime minister, but after further wrangling over proposed legislation concerning the budget and labor laws, he was defeated in a motion of censure and resigned in April 1987. President Soares dismissed the Assembly.

Early general elections in July 1987 resulted in a victory for the Social Democrat Party, which secured 148 seats of the 250, becoming the first party since 1974 to win an absolute majority in the Assembly of the republic. The socialists took only 60 seats. The PRD suffered a major reversal, gaining only 7 seats. General Eanes announced his resignation from the presidency of the party, and Cavaco Silva returned as prime minister and proposed radical economic change. The most contentious issue was that of labor laws, especially regarding reforms that would allow employers to dismiss redundant personnel. In March 1988, 1.5 million workers, fearing for the security of their jobs, took part in a short general strike. Labor unrest continued, affecting most sectors of the economy. Nevertheless, the government's legislation was passed by the Assembly.

In October the Social Democrat Party and the opposition socialists reached agreement on constitutional revisions. The constitution of 1989, approved by a large majority, did away with the Marxist concepts of collectivization and nationalization and state controls. It opened the way for privatization of the companies nationalized in 1975 and of television, the press, telephones, the post office, health care and transportation. It opened up the free market as Cavaco Silva had wished (and part of his 1987 campaign promises).

In the election to the European Parliament in June 1989, the PSD retained most of the seats, but in municipal elections held in December the party suffered a reverse, losing Lisbon and other major cities to the PS, supported by the PCP and the Greens (the environmentalist party). Jorge Sampaio, the PS secretary-general, became mayor of Lisbon. In January 1990 there were cabinet reshuffles, ministerial misconduct and resignations, and a new ministry of environment was established.

Mário Soares won another five-year term in the presidential elections held 13 January 1991. He secured an outright victory over four other candidates by receiving over 70 percent of the vote in spite of a scandal involving the socialist governor of Macão, who was accused of taking bribes from a German firm, hoping to secure a consultancy contract for the construction of an airport there.

Legislative elections were held in October 1991, and the PSD retained its absolute majority. In February the secretary-general of the PS, Sampaio, was replaced by António Guterres. The year 1992 saw large-scale protests by university students against the entrance examination system, the resignation of the minister of education, strikes by public service workers demanding pay increases and doctors protesting the government's plan to transfer some health services to the private sector. Soares' increasing use of the presidential veto to block legislation led to increased tension between him and the prime minister, Cavaco Silva. The year 1993 also had its problems. The government was embarrassed by accusations of corruption when EU funds destined for certain projects in Portugal were missing. Shortcomings in the health service also attracted attention. The minister of health resigned, and the minister of environment was forced out when he made offensive remarks concerning high levels of aluminum found in the water of a hospital in Évora, which resulted in the death of some patients. Further, a former secretary of state for health was sent to prison for corruption in awarding hospital contracts back in 1986. Also in 1993 there were violent scenes at Lisbon airport when employees of Air Portugal (TAP), angry over the carrier's proposal to freeze wages and lay off 2,500 redundant workers, demonstrated, and the riot police were called in. Student demonstrators, too, protesting against proposals to raise university fees, clashed with police.

Amnesty International expressed concern about torture by police and prison officials.

Strike action, scandals and investigations of corruption continued in 1994, disconcerting the government. In that year the PS won the majority of seats to the European Parliament in Strasbourg. In 1995 a new code of conduct for politicians and public officials was approved by the Assembly, involving matters pertaining to the financing of political parties and declaration of personal assets. After a five-year investigation, the PS was embarrassed by the announcement that twenty-three senior officials of the socialist union (UGT), including the secretary-general and his predecessor, were to stand trial for charges of fraud involving misappropriations of the European Social Fund. It was also discovered in that year from new evidence that the plane crash that killed Sá Caneiro back in 1980 was caused by a bomb on board.

ELECTIONS 1995 AND 1996

Nevertheless, in the next general election held in October 1995, the PS, advocating social reform and greater integration into the EU, took 112 of the 230 seats in the Assembly. António Guterres was appointed prime minister. The PSD won 88 seats in the election, 15 seats were taken by the United Democratic Coalition (CDU), an electoral coalition of the Communist Party (PCP) and other minor left-wing parties, and another 15 seats were obtained by the center-right Popular Party (PP), formerly known as the CDS.

In November 1995 Jorge Sampaio, former secretary of the PS, resigned as mayor of Lisbon and declared his candidacy in the presidential elections. In the January 1996 election, Sampaio received 53.9 percent of the votes cast, while Anibal Cavaco Silva, the other candidate, secured 46.1 percent and retired from politics. Squabbles and disputes characterized much of the year, with resignation of ministers over such matters as Sunday opening hours for stores, accusations of tax evasion, scandals involving the penetration of secret service agents into "subversive" left-wing trade unions and the bugging of politicians' and officials' telephone lines.

In August 1996 the prime minister announced proposals to radically reform the country's political system, reducing the number of deputies to the legislature, ending the monopoly of major political parties on the electoral system and establishing provisions for the holding of referenda to give the populace more say in policy. Agreement between the ruling and opposition parties was also reached on constitutional reform in early

1997 and on the gradual establishment of a professional army. Bitter controversy arose from proposals to liberalize the restrictive abortion laws. Evidence came to light in 1997 that between 1939 and 1942 the Salazar government had received gold worth about 517 million Swiss francs from the Nazi government of Germany, and Portugal had thus purchased gold stolen from Belgium and Holland. The Central Bank of Portugal set up an inquiry into the matter, headed by Mário Soares.

RELATIONS WITH SPAIN

Old quarrels and fears of Spanish hegemony on the Iberian Peninsula are not forgotten. In 1985 Portugal celebrated the 600th anniversary of the Battle of Aljubarrota. After centuries of intermittent warfare, mistrust and diplomatic wrangles, however, closer economic ties in the past few decades have brought benefits. Iberian free trade policies led Portugal to increase trade with Spain that surpassed its former transactions with Great Britain. After 1985 Spanish capital investment in Portugal reached levels that were greater than Spain's dealing in all other countries. Spanish tourists, attracted by the low prices, outnumbered all other tourists, new highways and bridges linked the two countries and Spanish firms poured in capital to benefit from the lower wages—as much as 50 percent lower—than at home.

In late 1996 Portugal and Spain agreed to increase cooperation regarding problems such as drug trafficking, organized crime and illegal immigration, but a year later relations were strained when the Portuguese released a Basque terrorist suspect on insufficient grounds of guilt instead of extraditing him to Spain as the Spanish requested. In September 1997 agreement was reached between the two countries on the allocation of responsibilities under NATO, and in October at a summit meeting between the Portuguese and Spanish prime ministers in Madrid, agreement was reached on compensation to be paid to Spaniards who had property confiscated during the 1974 revolution.

Since signing the Schengen Accord, the formal frontiers between Portugal and its only neighbor have disappeared. There are no longer tedious customs declarations or passport controls.

EXPO '98

On 21 May Expo '98 opened in Lisbon with pavilions and exhibits from 155 countries and international organizations taking part in the four-month, $3.4 billion extravaganza. This was the 500th anniversary of

Vasco da Gama's epic voyage to India, and it raised Portugal's international profile by attracting over 10 million visitors with its theme "The Oceans: A Heritage for the Future," coinciding with the United Nations "Year of the Oceans."

It was built around the Olivais Dock, until recently a polluted industrial area of dilapidated warehouses and a disused oil refinery, and after the affair Lisbon was left with Europe's largest oceanarium, a new rail terminal, a trade fair center flanked by a beautiful riverside walkway and an expanded metro system. The fast-developing area around the expo site, which stretches about three miles along the Tejo River, has attracted some business away from the congested core of the city and will provide new homes for an overcrowded metropolis.

OECD

Economic cooperation began in April 1948, when a group of sixteen European countries founded the Organization for European Economic Cooperation (OEEC) to work together for postwar recovery. Portugal was one of them. The Organization for Economic Cooperation and Development (OECD) succeeded the OEEC and was established on 30 September 1961 in order to broaden the scope of cooperation and promote economic growth in member countries' expanding world trade. The principal organ of the OECD is its council, made up of representatives from all member nations. According to its report of 1998, Portugal's economic outlook is favorable. Inflation and long-term interest rates have fallen close to the levels prevailing in the best-performing EU countries. In the area of health and longevity Portugal has made strides forward but still has a way to go to catch up with other European countries. Extreme poverty in some places has slowed down what may have been more rapid progress, and relatively low levels of education also contribute to health problems.

ELECTIONS 1999 AND THE COMING CENTURY

In the election for the European Parliament in June 1999 the Socialist Party (PS) won with nearly 44 percent of the vote. The PS failed by one seat to gain an absolute majority in the National Assembly elections held on 10 October 1999, winning 115 out of the 230 seats. Both the left-of-center Socialist Party and the right-of-center Social Democratic Party are firmly rooted to the middle of the political spectrum and show only minor differences on major issues.

Large-scale privatization programs have been in progress in Portugal since 1989, involving twenty-two companies in 1996–1997. Programs for 1998–1999 focus on airports and air navigation, motorways and tobacco—the latter, like cement manufacturing, pulp and oil, is already in progress.

Portugal will continue to benefit from closer ties with Europe, and now with the common European monetary system and the Eurodollar, the country will gradually reach a standard of living and literacy on a par with major European countries. The economic expansion, which began in 1994, gained further strength in 1997 due to falling interest rates, falling unemployment and disinflation.

Tourism will continue to play an increasingly larger role in the economy as the coastline and coastal hinterlands along the Atlantic, especially south of Lisbon in the Alentejo, develop their own tourist industries. The current rapid development of new arterial highways and improved air transport are bringing the country closer to Europe and into greater contact with its own internal structure. Optimism in the Portuguese ability to move forward into the twenty-first century is manifest. There has been a rise in self-employment, in part, reflecting stronger entrepreneurial confidence. Attention in future years will probably focus on bringing the country's level of skilled jobs and educational achievements closer to the European average. In the last three decades the country has shown a remarkable ability to adjust to changing circumstances.

The government's tight fiscal policies of maintaining price stability and other measures, such as improvements in public finances, have allowed it to meet the criteria for economic and monetary union (EMU). After 1999 the escudo will gradually be replaced by the Eurodollar that is now becoming the common European currency.

Notable People in the History of Portugal

Afonso Henriques or Afonso I (ca. 1105–1185). Resisting the domination of the neighboring kingdom of León, Afonso secured the independence of the county of Portucalense. Expanding his lands southward, he defeated the Moors in several battles, styled himself king and with the help of crusaders captured Lisbon in 1147. By the time he died, he had firmly established the independence of Portugal and founded a Burgundian dynasty destined to endure until 1385.

Afonso III (1210–1279). Conquered the southernmost province of Algarve in 1249, completing the Portuguese reconquest from the Moors and moved the capital from Coimbra to Lisbon. During his reign Portuguese replaced Latin as the court's written language. He introduced administrative reforms, encouraged much resettlement, promoted commercial and cultural development and broadened internal support for himself by summoning representatives of the towns to the Cortes for the first time in 1254.

Albuquerque, Afonso (ca. 1462–1515). Navigator, statesman and founder of the Portuguese empire in the Orient. In 1503 he made his first trip to the East. King Manuel appointed him governor of all Portuguese possessions in Asia, where he succeeded Francisco Almeida. Albuquerque captured the Indian district of Goa in 1510 and went on to complete the conquests of Malabar, Malacca and the Sunda Islands. He maintained strict military discipline in the territories under his control. A biography containing his collected papers was written by his son Braz Albuquerque in 1557.

Almeida, Francisco de (ca. 1450–1510). Portuguese soldier. In 1505 King Manuel appointed him the first viceroy of India, where he strove to exclude the Muslims and Venetians from commerce with the East. On his way to India he captured Kilwa and Sofala and destroyed Mombasa on the East African coast. He then established himself at Cochin in India. In 1509 he ravaged the Muslim port of Goa and other seaports on the coast of India and completely destroyed the Muslim fleet at Diu.

Beresford, William Carr (1768–1854). Served through Peninsular War and distinguished himself at Coruña. He completely reorganized the Portuguese army, of which he was made marshal in 1809. As commander in chief of the army and with only a weak junta for the government, he ran the country, but his odious rule and involvement in the suppression of a liberal conspiracy in 1817 forced him out of power.

Cabral, Pedro Alvares (ca. 1467–ca. 1520). Portuguese navigator. In 1500 with thirteen vessels and more than 1,000 men, Cabral left Lisbon under orders to proceed to India by the route discovered in 1497–1498 by Vasco da Gama. Driven far to the west, he encountered the coasts of Brazil, which he claimed for Portugal. He succeeded in reaching Calicut, India, where he negotiated a commercial treaty and established a trading post.

Camões, Luis de (ca. 1525–1580). National poet of Portugal. A humanist scholar, he was also a soldier and lived a life of high adventure at home, in Morocco and in the Eastern empire. He is best known for his epic poem *Os Lusíadas* (*The Lusiads*), a chronicle of Portuguese history up to and during the period of exploration and conquest and the outstanding literary expression of Portugal's golden age. Although he died in poverty and obscurity, the day of his death, 10 June, is now commemorated as the day of the Portuguese people.

Castro, Inês de (ca. 1320–1355). Galician noblewoman, mistress of Prince Pedro, whose unhappy fate has been the subject of tragedies and poems.

King Afonso feared that this union might affect the claim to the throne of his grandson and had Inês murdered. She is buried at Alcobaça beside her royal lover.

Covilhã, Perdo de (ca. 1450–ca.1545). He undertook a dangerous overland mission to investigate the source of the spice trade and sent back a report to the court. De Covilhã, the very model of a swashbuckling soldier and resourceful diplomat, and de Paiva set out in 1487 to Aden (where they separated—de Paiva to Ethiopia and de Covilhã to the Malabar coast, where Arab merchants held the trade monopoly). Back in Cairo he learned that de Paiva had died. King João ordered him to Ethiopia, where, prevented from leaving, he served four emperors and died there, an old man with many children.

Dias, Bartolomeu (ca. 1450–1500). Portuguese navigator. Dias set sail from Lisbon in August 1487 and in February 1488 was the first European to round the southern end of the African continent, continuing as far as the estuary of what was later named the Great Fish River. Opening a sea route from Europe to the Far East, Dias explored about 1,260 miles of previously unknown African coast. He perished in a storm off the Cape of Good Hope, which he had discovered.

Dinis, the Farmer King (1261–1325). Son of Afonso III and father of Afonso IV, Dinis led a rebellion against his father (1277–1279). He encouraged shipbuilding, agriculture, commerce and literature, founded the universities of Lisbon (1290) and Coimbra (1307) and was the most successful of Portugal's medieval kings, encouraging the nobles and military orders to pursue farming as opposed to war. He placed uncultivated land in the hands of small farmers to make it productive, and through his efforts Portugal was able to raise crops for export.

Eanes António dos Santos Ramalho, General (1935–). President of Portugal from 1976 to 1986 during the formative years of the fledgling democracy. A nonparty candidate, he was supported by the Socialist Party, the People's Democratic Party, and Social Democratic Center Party. He was reelected on 7 December 1980. Legally barred from a third term, he was succeeded by his former prime minister, Mário Soares.

Eça de Queirós, José Maria (1845–1900). Studied law at Coimbra. A realist whose novels and essays portray Portuguese society in the last decades of the nineteenth century, his themes dealt with the backwardness, poverty and ill health of the country attributed to the clergy or the superstitious ignorance of women, with a connection between the two.

Egas Moniz, António Caetano (1874–1955). Professor of neurology at Lisbon University, awarded the Nobel Prize for pioneering work in medicine (with Walter Hess, 1949). As foreign minister he headed the delegation to the Versailles Peace Conference (1918–1919).

Gama, Vasco da (ca. 1468–1524). Portuguese navigator. Commissioned by King Manuel I to make the journey by sea to India, he sailed from Lisbon (1497) with four vessels, rounded the Cape of Good Hope, reached Melindi on the east coast of Africa and thence sailed to Calicut (May 1498)—the first voyage from Western Europe around Africa to the East. On his second journey (1502–1503), he founded Portuguese colonies at Mozambique and Sofala and was later made viceroy of Portuguese Asia (1524).

Gulbenkian, Calouste Sarkis (1869–1955). Turkish Armenian oil billionaire and philanthropist, he moved to Lisbon from Paris in World War II with his considerable collection of art and artifacts. He bequeathed to the country, along with a superb museum, an impressive charitable foundation to support artistic, educational and scientific enterprises.

Henrique (Henry) the Navigator (1394–1460). A son of João I and Philippa of Lancaster, Master of the Order of Christ, he was the guiding spirit of the Portuguese discoveries, devoting much of his life to the cause of exploration in the Atlantic Ocean and the coast of Africa. He worked to improve the ships, their instruments and maps. By his death in 1460, the Portuguese had rounded the bulge of West Africa and reached the Guinea coast.

Herculano de Carvalho e Araujo, Alexandre (1810–1877). Foremost Portuguese historian of the nineteenth century and author of novels, poetry and short stories. His major contribution to Portuguese history was his use of primary sources of documentation, avoiding the accepted ideas of divine intervention in the affairs of the world which brought him under attack from the pulpit.

João I (1357–1433). A son of Pedro III, he founded the dynasty of Avis. He and his general, Nuno Alvares Pereira, won the Battle of Aljubarrota against the Spanish in 1385 and assured the continuing independence of Portugal from the Castillian crown. He later married Philippa of Lancaster and had the great abbey of Batalha constructed in fulfillment of a vow.

João IV (1604–1656). Eighth duke of Bragança and one of the greatest landowners in Portugal of his time. Capable and prudent, he was chosen by the nationalists to lead the country through the revolution of 1640, which restored Portuguese independence from Spain.

João V (1689–1750). Ruled during the heyday of Brazilian trade and gold production. He was devoted to pomp and luxury and lavished great sums of money on construction, the chief example being the luxurious palace, monastery and library of Mafra.

Magalhães, Fernão de (Magellan) (ca. 1480–1521). Portuguese navigator and explorer, the first European to cross the Pacific Ocean. After being turned down by the Portuguese court, he offered his services to the king of Spain and sailed from Sanlucar de Barrameda to try to reach the Indies by sailing west. He did not survive the journey, and only one of his five ships sailed around the world and reached home.

Manuel I (1469–1521). Unified the administrative and fiscal structure of the country and established Portuguese commercial power with trading posts in the East Indies, Asia and Africa. During his reign culture flourished, and Lisbon became the focal point of world trade with some 250 sailings to India. The Manueline style of architectural design, with maritime motifs, was named after the king. A blight on his reign involved the expulsion of Jews from Portugal in 1497.

Pessoa, Fernando (1888–1935). Avant-garde poet and prose writer of international reputation. Greatest literary figure in Portuguese modernism, he was raised in South Africa and educated in English. After Camões he is considered to hold the most important place in the minds and consciousness of the Portuguese.

Philippa of Lancaster (1359–1415). Daughter of John of Gaunt, duke of Lancaster, married João I in 1387. Mother of King Duarte, the influential

Pedro, Henrique the Navigator, the less conspicuous João and the unfortunate Fernando. A gentle queen, she is reputed to have had a civilizing influence on the manners and customs of the Portuguese court. She is buried beside João in the abbey of Batalha.

Pombal, Marques de (1699–1782). Portuguese statesman and virtual ruler of the country during the reign of King José. After the devastating Lisbon earthquake in 1755, Pombal organized the relief efforts and planned its rebuilding. He was made chief minister in 1756, and his powers were nearly absolute. He abolished slavery in Portugal, reorganized the educational system, agriculture, the army and commerce and published a new code of laws. He expelled the Jesuits from the country and kept the nobility in line. Created a marques in 1770, his power ended when the king died.

Salazar, António de Oliveira (1889–1970). Professor of economics at Coimbra University, he entered the government in 1928 as minister of finance and in July 1932 became premier with dictatorial powers. He drafted the constitution of the fascist Estado Novo (New State), put into effect in 1933. He maintained order with a powerful secret police (PIDE), a large army and the paramilitary Portuguese Legion. In foreign affairs Salazar sought close relations with Spain, Britain and the United States. In his last years he was caught up in the futile and costly attempt to repress rebellions in the African colonies.

Sancho I (1185–1211). Son of Afonso I, Sancho I continued the reconquest and resettled depopulated areas, welcoming foreigners and building towns, castles and roads. He gave vast territories to the military orders and sought to strengthen the crown against the nobility and the church, establishing royal commissions to recover illegally held church lands. He was also a poet and died a very wealthy man from trade.

Sebastião (1554–1578). King of Portugal, lost his life—and almost ruined his country—in a crusade against Morocco. He reversed João III's policy of withdrawal from North Africa and in 1578 assembled an army to fulfill his dream of defeating Islam. Sebastião and most of his men were killed or captured, and the prisoners were sold back for ransom, depleting the financial resources of the country. He left no heir, and the crown passed to Spain, which ruled Portugal for the next sixty years.

Soares, Mário (1924–). Lawyer, historian and politician, ex-leader of the Portuguese Socialist Party. During the 1950s and 1960s, in the forefront of the democratic opposition to the regimes of Salazar and Caetano, Soares was imprisoned twelve times and exiled to São Tomé. After the military coup of 1974, he returned to Portugal and served as foreign minister (1974–1975) and minister without portfolio (1975). When the socialists won the elections of 1976, Soares became prime minister and again in 1983. He was elected president in 1986 and 1991.

Viriatus (?–139 B.C.). A legendary Lusitanian shepherd-hero from the mountains of the Serra da Estrêla who gathered a guerrilla army, fought and often defeated the Romans for twenty years. After his death through treachery, he became the national symbol of resistance.

Wellesley, Arthur, duke of Wellington (1769–1852). Arrived in Portugal with an expeditionary force in 1808 and defeated the occupying French army at Roliça and Vimeiro. Returning to Portugal the following year, he dislodged the French under Soult from Oporto. In 1810 he stopped the third French advance on Lisbon under Messéna at Buçaco and again at his defensive lines of Torres Vedras. He pursued the retreating French, winning again at Fuentes de Oñoro and Albuera, eventually pushing them back across the Pyrenees. He was created duke of Wellington in 1814.

Xavier, Francis (1506–1552). Cofounder of the Society of Jesus, he was invited to Lisbon by João III and helped to establish Jesuit schools in Portugal that influenced education for the next two centuries. Known as the Apostle of the Indies, he spread Christianity throughout much of the eastern Portuguese empire and Japan before succumbing on a small island near Macão in 1552 on his way into China. In 1622, he was canonized.

Appendix A: Monarchs and Heads of State

HOUSE OF BURGUNDY

Afonso I	1128–1185
Sancho I	1185–1211
Afonso II	1211–1223
Sancho II	1223–1248
Afonso III	1248–1279
Dinis	1279–1325
Afonso IV	1325–1357
Pedro I	1357–1367
Fernando	1367–1383
(Interregnum)	1383–1385

HOUSE OF AVIS

João I	1385–1433
Duarte	1433–1438
Afonso V	1438–1481

João II	1481–1495
Manuel I	1495–1521
João III	1521–1557
Sebastião	1557–1578
Cardinal Henrique	1578–1580

SPANISH (HABSBURG) KINGS

Felipe I	1580–1598 (Felipe II of Spain)
Felipe II	1598–1621 (Felipe III of Spain)
Felipe III	1621–1640 (Felipe IV of Spain)

HOUSE OF BRAGANÇA

João IV	1640–1656
Afonso VI	1656–1668 (deposed, d. 1683)
Pedro II	1668/1683–1706
João V	1706–1750
José I	1750–1777
Maria I	1777–1799 (incompetent to rule, d. 1816)
João VI	1799/1816–1826
Pedro IV	1826–1828 (abdicated, d. 1834)
Miguel	1828–1834 (deposed, d. 1866)
Maria II	1834–1853

HOUSE OF SAXE-COBURG-GOTHA

Pedro V	1853–1861
Luis	1861–1889
Carlos	1889–1908
Manuel II	1908–1910 (deposed, d. 1932)

HEADS OF STATE (PRESIDENTS)

First Republic

| Teófilo Braga | 1910–1911 |
| Manuel de Arriaga | 1911–1915 |

Teófilo Braga	1915
Bernardino Machado	1915–1917
Sidónio Pais	1918
Admiral João do Canto e Castro	1918–1919
António José de Almeida	1919–1923
Manuel Teixeira Gomes	1923–1925
Bernardino Machado	1925–1926
Commander José Mendes Cabeçadas	1926
General Manuel Gomes da Costa	1926
General António Oscar de Fragoso Carmona (with António de Oliveira Salazar, premier (1932–1968)	1926–1951
General Francisco Craveiro Lopes	1951–1958
Admiral Américo Tomás (with Marcelo Caetano, premier 1968–1974)	1958–1974

Second Republic

General António Spínola	1974
General Francisco da Costa Gomes	1974–1976
General António Ramalho Eanes	1976–1986
Mário Soares	1986–1996
Jorge Sampaio	1996–

Appendix B:
Portuguese Colonies

The Portuguese are found throughout the world—their customs and language span the oceans and cling to many distant lands.

AFRICA

The Community of Portuguese-Speaking Countries (CPLP) comprises Angola, Cape Verde, Guinea-Bissau, Mozambique, São-Tomé e Príncipe, Brazil and, of course, Portugal. In July 1996 Portugal hosted the inaugural meeting of the CPLP as a linguistic and cultural organization, but it also hoped to promote closer political and economic ties. Its headquarters was established in Lisbon. In the African ex-colonies, Portuguese vies with the local languages as an official means of communication (in Creole form in Guinea-Bissau). In São Tomé e Príncipe (two volcanic islands, Africa's smallest nation), Portuguese is the primary language of the people.

Roman Catholicism, a legacy of Portuguese missionaries, has also persisted in Africa among about 38 percent of the population in Angola, 30 percent in Mozambique and 5 percent in Guinea-Bissau, where Muslim influence has been strong.

Apart from the slave trade, the Portuguese possessions in Africa attracted little attention in the eighteenth and nineteenth centuries. The liberal government abolished the trade in slaves in 1858, although at that time government forces in Africa were inadequate to enforce the decree, and it continued for another thirty years or so. The country was barely able to maintain the toehold it held on African soil, although the Septembrists under Sá da Bandeira envisaged an African empire to replace that lost in Brazil. By the mid-nineteenth century, most of the Guinea coastal areas had been lost to France. After 1870 Portugal took more interest in Africa to maintain its status in the world and sent exploratory expeditions inland from its coastal enclaves. Mozambique was the most neglected of the overseas territories until the opening of the Suez Canal enhanced its commercial value.

At the Berlin Congress of 1885, summoned by Bismarck to establish demarcation lines among the competing powers in Africa, Portugal was mostly ignored and excluded from the Congo region, where it had been installed for four centuries. Some progress was made in establishing Portuguese lines of demarcation in Angola, however, but further expansion to the east aroused British hostility.

Some Portuguese would have liked to see a kind of commonwealth of Portugal with the former colonies as autonomous units in a big, happy, Lusophone empire. But the country could not afford it nor tried; its former colonies are some of the poorest nations in the world. Life expectancy in all of these countries is low. In Angola it is forty-four years for males and forty-eight for females. Infant mortality is high, and there are few doctors and hospital beds in relation to the population. In Mozambique there is one doctor for about every 36,000 persons. Literacy is also low in the ex-colonies, somewhere around 30 to 40 percent of the population.

Large-scale colonization did not begin in Angola until the twentieth century, when hundreds of thousands emigrated there from Portugal. During the Salazar dictatorship the foreign orientation of the government was to hold on to the colonies, which were claimed to be an integral part of Portugal. A guerrilla war led to independence in 1975.

After independence, civil war in Angola killed thousands of blacks, drove most whites to emigrate and completed economic ruin. Portugal expressed willingness to participate in the reconstruction of the economy of Angola in 1988 and played a significant part in the peace process. Meetings between UNITA and the Angolan government were held in Lisbon, culminating in the peace accord of 1991. After a resumption of hostilities in 1993, UNITA rejected Portugal's status as observer but then in 1994 again welcomed the possibility of Portugal in further mediation. A new peace agreement was signed in November of that year, but allegations that the Portuguese had given technical assistance to the government of Angola undermined its claim to neutrality. During a five-day visit to Angola in 1997 the Portuguese prime minister stressed the need for long-term, bilateral cooperation.

Revolt against Portuguese rule in Mozambique began in 1964, when guerrillas of the Mozambique Liberation Front (FRELIMO) struck out of Tanzania. Only 65,000 whites were resident in Mozambique when it achieved independence in 1975 and moved to establish a Marxist state. Hostilities broke out between the government and the rebel Mozambique National Resistance (MNR). The exodus of most whites, who formed the technical and professional class, weakened the nation's economy. The ruling party formally abandoned Marxist-Leninist policies in 1989.

In the quest for peace in Mozambique, Portugal also played a role. Relations between the two countries deteriorated in 1989, when a Mozambican diplomat was expelled from Portugal after implication in the assassination in Lisbon of a Mozambican resistance leader. Friendly relations were restored in 1990, when President Chissano paid an official visit to Lisbon, and in January 1992, Portugal received an invitation to attend the peace talks as an observer, which culminated in a treaty signed in Italy.

BRAZIL

Brazil is the fifth largest country in the world; its official language is Portuguese, although German and Italian are spoken by many Brazilians, especially those living in the cities of the south. Portuguese, Africans and mulattoes make up the vast majority of the population, and nearly 75 percent of the inhabitants are Roman Catholic.

Although independent since 1822, Brazil maintains strong economic and social ties with Portugal. There is also a mutual agreement for citizens of one country to obtain citizenship in the other, and yearly joint consultations occur between their respective foreign ministers. Brazil remains a market of considerable, long-term economic importance for Portuguese investment, which amounted to about $1 billion in 1999.

EAST TIMOR

Timor is the largest and easternmost of the Lesser Sunda Islands in the Malay Archipelago. Dili is the capital of East Timor Province. Traditional religions predominate, and there are small Muslim and Christian communities. Most of the people are of mixed Malay, Polynesian, and Papuan descent. The Portuguese founded settlements on Timor in the early sixteenth century, and Dutch traders first landed on the island in 1613. The Portuguese and Dutch competed for influence until a series of agreements, the last in 1914, established boundaries between their holdings. Dutch Timor, centered at Kupang in the west, became part of the Republic of Indonesia in 1950. Portuguese Timor was forcibly annexed by Indonesia in late 1975. When Timor was occupied by Indonesian forces, the return of troops and European settlers to Portugal aggravated Portugal's own problems of unemployment and political unrest. UN-sponsored negotiations began in 1983 but fared poorly, and Portugal registered a formal complaint in 1988, when President Suharto of Indonesia visited East Timor. Under UN supervision, talks between the Portuguese and Indonesians began again in 1992 but ended without agreement. Discussion continued intermittently, with Portugal condemning police brutality in East Timor and granting political asylum to East Timorese who managed to flee. In May 1997 the Portuguese government formally protested to the UN the Indonesian handling of elections in East Timor with attendant outbreaks of violence. Diplomatic relations with Indonesia were reestablished in 1999, and Portugal has offered to fund East Timor's annual budget during its transition to an autonomous region or independent state. The former governor of East Timor, Mario Carrascalão, in favor of independence for the 800,000 people there, fled to Lisbon 28 April 1999 fearing for his life after receiving threats from pro-Indonesian factions. An overwhelming number of East Timorese voted for independence in a referendum held on 30 August 1999, but continuing civil strife resulted in occupation by UN peacekeepers.

MACÃO

Macão, an area of six square miles, is an enclave, a peninsula and two small islands at the mouth of the Canton River in China. The population is about 95 percent Chinese. Portugal granted broad autonomy to Macão in 1976. In May 1985 President Eanes visited Beijing, and it was announced that the Portuguese and Chinese governments would negotiate the future of Macão. The first round of negotiations took place in 1986, and in April 1987 the two countries signed an agreement whereby Portugal would transfer the administration of Macão to the Chinese 19 December 1999. Before that date Portuguese passports would be available to certain Macão residents. In 1997 President Sampaio urged respect for the Portuguese cultural identity in Macão, which the Chinese promised to maintain as a capitalistic system after 1999. Macão, like Hong Kong, was guaranteed fifty years of noninterference. The modern world left Macão behind as Hong Kong became the commercial and financial hub of East Asia, allowing it to degenerate into a somewhat seedy backwater of only tourist interest. A revival under Chinese authority will transform it into a new and different kind of enclave. How much and for how long the unique combination of cultural features that made up Macão will persist are anyone's guess. Meanwhile, how many residents of Macão's more than 100,000 Portuguese with EU passports will choose to remain is an open question. The residents have endeavored to maintain the distinct cultural heritage of the oldest European settlement in Asia by constructing museums and revamping old sites of historical importance. The charm of Oriental and Western blend has, in some respects, turned to a lethal mix as control over gambling and vice is fought for by rival gangs. Portugal objects to China's plans to send in troops to restore order amid the turf war waged by Macão's gangsters over profits at the casinos, the mainstay of the economy.

Glossary

auto-da-fé. "Act of faith," euphemism for a death sentence.

azulejos. Tiles originally polychrome in Portugal but later mostly blue and white and depicting scenes of history or designs.

caciques. Local political overseers.

caravel. Fifteenth- and sixteenth-century lateen-rigged sailing ship.

castro. *See* citânia.

citânia. Prehistoric, often hilltop and fortified, settlement.

conselho. Borough.

Cortes. Parliament.

estado novo. New state.

forais. Charter.

infante. Prince or infanta princess.

judiaria. Jewish ghetto.

junta. Political or military group or council.

manuelino. Architectural style (Manueline) from the reign of Manuel I.

Moçarabe (Mozarab). A Christian under Moorish rule. Also refers to their architecture.

Mudejar. A Muslim under Christian rule. Also refers to their style of decoration and architecture.

praça. Plaza or square.

serra. A mountain range.

taifa. Independent, small Muslim kingdom.

Acronyms

AD	Democratic Alliance (Aliança Democrática)
CDS	Christian Democratic Party of the Social Democratic Center (Partido do Centro Democrático Social)
CDU	United Democratic Coalition (Coligação Democrático Unitário)
COPCON	Operational Command for the Continent (Comando Operacional do Continente)
CPLP	Community of Portuguese-Speaking Countries
CR	Council of the Revolution (Conselho da Revolução)
DGS	General Directorate of Security (Direcção-Geral de Segurança)
EEC	European Economic Community
EFTA	European Free Trade Association
EMU	European Monetary Union
EU	European Union
FRELIMO	Front for the Liberation of Mozambique (Frente de Libertação de Moçambique)
GATT	General Agreement on Tariffs and Trade

GNR	Republican National Guard (Guarda Nacional Repúblicana)
IMF	International Monetary Fund
MFA	Armed Forces Movement (Movimento das Forças Armadas)
MNR	Mozambique National Resistance
NATO	North Atlantic Treaty Organization
OECD	Organization for Economic Cooperation and Development
OEEC	Organization for European Economic Cooperation
PAIGC	African Independence Party of Guinea and the Cape Verde Islands (Partido Africano de Independéncia para a Guiné e Cabo Verde)
PCP	Portuguese Communist Party (Partido Comunista Português)
PIDE	International Police for the Defense of the State (Polícia Internacional e do Defesa do Estado)
PPD	People's Democratic Party (Partido Popular Democrático)
PRD	Democratic Renewal Party (Partido Renovador Democrático)
PRP	Portuguese Republican Party (Partido Republicano Português)
PS	Portuguese Socialist Party (Partido Socialista)
PSD	Social Democrat Party (Partido Social-Democrata)
UGT	General Union of Workers (União Geral dos Trabalhadores)
UN	United Nations
UNESCO	United Nations Educational, Scientific and Cultural Organization
UNITA	National Union for the Total Independence of Angola (União Nacional para a Independéncia Total de Angola)
WHO	World Health Organization
WTO	World Trade Organization

Bibliographic Essay

For English readers, the following materials and their bibliographies will be helpful as supplementary readings.

GEOGRAPHY

Geographical treatments of the country may be found in the works of Dan Stanislawski, *Individuality of Portugal: A Study in Historical-Political Geography* (Austin, 1959; Westport, CT, 1969), who emphasizes differences between Portugal and Spain in geography, geology and culture. See also Ruth Way and Margaret Simmons, *Geography of Spain and Portugal* (London, 1962).

GENERAL HISTORIES

A succinct account of Portuguese history is contained in A. H. de Oliveira Marques, *History of Portugal*, 2 vols. Vol. I: from Lusitania to empire; Vol. 2: from empire to corporate state (New York, 1972). Another outstanding work of a general nature from Roman times to Salazar is Harold Livermore's 500-page *A History of Portugal* (Cambridge, 1947) and his revised and shortened version, *A New History of Portugal* (Cambridge, 1967). Requiring considerably less studious concentration are Charles E.

Nowell's *Portugal* (Princeton, 1973) and José Hermano Saraiva, *Portugal: A Companion History* (Manchester, 1997). A cultural overview is J. P. de Oliveira Martin's, *A History of Iberian Civilization* (New York, 1930). David Birmingham, *A Concise History of Portugal* (Cambridge, 1993) is mainly dedicated to the period after the restoration in 1640. For integrated Portuguese and Spanish history see Stanley G. Payne, *A History of Spain and Portugal*, 2 vols. (Madison, WI, 1973) and William C. Atkinson, *A History of Spain and Portugal* (London, 1960).

ANCIENT HISTORY

For a survey of prehistoric Portugal see H. N. Savory, *Spain and Portugal: The Prehistory of the Iberian Peninsula* (London, 1968) and J. M. Anderson and M. S. Lea, *Portugal 1001 Sights: An Archaeological and Historical Guide* (Calgary, 1994). More specific and technical is Richard J. Harrison's *The Bell Beaker Cultures of Spain and Portugal* (Cambridge, MA, 1977). An excellent comprehensive introduction to the Roman period may be found in the work of Jorge de Alarcão, *Roman Portugal* (Warminster, England, 1988).

MIDDLE AGES

Hugh Kennedy's *Muslim Spain and Portugal* (Harlow, 1996) contains many references to Portugal and the Muslim political system. A. H. de Oliveira Marques, *Daily Life in Portugal in the Late Middle Ages* (Madison, WI, 1970) presents an analysis of the period, and Bailey W. Diffie's *Prelude to Empire: Portugal before Henry the Navigator* (Lincoln, NE, 1960) presents a synthesis of the medieval foundations of Portuguese maritime expansion.

AGE OF DISCOVERY

A very readable account of the period from João I to Manuel I is by Christopher Bell, *Portugal and the Quest for the Indies* (London, 1974). C. R. Boxer, *The Portuguese Seaborne Empire 1415–1825* (Harmondsworth, 1970) is an important work demonstrating how Portugal pioneered the overseas expansion of Europe. See also C. R. Boxer, *Portuguese Merchants and Missionaries in Asia* (London, 1988). For early relations between Portugal, Brazil and Angola see Boxer's *The Golden Age of Struggle for Angola and Brazil* (Berkeley, 1962). Bailey W. Diffie and George Winius, *Foundations of the Portuguese Empire, 1415–1850* (Minneapolis, 1977) provides a well-balanced treatment of Portugal's pioneer role in the age of expansion. Alfred Hower and Richard Preto-Rodas, eds., *Empire in Transition: The Portuguese World in the Time of Camões* (Gainesville, 1985) is a collection of essays dealing with sixteenth-century Portugal. See also John Ure, *Prince Henry the Navigator* (London, 1977). John Hemming, *Red Gold: The Conquest of the Brazilian Indians, 1500–1760* (Cambridge, MA, 1978) is an even account of the sixteenth-century exploration and conquest. Also of note is A.J.R. Russell-Wood, *The Portuguese Empire 1415–1808* (Manchester, 1992), a thematic approach to the period.

OVERSEAS EMPIRE

Portuguese Africa has been the subject of much comment in recent decades such as D. Wheeler and R. Pélissier, *Angola* (London, 1971) and the brief survey of Ronald H. Chilcote, *Portuguese Africa* (Englewood Cliffs, NJ, 1967). The work by F.C. Egerton, *Angola in Perspective* (London, 1957) presents the Portuguese position. See also Eduardo Ferreira, *Portuguese Colonialism in Africa* (Paris, 1974), Marilyn Newitt, *Portugal in Africa* (London, 1981), James Duffy, *Portuguese Africa* (Cambridge, MA, 1968) and William Minter, *Portuguese Africa and the West* (Harmondsworth, 1972), which gives a history of relations between Africa and the West with emphasis on Portugal's oppressive government. Note also R. J. Hammond, *Portugal and Africa 1815–1910, a Study in Uneconomic Imperialism* (Stanford, 1966). Franco Nogueira, *The United Nations and Portugal* (London, 1963) is an account of Portugal's reaction to Article 73 of the UN, which condemned colonial policy.

Of enduring importance to Portugal, Brazil has been the subject of many works. See, for example, Caio Prado, *The Colonial Background of Modern Brazil* (Berkeley, 1967) and Bailey W. Diffie, *A History of Colonial Brazil* (Malabar, 1987). C. R. Boxer, *Salvador de Sá and the Struggle for Brazil and Angola, 1602–1686* (London, 1952) is a treatment of the Portuguese response to Dutch hegemony. From an economic point of view, see G. J. Ames, "The Carreira da India, 1668–1682: Maritime Enterprise and the Quest for Stability in Portugal's Asian Empire," *Journal of European Economic History* 20, no. 1 (1991): 7–28.

Portuguese trade with England is the subject of A. D. Francis, *The Methuens and Portugal 1691–1708* (Cambridge, 1966) and H. E. Fisher, *The Portuguese Trade* (London, 1971).

MODERN PORTUGAL

T. D. Kendrick, *The Lisbon Earthquake* (London, 1956) describes events in Lisbon that followed the disaster. Douglas L. Wheeler, *Republican Por-*

tugal (Madison, 1978) deals with the political history of Portugal from 1910 to 1926. A good account of Salazar and his policies is presented by Hugh Kay, *Salazar and Modern Portugal* (London, 1970) and Antonio de Figueiredo, *Portugal: Fifty Years of Dictatorship* (Harmondsworth, 1976). Mário Soares, *Portugal's Struggle for Liberty* (London, 1975) deals with life and politics under Salazar and Caetano. Written while Soares was in exile, this is an account of the times by one who was directly involved.

AFTER 1974

The revolution of 1974 and aftermath are well represented in Hugh Jenkins, ed., *Insight on Portugal, the Year of the Captains* (London, 1975), which presents a detailed account of the unfolding of the 1974 revolutionary events. In this connection see also Thomas Bruneau, *Politics and Nationhood: Post Revolutionary Portugal* (New York, 1984). Other books include Phil Mailer, *Portugal: The Impossible Revolution?* (London, 1977) and Robert Harvey, *Portugal: Birth of a Democracy* (London, 1978). Diamantino P. Machado, *The Structure of Portuguese Society* (Westport, CT, 1991) explains why fascism was doomed to failure in Portugal. Walter Opello, *Portugal from Monarchy to Pluralist Democracy* (Boulder, CO, 1991) presents a brief overview of earlier periods but concentrates on the political history of Portugal during and after the dictatorship of Salazar. Jean-Pierre Faye, *Portugal: The Revolution in the Labyrinth* (London, 1976) uses evidence compiled by the Russell Commission regarding the downfall of Major Otelo Saraiva de Carvalho, 25 November 1975 (including CIA participation). Hugo Gil Ferreira and Michael W. Marshall, *Portugal's Revolution: Ten Years On* (Cambridge, 1986) is an oral history of many of the officers who were involved in the overthrow of the Salazarian regime. Martin Kayman, *Revolution and Counter-Revolution in Portugal* (London, 1987) deals with the origins and failures of the revolution. Kathleen Schwartzman, *The Social Origins of Democratic Collapse: The First Portuguese Republic in the Global Economy* (Lawrence, KS, 1989) attempts to explain the collapse of the First Republic in socioeconomic terms. The role of the military is examined by Douglas Porch, *The Portuguese Armed Forces and the Revolution* (London, and Stanford, 1977). Jose Da Silva Lopes, ed., *Portugal and EC Membership Evaluated* (London and New York, 1993). Contributors analyze the net gains and losses to Portugal of EEC membership. For political history after the revolution, see L. S. Graham and D. L. Wheeler, eds., *In Search of Modern Portugal* (Madison, WI, 1983).

MILITARY HISTORY

An account of the Battles of Aljubarotta and Torres Vedras is given by David Chandler in *A Guide to the Battlefields of Europe* (Ware, England,

1965). For a description of the Battle of the Three Kings in Morocco, see Edward W. Bovill, *The Battle of the Alcazar: An Account of the Defeat of Dom Sebastian at El-Ksar el-Kebir* (London, 1952). For the Napoleonic period see Jac Weller, *Wellington in the Peninsula, a Military History* (London, 1962) and A. H. Norris and R. W. Bremner, *The Lines of Torres Vedras* (Lisbon, 1980). Anthony Brett-James, *Life in Wellington's Army* (London, 1972) presents an interesting compilation. R. E. Vintras, *The Portuguese Connection: The Secret History of the Azores Base* (London, 1974). Here a member of Churchill's war cabinet tells how old treaties with Portugal were invoked to establish bases on the Azores in World War II.

ARTS AND LITERATURE

For a solid treatment of early modern Portuguese art see Robert Smith, *The Art of Portugal 1500–1800* (New York, 1968).

Works on architecture include George Kubler, *Portuguese Plain Architecture; Between Spices and Diamonds, 1521–1706* (Middletown, CT, 1972), Júlio Gil, *The Finest Churches in Portugal* (Lisbon, 1988) and by the same author, *The Finest Castles in Portugal*, trans. George F. W. Dykes, 3d ed. (Lisbon, 1996), the latter two illustrated with fine photography. The chapter by J. B. Bury in the *Blue Guide Portugal* (London, 1989) is of interest.

For literature see A.F.G. Bell, *Portuguese Literature* (Oxford, 1922, 1970) and Ronald W. Sousa, *The Rediscoverers: Major Writers in the Portuguese Literature of National Regeneration* (University Park, PA, 1981). Maria I. Barreno et al., *The Three Marias: New Portuguese Letters*, trans. Helen R. Lane (Garden City, NY, 1975). A bibliography based on the collections of Indiana University is compiled by Hugo Kunoff, *Portuguese Literature from Its Origins to 1990* (Metuchen, NJ, 1994).

RELIGION

L.M.E. Shaw, "The Inquisition and the Portuguese Economy," *Journal of European Economic History* 18, no. 2 (1989): 415–31. Manfred Barthel, *The Jesuits* (New York, 1984). John W. O'Malley, *The First Jesuits* (Cambridge, MA, 1993).

MISCELLANEOUS

P. Th. Rooney, "Habsburg Fiscal Policies in Portugal 1580–1640," *Journal of European Economic History* 23, no. 3 (1994): 545–62. G. Clarence-Smith, *The Third Portuguese Empire* (Manchester, 1985). Carl A. Hanson, *Economy and Society in Baroque Portugal 1668–1703* (Troy, NY, 1981). *Portugal: A Country Study*, 2d ed. (Lanham, MD, 1994) is part of a series of area handbooks put out by the Federal Research Division of the Library of Congress.

Hugh Muir, *European Junction* (London, 1942) provides an eyewitness account of life in Lisbon at the beginning of World War II.

Madelena Barbosa, "Women in Portugal," *Women's Studies International Quarterly* 4 (1981): 477–80 is an interesting, but old, article, as much has progressed since it was written. Caroline B. Brettell, *We Have Already Cried Many Tears: The Stories of Three Portuguese Migrant Women* (Cambridge, MA, 1982), a biographical discussion of three working-class women who emigrated from Portugal to France, gives a portrait of the status of women in Salazarist Portugal and the effects of migration.

OECD Economic Surveys 1997–1998: Portugal (Paris, 1998). The international body of OECD makes available all information relevant to the formulation of national policy in every major field of economic activity. *The Statesman's Year-Book*, 135th ed. New York, 1998–1999) is the essential political and economic guide to all the countries of the world.

Four volumes were published for Expo '92, the Sevilla international exposition. Vol. 1, *Portugal and the Discoveries: The Meeting of Civilizations* shows the pioneering skill of early Portuguese mariners. Vol. 2, *Portugal: Building up a Country* discusses the archaeological heritage and domestic and overseas cross-cultural contacts. It includes a chronology. Vol. 3, *Portugal: Language and Culture* discusses the literary and artistic heritage of the country, and vol. 4, *Portugal Today* reports on the country in general, including landscape, architecture and the way of life.

Index

About the Author

JAMES M. ANDERSON is Professor Emeritus at the University of Calgary, in Alberta, Canada. He has spent many years in Portugal and Spain both as a Fulbright Scholar and the recipient of Canada Council and other grants. He is the author of six books and numerous articles in Iberian studies.